I0129449

Queer Activism in India

Naisargi N. Dave

QUEER ACTIVISM IN INDIA

A Story in the Anthropology of Ethics

Duke University Press | Durham and London | 2012

© 2012 Duke University Press

Designed by Amy Ruth Buchanan

Typeset in Scala by Keystone
Typesetting, Inc.

Library of Congress Cataloging-in-
Publication Data appear on the last
printed page of this book.

All rights reserved

contents

acknowledgments

This book was inspired and helped along by so many people. I hope that in dedicating this book to several of them I am not diluting my thanks, but expressing the depth and breadth of my gratitude. This book is, first of all, for PRISM and Sangini. Thank you for letting me into your lives and your work. I hope that you read in these pages my absolute respect and admiration for you. Specifically in Sangini I want to thank Betu, Cath, and Maya; in PRISM, Akshay Khanna, Gautam Bhan, Jaya Sharma, and Lesley Esteves. Jaya and Lesley, this book is, in part, a love letter to you; a very long, rambling, and weird love letter, I know, but a love letter all the same. I can't thank you enough for all you've done for me and meant to me and for how you've changed the world. Other activists and thinkers and friends in India I wish to thank are Alok Gupta, Arvind Narrain, Ashwini Sukthankar, Chayanika Shah, Chatura, Deepa Nair, Elavarthi Manohar, Farah Vakil, Geeta Kumana, Geeti Thadani, Jasmin Jagada, Maya Sharma, Nivedita Menon, Ponni Arasu, Pramada Menon, Ranjana Padhi, Shaleen Rakesh, Shalini Mahajan, Shobha Aggarwal, Sonali Gulati, Tarunabh Khatain, Tejal Shah, Vikram Doctor, and Vinay Chandran.

Ann Arbor is a dear place to me for everything I learned there and for all the time I spent within its intimate square mileage. This book is also for my former adviser, Jennifer Robertson, who is even still my model teacher, scholar, and mentor; thank you, for everything. I remain indebted to my other dissertation committee members, Sumathi Ramaswamy, Alaina Lemon, and Miriam Ticktin. I am honored to have learned from you. Sumathi, I owe you a particular note of thanks for all of your guidance. I extend my fondest thanks to other friends and teachers from my days at the University of Michigan: Bhavani Raman, Bruce Mannheim, Chandan Gowda, Edward Murphy, Francis Cody, Genese Sodikoff, Jill Constantino, Karen Hebert, Lee Schlesinger, Marina Welker, Michael Baran, Sharad Chari, and Tom Fricke.

Somehow I wound up with this wonderful job in a great city and surrounded by dream colleagues. At the University of Toronto, and in Toronto more generally, I want to thank Amira Mittermaier, Andrea Muehlebach, Andrew Gilbert, Bonnie McElhinny, Francis Cody, Girish Daswani, Holly Wardlow, Janice Boddy, Jennifer Jackson, Jesook Song, Joshua Barker, Kajri Jain, Lisa Forman, Michael Lambek, Sandra Bamford, Ritu Birla, and Tania Li. I also thank my students, undergraduate and graduate, who make me feel very lucky to spend my days the way I do.

There are many people beyond my India, Michigan, and Toronto worlds who have helped me immeasurably and taught me a great deal. My sincerest thanks to Carla Roncoli, Gayatri Reddy, Kamala Visweswaran, Lawrence Cohen, Nita Karpf, Martin Manalansan, and Tom Boellstorff. I wish I could thank by name all the people who have been anonymous along the way, but you know who you are; please also know how grateful I am. I am also very grateful to the Association for Queer Anthropology (AQA) for all the warmth and intellectual excitement I find within its spaces.

Where to include three of my favorite friends—India or North America, the academy or outside of it—I do not know, and so for them, a paragraph all their own. Sunila Kale, Surabhi Kukke, and Uzma Rizvi, thank you for all the fun and love and laughing.

And to Madeleine Findley, every word of this book's first iteration was written because of you.

The research and writing of this book have been supported by a Dissertation Research Grant from Fulbright-Hays, a Rackham Humanities Fellowship at the University of Michigan, a Foreign Language and Area Studies Fellowship at the University of Michigan, and a Start-Up Grant from the Connaught Foundation at the University of Toronto. I was also helped tremendously by the American Institute of Indian Studies in New Delhi and Chicago. I thank all of these institutions for their support. Portions of this book have been published previously in *Signs: Journal of Women in Culture and Society* (Dave 2010), *Cultural Dynamics* (Dave 2011b), *American Ethnologist* (Dave 2011c), and *Law Like Love: Queer Perspectives on Law* (Dave 2011d). This book has benefited greatly from critical feedback at the Department of Anthropology at Cornell University; the Department of Anthropology at McMaster University; the Jackson School of International Studies at the University of Washington; the Public Texts Seminar Series at Trent University; the Center for South Asian Studies at the University of Michigan; the Department of Global Development Studies at Queen's University; the Yale Research Initiative on the History of Sexualities at Yale University; and the "Ethnographies of Activism" workshop at the London School of Economics. Thank you to my hosts and to those audiences for helping me to refine my arguments and see new things in my material. I had two reviewers for this manuscript. One made himself known to me (thank you, Martin Manalansan) and another was anonymous. Both provided exceptionally helpful feedback and I am deeply indebted to them. Thank you to my research assistant, Kevin Nixon, for helping me in the last stages of this book's preparation. Thank you to the artist, Dhruvi Acharya, for allowing me to use her striking watercolor, *Women*, on the cover of this book. Finally, I wish to thank my editors at Duke University Press, Valerie Millholland, Gisela Fosado, Rebecca Fowler, Jeanne Ferris, and Susan Albury. I am very fortunate to have had their support and the benefit of their expertise.

In the spirit of my nascent turn to posthumanism, I wish to thank Phoebe and Basil, and to do so without the slightest trace of embarrassment whatsoever. This book is in part for Vihaan Dave, my little nephew, son of my not-so-little little brother, Prerak Dave, and my talented and generous sister-in-law, Kshipra Dave. I am tempted to say that I hope Vihaan is inspired by this book to become a lesbian and move to Canada, but then my mother would be very peeved with me. And so to my mom, Parthivi, who still finds the very notion of anthropology amusing but, I suspect, is also secretly proud of my unorthodox choices in life. And to my dad, Nitin, who could not conceal his delight if he tried. They have both given me very much, and I am grateful.

introduction

"Where do we go now?" Gautam wondered aloud. His expression was of optimism and loss, touching on both but settling on neither. We were all sitting, the dozens of us, on the floor of a gallery and performance space on the second floor of a building in New Delhi's Connaught Place. It was a familiar and comfortable scene, even if some of the faces were new. A group of college-aged gay boys, in their neatly pressed kurtas and colorful scarves, sat affectionately, with heads in each other's laps and holding hands. A young dyke stood in the back, leaning coolly against the door-frame amid all our discarded sandals, lowering her eyes with a shy smile when someone made flirtatious reference to her good looks.

A collective called Nigah had been holding a bilingual, biweekly Queer Café here since 2009. On this particular night at the Café in the summer of 2011, Nigah was commemorating the anniversary of India's first known gay protest, held on August 11, 1992. Protesting against police harassment of gay men, activists had assembled outside Delhi's police headquarters. Some of those activists spoke at Nigah's commemoration event. They re-called excitement, outrage, and euphoria—not knowing exactly what would follow, or even how this moment had happened, but knowing that the world was becoming something different. Someone pointed out that only a few storefronts away from us there had been another extraordinary event,

1. Delhi's first Gay Pride parade, June 29, 2008. Photograph by Maurizio Cecconi, www.puta.it.

in December 1998. The famous Regal Cinema was then showing a little-watched art house film called *Fire* about two sisters-in-law who reluctantly, but desperately, fall in love. Right-wing activists attacked the theater and the film, claiming that there are no lesbians in India; lesbians responded by vocally and spectacularly being, emerging dramatically as a critical counterpublic. For those who had also been at the protest in 1992, it was once again the unimaginable unfolding.

Delhi's first Gay Pride parade was also held nearby, in June 2008. The marchers were anxious at first, outnumbered probably ten to one by police and journalists. But the group of revelers soon swelled to a euphoric, drum-beating, slogan-shouting thousand, outnumbered no more (see figure 1). Then of course there was the event that sparked Gautam's query: the Delhi High Court's decriminalization of adult, consensual, same-sex sex in July 2009, which set off joyous celebrations of an entirely new order, even among those activists skeptical about legal change.[1]

All of these events share two things at least. One is a sense of enormous possibility, of a new social world becoming. The other is a sense of closure, of potentials seemingly realized, of questions now answered—indeed, of where-do-we-go-now. This book is about that affective experience of radical emergence, in which lives and worlds play to great consequence between potential and closure. I thus trace the moments through which queer activism in India, and lesbian activism in particular, has variously emerged, and what was lost and found through these critical events. But queer activism's most spectacular moments are just that: spectacular moments. And what they often obscure are the practices of reflection and intimate relationality that define activism at all. I argue in this book that activism is ethical practice, an effect of three affective exercises: the problematization of social norms, the invention of alternatives to those norms, and the creative practice of these newly invented possibilities. In other words, I theorize activism as critique, invention, and creative practice. This book examines how these practices live, die, change, and unfold in their inevitable confrontation with the normalizing imperatives of political engagement. Norms, though, are not the other to ethics, nor is closure the other to potentiality: limitations are the very condition of possibility for once unthinkable social emergences—like queer activism in India.

Beginnings to a Question

I began this research in the summer of 1999, six months into the heady aftermath of the right-wing campaign against *Fire*. In July of that year, CALERI, or the Campaign for Lesbian Rights—a collective born out of progressive counterprotests to the anti-*Fire* riots—was in the final stages of editing its inaugural manifesto, *Lesbian Emergence*. During that month, I spent several evenings at a no-frills rooftop coffeehouse (also in Connaught Place), observing and tentatively participating in CALERI's vigorous debates over language and strategy. When I left India that summer, my plan was to conduct a comparative research project analyzing the strategic and philosophical differences between CALERI—this autonomous, self-described radical collective aspiring to lesbian visibility and the attainment of equal rights —and another lesbian group in Delhi called Sangini—an internationally funded help-line-cum-support group whose directors and members resisted public protest in the interest of maintaining a "safe space" of anonymity for those many Indian women whose familial and economic circumstances prevent them from being out.

But when I arrived in India for my main fieldwork period at the end of 2001, CALERI had, for all intents and purposes, become defunct. Two of its founders had emigrated to the United States for advanced studies, while several others had left the collective due to the strains and conflicts endemic to political organizing. In CALERI's place had arisen a new collective. Called PRISM (People for the Rights of Indian Sexual Minorities), it was another resolutely nonfunded collective, comprising men, women, and transsexuals; straight, queer, and nonidentifying—all united in the cause of public queer advocacy (see figure 2). My flat was just a kilometer away from the home of two of PRISM's cofounders, Lesley and Jaya—a lesbian couple who I had become friends with in an earlier summer—and I spent many days and nights with them, outside of PRISM meetings, basking in their exceptional hospitality. Their home was indeed an exceptional place, something of a queer halfway house and cooperative. Friends and strangers from across the country and abroad would come and go, seeking solace from heartache, marriage pressures, unwelcoming and abusive families, and all forms of loneliness.

As these people passed through, they would inevitably, if with some initial reluctance, become active participants in the spirited political debates that formed the center of our lives there—whether PRISM should apply for funding, and what compromises would result from doing so; the limitations and possibilities of identity-based politics; whether the "Indian" in People for the Rights of Indian Sexual Minorities made too much of an appeal to nation and culture; whether the phrase "Sexual Minorities" limited PRISM's vision only to gays and lesbians, rather than to society as a whole. These committed and sometimes accidental activists would become for me and for one another something similar to Kath Weston's (1991) idea of a "chosen family"—queer parents, brothers, sisters, and daily companions. And through these collective practices—simultaneously affective and disciplining—emerged a grappling with the question "how might we live as queer Indians?," which served as the moral foundation for the group's political life. If my responsibility, as an ethnographer, friend, and co-believer, was to understand what it meant to be an Indian queer activist at this point in history, asking how organizations function or how their strategies compare, did not feel sufficient. These were affective politics, through and through.

So I started asking about activists themselves: Why are activists, activists? Why do (these) activists act? The answers I started to come to seemed to exist within the realm of the ethical. These activists act because, collectively, they nurture ethical ideals about what the world could look like. They act out of conflicted, sometimes uncomfortable, beliefs in the possibility of

2. A PRISM member setting up for a women's movement rally in Delhi. Every pair of silhouettes represents a lesbian double suicide. The sign tells of two women in Gujarat who threw themselves under a train in November 2002 rather than be parted by arranged marriage. Photograph by the author.

justice. They act in part because they desire new freedoms that they can as yet only imagine, but strive to enable. The opportunity to live, argue, love, and work among them thus left one thing, however inchoate for me at the time, in little doubt: that for these activists, and for the others in their larger constellation, queer activism is centrally about the search for, and the cultivation of, ethics.

It was only many months later—reading my notes on my life with PRISM alongside works on the nexus of ethics, politics, and aesthetics—that I came to a workable understanding of what this activism as ethics might be. Previously keeping me from considering PRISM's labor as "ethical" was the oppositional role that morality played in the lives of most of these activists, and of queer people more generally: that is, morality as norms for "proper" gendered, sexual, and familial comportment, and a structure for the maintenance of existing relations of power. Michel Foucault's (1985) subtle distinction between "ethics" and "morality" (see also Mahmood 2005, 28) encouraged me to see ethics as the *undoing* of social moralities. Activism then became clearer as a kind of ethical practice, distinguished from moralism by its creatively oppositional relationship to the normalization of life and words.[2] Activism as ethical practice, as I saw it in PRISM's lifeworld, is the creative, practical struggle against the drive to normalization ("normalization" in the sense of a narrowing of possibilities); or, to use a Deleuzian phrase, PRISM's activism was a creative struggle to forever become molecular rather than to be molar (Deleuze and Guattari 1987, 303). However I might put it, this life felt like an ethics.

Ethics and Queer Politics

Foucault—in the ethical turn of his work, which began between the first two volumes of his history of sexuality—advanced two notions of the ethical that Ewa Ziarek (1995) has distinguished as the juridical and the aesthetic. In *The Use of Pleasure*, Foucault is concerned with delineating the moral apparatus of the ancient Greeks, which, unlike Christian morality, focused on the proper use of pleasure rather than the proper regulation of sin. The ethical practice required by such a moral framework was a set of techniques —primarily bodily, such as fucking and preening—performed on and through the self in order to create the self as a morally recognizable subject, one who used pleasure fully and properly to achieve a life of brilliance and happiness. In an influential anthropological application of Foucault's work on ethics, Saba Mahmood (2005) demonstrated that Egyptian women's practices of piety were ethical practices performed in order to become morally recognizable subjects according to the dictates of Islam.[3] This is a juridical ethics—practices and techniques that work to more deeply inhabit law rather than to undermine it.

It was a more politically programmatic, more forthrightly queer Foucault who began to advance an aesthetic mode of ethical self-fashioning (Ziarek 1995, 187) that emphasized invention and creativity over the inhabiting of already given norms for proper behavior. Beginning in the late 1970s, Foucault began relating his work on the aesthetics of existence to the place of ethics in contemporary gay and lesbian politics. "It's up to us to advance into a homosexual ascesis," he said in 1977, "that would make us work on ourselves and invent (I don't say discover) a manner of being that is still improbable" (Foucault 1988, 116; see also Foucault 1994, 137). This "homosexual ascesis" was neither asceticism nor a form of identity politics; it was neither renunciation of the existing nor adherence to a new code of what homosexuality is and must be. Foucault's radical ethics for the contemporary world was precisely a "rethinking of the ethical relation of the self *beyond identity and moral law*" (Ziarek 1995, 181, emphasis added). Rather than thinking of ethics as another form of subjection to mandated ways of being, Foucault understood homosexual ascesis as "the work that one performs" (1994, 137)—the "work at becoming homosexuals"—rather than "be[ing] obstinate in recognizing that we are" (136).

But what precisely is this "becoming," this "work," and how does it relate to the Indian queer activism I describe and analyze in this book? First, it is useful to think, along with Foucault scholar Arnold Davidson (2005), of ascesis as a form of philosophical labor. In the first chapter of *The Use of Pleasure*, Foucault defines philosophy itself as "an 'ascesis' . . . an exercise of oneself in the activity of thought" and "the endeavor to know how and to what extent it might be possible to think differently, instead of legitimating what is already known" (1985, 9). Davidson argues that the linking of ascesis with philosophical labor is nowhere more vibrantly brought out than in Foucault's discussion of the radical potential of contemporary queer practice (Davidson 2005, 133). That argument is borne out in Foucault's comments in a 1981 interview: "Another thing to distrust is the tendency to relate the question of homosexuality to the problem of 'Who am I?' and 'What is the secret of my desire?' Perhaps it would be better to ask oneself, 'What relations, through homosexuality, can be established, invented, multiplied, modulated?' The problem is not to discover in oneself the truth of one's sex, but, rather, to use one's sexuality henceforth to arrive at a multiplicity of relationships" (1994, 135).

Within this articulation of a homosexual ascesis—or, as we might put it, a radical ethic—there are three things that pertain directly to an understanding of Indian queer activism.[4] First is a commitment to philosophical exercise, to think differently, to ask new questions of oneself in order to analyze and surpass the limits upon what can be said and done. It is this aspect of ethical practice that Foucault refers to as "problematization," or a critical reflection upon norms (Faubion 2001, 97). Second is the emphasis not on liberation from power or on a reversal of existing structures, but on the imaginative labor of inventing heretofore unimaginable possibilities. Third is the inherently relational quality of this ethic—an inhabiting of one's distance from moral norms such that the very remove from institutional power serves as the condition of possibility for the creative practice of multiple affective and relational forms.

I see critique, or problematization, in PRISM's relentless but joyful scrutiny of its own reliance on normative models of identity and atomistic politics, a scrutiny that demands the scrutinizer's own constant undoing. In that promise of alternative sociality as queer family, friends, lovers—as queers at all—I find the imaginative labor of inventing new possibilities. Finally, in PRISM's home—that space of invention in which the enforced remove from family, law, and nation serves as the necessitating factor, as well as the condition of possibility, for the creative practice of new forms of care and relationality—I see the affective exercise of creative practice in order to live differently.

It is this set of exercises—problematization, invention, and creative relational practice—that I argue in this book constitute activism.[5] Lesbian and gay activism in India is a case in point, but with its own contextual and relational challenges—challenges that this ethnography explores. One of the factors that uniquely inflects queer activism is tied directly to what it must invent in order to be: that is, affective, cohesive sociality (see Muñoz 2009, 11). To desire the same sex in (near) solitude has been a central fact of queer life before, and even after, an activism emerged in its name. Queer activism requires sociality, but, as we see with PRISM, that sociality takes the form of a commons in which the radical, creative possibilities that the commons enables must also, to some extent, be enclosed within itself in order for those possibilities to thrive, thus always reproducing certain disciplinary apparatuses.⁶ This is one of many tensions between an ethics of denormalization and our longing for, and recourse to, norms.

I use "ethics" in this book to refer to those practices that emerge from within subjections as a creative, disruptive response to normalization. By "normalization," I refer to a narrowing of possibilities to conform to institutionally legitimized norms such as identity, community, national belonging, and the language of law and right. But I don't assign ethics a positive value and normalization a negative one. Ethics is activism, but so are the norms against and through which those critical practices emerge. I argue that the key problem for understanding lesbian and gay activism in India is: how does ethical practice emerge from, confront, and partially reproduce the normalizing processes that work to render that which is most potentially radical about activism—that is, its ethical impulse—commensurate with existing norms (see Povinelli 2001)? And then there is the related question: how is all this felt, and how does that matter?

Affect and Activism

By emphasizing activism as ethical practice, I hope to address its structures of feeling, the formative but embryonic aspects of what moves us in the world. I draw here on Raymond Williams, who describes structures of feeling as "the actual alternative to the received and produced fixed forms . . . a kind of feeling and thinking which is indeed social and material, but each in an embryonic phase before it can become fully articulate and defined exchange" (1977, 131). Structures of feeling matter for Williams because they are lived and because, though not yet institutionalized, they nevertheless give shape to experience and action (131–32). They give us a glimpse, in other words, of becoming.

In this book I take structures of feeling as fields of possibility, spaces in which material constraints do indeed structure imagination—but, because those imaginings are nowhere manifest (not even, fully, in language), they are not yet determined or limited by existing norms. Activism begins within fields of possibility, in the form of an emergent sense that something is now possible. Or, as Lisa Duggan and José Muñoz might argue, activism begins with "educated hope," a "thinking beyond the narrative of what stands for the world today by seeing it as not enough" (2009, 278–79). This, I argue, is what renders activism centrally and foundationally affective.

My thinking about affect is also informed by Brian Massumi. He defines affect as intensity, with intensity defined as a quality of experience that is yet inassimilable to sociolinguistic fixing (2002, 27–28). Insofar as we embody simultaneously yet-inassimilable and assimilated (that is, named and qualified) experiences, affect is a realm of potential, a realm where opposites coexist, where multiple potentials are immanent. Another way to put it is that affect is the simultaneous participation of that which is still autonomous of fixing in that which is already delimited (or: the virtual in the actual world) (Massumi 2002, 35). Activism begins, then, precisely as the virtual in the actual world, the previously unthinkable that is now a flickering possibility, just on the verge of entering upon the world of norms. To study activism is to study the relationship between the virtual and the actual, the as-yet-inassimilable and the assimilated. It is just such a project that Deborah Gould undertakes in her ethnography of Act Up (2009; see also 2010).

In this book, I analyze the processes of mediation through which new affects are produced—what are those loosely collective moments in the lives of people through which we come to believe that something previously unthinkable is now possible? How do such immanent imaginings become articulable and articulated dreams and strategies? What different forms do activism and affect take when dreams of transformation confront the norms, institutions, and molarities of political engagement? What this amounts to is an ethnography of how affect becomes experience, and how social actors—such as the activists in this book—come to experience the world as a series of different limits, limits that serve as the norms against which new critiques and problematizations arise, and within which dreams of possibility are variously kindled and assimilated.

Transnational Affects

Indian lesbian and gay politics has been shaped by transnational circulations of people and agendas, from peripatetic scholars like the founder of Indian lesbian activism, Giti Thadani, to the Swedish agency that funded Indian lawyers to fight for the decriminalization of same-sex sex in India. Furthermore, the emergence of collectivized gay and lesbian politics in India in the late 1980s and early 1990s coincided neatly (and not coincidentally) with the liberalization of India's economy in 1991 and the acceleration of the global fight against HIV/AIDS. The history of queer activism in India is, in other words, inseparable from the history of neoliberalism, nongov-

ernmental organizations (NGOS), the politics and anti-politics of development, and the agendas of a modernizing state and a transnational public
health apparatus (see Agrawal 2005; Baviskar 2004; Escobar 2008; Ferguson 1990; Akhil Gupta 1998; Kamat 2002; Li 2007; Moore 2005; A. Shah
2010; A. Sharma 2008; Tsing 2004). The NGO-ization of grass-roots politics (or the NGO-driven invention of social issues out of seemingly nothing
at all) has been a popular theme in scholarship on South Asian social movements, and I deal with these debates in chapter 3 as they pertain to Indian
queer activism. Here, I will simply characterize my own approach.

The existing ethnographic literature on NGO-ization in India spans a
short spectrum from hostility toward NGOS for their co-optation of grass-
roots struggles (see, for example, Kamat 2002) to a tentative, critical acknowledgment of the political possibilities that distant institutional agendas create for local actors (see, for example, K. Misra 2003 and 2006; A.
Sharma 2008). Within this spectrum, Amita Baviskar's work exemplifies
an attention to the visceral, affective dimensions of activism in its struggle
between local realities and global influence. She writes about the Narmada
Bachao Andolan, a movement that sought to halt the construction of a dam
in western India that would displace tens of thousands of tribal people, or
adivasis, in the name of development (Baviskar 2004). As it turned out, this
massive uprising on behalf of tribals and against development was engi-
neered primarily by middle-class, urban activists, and Baviskar pays close
critical attention to the conflicts that ensued as the movement's leaders
engaged in a series of difficult, strategic compromises in order to make
tribal struggles intelligible to the urban Indians and international allies of
their own milieu who had the power to influence the fate of the adivasis.
Her ethnography ends bleakly, with construction proceeding, waters rising,
and Andolan activists retreating to their urban lives. A polemicist might
have reached a swift and damning conclusion about the movement. But
Baviskar suggests that the debris of struggle demands complex reflection:
"when we assess how the Andolan changed the world, which it surely has in
profound ways, we will also have to ask: how did it change the world of the
poor adivasis who formed its core? For a flickering moment, the Sangath [a
village level organization led by adivasis] made it possible to imagine other
worlds where adivasis could be powerful and respected. And the Andolan
made it possible to believe that mere adivasis . . . could bring dam construction to a grinding halt" (Baviskar 2004, 279).

It is this sort of attention to the complexity of social action—its strategic calculations, its violences, its animating hopes, and its imaginative inventions—that I try to bring here. Rather than making arguments about aggressive global impositions upon local struggles or, at the other end, the seamless creation of a transnational public sphere of solidarity and common interest (Guidry, Kennedy, and Zald 2000; Keck and Sikkinik 1998; Nash 2005), we might, as Anna Tsing suggests, look for points of friction: "the awkward, unequal, unstable, and creative qualities of interconnection" (2004, 4; see also A. Sharma 2008, xviii) that prove "key to emergent sources of fear and hope" (Tsing 2004, 11).[7] My interest is in the sometimes ephemeral, but always consequential lived experience of radical social action.

Queer Politics as Invention

Among my arguments in this book is that queer, and especially lesbian, activism in India is much more an activism of invention than of resistance. Resistance has been a key analytic in anthropology since the 1970s. Influenced by practice theory as well as the contributions of feminist, agrarian, and Subaltern Studies, anthropology turned away from totalizing narratives of dominance and subordination in favor of recovering the "small voices" (Guha 1997b) of resistance in field sites and archives (see Gal 1995). For anthropologists of South Asia, the turn to recovering spaces and voices of resistance was a welcome intervention, especially given the amount of work demonstrating the subordination of women, tribals, scheduled and backward castes, and peasants. The founding of the Subaltern Studies Collective in 1982 was central in raising critical questions for South Asian historiography around agency, ethnographic and historiographic method, and the multiplicity of routes of power. An oft-cited fault of the project, however, was its seeming indifference to women as agentive subalterns and to gender and sexuality as critical sites of power's fraught congealment (Chatterjee 1990; Guha 1987; Spivak 1988).

Work such as that of Gloria Raheja and Ann Gold (1994) was key in shifting the focus to women's resistance to hegemonic norms in Indian social life. In their ethnography of rural North Indian women's expressive genres, Raheja and Gold build on Subaltern Studies and follow James Scott (1990) in searching for the "hidden transcripts" of subaltern agency. To listen to the songs women sing and the jokes and stories they tell, Raheja and Gold argue, offers a corrective to both colonial historiography and

Western feminist scholarship: Indian women do not only suffer, but they also imaginatively critique; they do not succumb to dominant ideology but provide "alternative moral perspectives" (1994, 25); they do not fear pleasure but demonstrate an "exuberant sexuality" (1994, 27). Raheja and Gold's understanding of resistance is similar to the radical ethics that I consider central to queer activism in India: problematization of norms, the imaginative invention of new possibilities, and the attempted practice of new relational forms. But there are two main ways in which lesbian activism is unique from other activisms and renders "resistance" an insufficient analytic.

What we seek and demonstrate in accounts of everyday acts of resistance are the fault lines those acts reveal in the moral and institutional apparatus that subordinates the resisters. But implicit here is the idea that those who resist have some collective knowledge of that apparatus. In the case of women qua women, this holds true. The apparatus that subordinates women is everywhere visually, orally, and physically operative, its roots deep and culturally legitimized. Women are taught from the beginning of life how to be women and how to inhabit their gender, and such ubiquitous artifacts as the worship of satis, prayers for the birth of sons, laws regarding inheritance and rape, and dowry murders made to look like kerosene accidents are only the most visible of the pedagogic tools. Heteronormativity, however, has been such a deeply naturalized aspect of social life that it requires no system of accomplishment and reward. The moral and institutional apparatus that demands hetero-desire and punishes homo-desire has long been uniquely invisible.

Tied to the invisibility of lesbian oppression is the second unique feature of its activism. Difference among other subaltern groups is congenitally or spatially determined and collectively enforced through practices of social segregation—such is the case for women, tribals, scheduled and backward castes, the uprooted poor, and even hijras.[8] But lesbians are excluded from all social and cultural recognition, so that even the comfort of collective anger, the possibility of resistance, and the knowledge of what to resist and with whom is unavailable (see Fernandez and Gomathy 2005). Women know they suffer as women, the poor know they suffer as poor, and hijras know they suffer as hijras; their very subordination is enforced through practices of segregation with others like themselves. The upshot is that most subaltern groups must and do plot, practice, sing, joke, and rage

together. It is the very unknowingness of any lesbian possibility or prohibition, the sense of absence from culture and history, the lack of a class within
which cooperation is possible, that has—until the recent advent of the
movement I write about here—almost completely defined the emergent
space of same-sex desire in India.[9] Acts of same-sex love are not acts of
resistance—they are experienced as acts of social and cultural invention.

In the PRISM household, for example, the very heart of political action
rested in the commitment to invent new ways of being where no such things
were known to exist. It was a politics resembling Foucault's notion of an
aesthetics of resistance: that without the invention of possibilities for pleasure
and love there can be little resistance and little to resist for. For most lesbians and gay men in India, it is not enough to engage in solitary semiotic
struggles, reading themselves into dominant texts (but see Muraleedharan
2005).[10] They simultaneously seek and create new forms of relationality
and belonging from within which such acts accrue meaning and value.

In focusing on the inventiveness of queer politics, I find it useful to
think of those politics not as constituting a social movement or as a series
of acts of resistance, but as constituting what Elizabeth Povinelli (2001)
calls a radical world. Radical worlds are always in process, linked through
their shared existence in a field of possibility. To think of queer activism this
way enables engagement with the processes by which what is possible approaches its social limits. I thus share Povinelli's concern with "the delicate
and dramatic ways in which institutionalized conventions . . . commensurate social worlds—how they make radical worlds unremarkable" (Povinelli
2001, 320). To transform something as radical as lesbian desire in India
into the unremarkable seems like an extraordinary task, but—as I will show
in this book—every aspect of political engagement in democracy, from the
community to the courtroom, plays a role in the commensuration of emergent worlds, or the containment of affect in intelligible forms. Viewed from
the side of activists, we can understand these processes of containment as
challenges of an intimate kind.

Queer in the Non-West

Almost twenty years ago, Weston (1993) noted that the anthropology of
lesbian and gay sexuality reproduces a division of political labor in which
the West is seen as the site of public political formations around sexuality
and the non-West as the site of private struggles over identity formation or

the negotiation of queer desire with local moralities. That division lingers. In the many important recent works on queer sexualities outside Europe and North America (Blackwood, Bhaiya, and Wieringa 2009; Boellstorff 2005a; Carrillo 2002; Lorway 2008; Manalansan 2002, 2003; Rofel 1999; Sullivan and Jackson 2001), anthropologists study queer lives for their management of queer sexuality against two social facts: first, the Western imperative to make of queerness a political identity; and second, the local reality of the incommensurability of queerness with religion or nation. The latter limitation is seen as making it either dangerous or unthinkable to conform to the former imperative—to forge a queer public—which points to a second layer of missed translation: that between Western queer norms and local moralities.

At the heart of both of these notions is the presumed alterity of non-Western sexualities from Western ones in anthropological thought. Weston tells us that this presumption stems from necessity. In order for same-sex sexuality to become a legitimate site of anthropological investigation, early scholars had to demonstrate that it was indicative not of individual psychosis (a subject for other disciplines) but of different cultural logics. The ethnocartography, as Weston calls it, of early lesbian and gay anthropology sought to show, through accounts of third genders and practices of ritualized homosexuality, that same-sex sexuality exists everywhere and is everywhere a site for discovery of culturally variable forms of social organization.[11] The anthropology of queer sexuality has, since its inception, necessarily been about the sexual alterity of cultural others.

A lesbian and gay anthropology of the non-West that could engage with questions of identificatory and behavioral similitude across cultures, rather than only alterity, was enabled at the conjunction of larger trends in the discipline—namely, understanding culture as an inherently translocal process and seeing globalization as an incitement to both sameness and difference. The primary rubric for explaining similarity across culture was, until the mid-1990s, that of cultural imperialism (see Tomlinson 1991). This theory of a top-down, West–East flow of capitalist cultural hegemony was the basis for political scientist Dennis Altman's now well-known "global gay" thesis, which critiqued the effacement of traditional sexual self-concepts in the non-West by a modern, western-style gay identity (1996). Intellectual historian Joseph Massad has echoed this thesis recently in the context of Arab sexualities, arguing that westernized gay activists, constituting the "Gay International," impose a homo-hetero binary on a far more capacious field of Arab sexual practices (2007). In both such narratives, sameness masks an originary difference (Rofel 1999).

Critical ethnographic studies of globalization had already moved anthropology away from such a same-or-different approach to identity. The new problematic, as Arjun Appadurai (1996, 32) characterized it, was precisely the tension between homogenization and heterogenization. With this intellectual purchase on processes and experiences of similitude, scholars of sexuality produced ethnographic accounts of a non-ethnocartographic sort: work that could take seriously the existence of lesbians and gays in the non-West. But these works still emphasized an underlying difference between Western queers and their non-Western counterparts: gay men in China "double" so that they can be gay but still Chinese (Rofel 1999); Indonesian *gay* and *lesbi* people "dub culture" so that they can be simultaneously queer and Indonesian; non-Western lesbians engage in "local mistranslations" (King 2002); gay Filipinos enact a "conjuncturalism of identities" (Manalansan 2002). Even with the acknowledgement of sexual and identificatory similitude across boundaries, we persist in claiming that culture is the difference between us, and that this difference is always central to sexual self-identification outside of Western Europe and North America.

Following from the presumption of cultural alterity is the idea that most non-Western queer people are preoccupied not with the politics of identity, but with commensurating their sexuality with culture, religion, or nation. Thus committed to understanding how this majority of queer people in non-Western sites live and negotiate their sexual identities, anthropologists have made separations between activists and nonactivists, or those who embrace Western politics and those who do not or, more importantly, cannot (Lorway 2008, 21). Tom Boellstorff, for example, does not focus on the Indonesian gay and lesbian political movement because it is "not indicative of how gay and lesbian lives are typically lived" (2005b, 6). Martin Manalansan cautions that "although there is need to take stock of what is happening to various national gay and lesbian movements, there is even greater need to be more mindful of those who fall outside those movements" (2002, 248). His notion of the "greater need" reveals a value system in which a supposedly more authentic cultural subject is analytically privileged over the less authentic queer activist. If anthropologists no longer see same-sex sexuality and its practitioners as "incarcerated" by culture (Appadurai 1988) as the ethnocartographers did, same-sex desiring subjects often remain, in anthropological renderings, incarcerated within the realm of the everyday.[12]

In this book I choose to focus on something extraordinary—lesbian activism in a time and place of often violent cultural conservatism—in part for what it tells us about something exceedingly ordinary: that what most activist and nonactivist lesbian women in India share is a desire to experience sexuality as potential and possibility. In this light, incommensurability is not the defining problem of the non-Western queer woman. Rather, it constitutes a desired field of possibility relative to moments in which she is made to commensurate her experiences to rules, cultural norms, or liberal political banalities. The lives of the Indian queer activists I write about are certainly not typical of the lives of most Indian gays and lesbians. But their lives have much to teach us about a central anthropological question: How are cultural norms newly imagined, deployed, and inhabited in and through the politics of sexuality?

On Queer Language

Nearly forty of us had gathered one late afternoon in an empty classroom of a Christian school in Hyderabad to talk about sexual rights organizing across Asia. We sat in a circle as fans turned slowly overhead and bright sun streamed thickly through the open windows. A group of three stood smoking near the door. A Nepali woman spoke in Hindi when it was her turn to introduce herself. She talked about her work with a counseling service in Kathmandu for women in distress. An activist from Delhi responded to her in Hindi, inquiring if she received calls from lesbians. In posing the question, the Delhi activist translated "lesbian" into the Sanskritic *samlaingik log*, literally "those of the same sex" or "homo-sexual."[13] My friend Gautam, who was sitting next to me, chuckled and wrote something in his notebook. I turned to him with an inquisitive look, and he slid the notebook into my lap, pointing with this pen to what he had written: "Translations. The queer language is always foreign."[14]

As was often the case in the field, the clearest of analyses was already made for me. Indeed, whether in Hindi, Sanskrit, Marathi, Urdu, or English, the words that are called up to talk about Indian homosexualities always seem to have a ring of the strange. English words like "gay" or "lesbian," which have been in circulation in India since the late twentieth century, are not, as I show in chapter 1, automatically felt as strange by those who assume them. The incommensurability of "lesbian" with "India" is something that is actively produced—by analysts invested in local cultural difference, nationalists invested in cultural integrity, or international donors and NGOS invested in a diversity of fundable niches. When activists then call up such "indigenous" substitutes as samlaingik log, those words feel foreign because they are—contrived markers rather than sites for passionate subjective attachment or collective mobilization (see Das Gupta 2006, 171).

Still, it is among the first tasks of any emergent movement that rallies around a yet-emergent identity to send its resident historians back in time, to drag out the submerged bodies that lie nearly forgotten under the thick stratum of official history's obfuscations. Lesbian and gay scholars in India have taken up this task with dedication, historicizing same-sex love as an integral and celebrated part of India's cultural traditions (Thadani 1996; Vanita and Kidwai 2001; Vanita 2005). Other scholars of India have contributed, locating evidence of same-sex desire in classical medical texts (Sweet and Zwilling 1993). Such archaeologies have uncovered a host of vernacular terms denoting same-sex sex, gender non-normativity, and their practitioners. Among those terms predating the colonial era are the *tritiya prakriti* (third nature) as defined in Indian medical texts in the sixth century BCE (Sweet and Zwilling 1993); *samlingbhogi* (enjoying, eating of the same sex) (Thadani 1996, 78); *dogana*, as an Urdu term from the early nineteenth century for a woman's female lover (Vanita 2005, 62); and *chapti* (rubbing, clinging) to describe what those lovers do (Vanita 2005, 62).[15]

The collective display of these terms tells us that homo-love and the people who make it have always existed in India. Still, none of these categories have been useful for contemporary sexual subjectivity. Activists have, however, recently invented new terms for a culturally located homosexuality, seeking language that can be both culturally intelligible and affectively inhabited. Lesbians in Bombay[16] have advocated the use of *jinsi* for sexuality and *humjinsi* to refer to same-sex sexuality; a lesbian collective in Bombay called itself Stree Sangam, meaning "a confluence of women." (Notably, they have since abandoned the imperative of cultural commensurability, changing their name to LABIA, or Lesbians and Bisexuals in Action.) Sangini, a group that was partly founded on a rejection of "lesbian," temporarily replaced that signifier with such Hindi phrases as *aisi mahila jo dusri mahilion ki taraf aakarshith hoti hai* (the kind of woman who is attracted to other women). Even untranslated, phrases like "women who love women" and "single women" have been advocated by some feminist and lesbian activists as more fluid substitutes for the politicized, sexually speciated category of "lesbian." As I discuss in greater detail in chapter 3, such activists argue that these oblique terms provide an important choice for women who can quietly take advantage of culturally available spaces of homosociality, or for women who don't want their other political commitments—like class or anticommunalism[17]—to be overshadowed by their "lesbian" identification.

Analysts, too, have invented and advocated new terms. Wary of imposing the modern identity labels of "gay," "lesbian," and "queer" on same-sex interactions in history, Ruth Vanita and Saleem Kidwai (2001, xxi) opt for "homoerotically inclined";[18] Suparna Bhaskaran (2004) speaks of the "*khush* sexualities" of the present; Jeremy Seabrook (1999) argues that India has no homosexuality at all and prefers terms such as men who have sex with men (hereafter MSM), *kothi* (effeminate, mostly non–English speaking men who are penetrated in sex[19]), and *panthi* (the masculine men who penetrate kothis)—terms that, he argues, connote behavioral fluidity rather than a Westernized psychosexual identity.[20]

Naming is clearly a contentious issue for scholarship on sexuality—especially for scholarship on non-normative sexualities outside of Europe and North America, where the presumption of radical cultural difference tends to overwhelm the possibility that Western terms can have any real salience for most people (Robertson 1998, 18–19; Das Gupta 2006, 168). The two critical questions around naming for this book are: how to address forms of same-sex sexual behavior that predate the invention of "gay" and "lesbian"; and how to refer to same-sex desiring women in the contemporary period (that is, since "lesbian" began circulating in India in the late 1980s) who are outside the communicative circles in which that term actually circulates. In both cases, I tend to use "lesbian," "gay," and "queer," for the following reasons.

As Vanita has noted for the historical question, the substitutes that analysts tend to use, such as "homoerotically inclined," are no more true to their historical context than "lesbian" or "queer"; people in the early nineteenth century did not refer to their sex lives as "alternative." Furthermore, we might try to use excavated indigenous terms such as dogana or samlaingik, but we do so without knowledge of the habitus in which they were deployed—a conflation of knowledge of vocabulary with knowledge of its usage. This is not to question the political and philosophical importance of these questions about terminology, many of which have been key in feminist scholarship as well (see Riley 1988), but to point out that our turns to the past can be just as problematic as uninterrogated presentism.

The second question is critical for writing about rural and semi-urban Indian women who have relationships with other women but speak only vernacular languages. First, it is misguided to assume from the start, as many people do, that such women cannot think of themselves as lesbian—this is only elitism dressed up as class sensitivity, and the examples in chapter 1 show that such a supposition is also just simply wrong. The analytical liberties I take in using "lesbian" doubles as a kind of solidarity.[21] For example, when I refer to two women in rural Kerala who jointly committed suicide the night before one of them was to marry, but who did not leave a note declaring that they were lesbians, I refer to them as lesbians and their suicide as a lesbian suicide. The term "lesbian," then, is one of writerly convenience but also of potentiality—instead of thinking of "lesbian" as a fixed thing that people are or are not, I see it as a practice of enunciation for a set of loosely recognizable behaviors and longings.

My use of "queer" in this book is also more than a term of convenience, one that doubles as an analytic as well as an assertion of solidarity. The umbrella term that activists used to refer to lesbians, gays, hijras, kothis, and transsexuals when I began fieldwork was "sexuality minorities." As I discuss in chapter 2, many activists began rejecting this phrase as too centered on sexual identity and not signaling their intersectional critique of all forms of limitation not limited to sex. "Queer," a term that has come to India largely through the migratory movements of young, cosmopolitan scholar-activists (just like "lesbian," "gay," and their activism more generally) then gained currency as a widely accommodating, radical political frame (Narrain and Bhan 2005, 3–4).

What has gained currency among activists does important analytic work for me, too. I understand "queer," with David Halperin, as "by definition whatever is at odds with the normal, the legitimate, the dominant . . . it describes a horizon of possibility whose precise extent and heterogenous scope cannot in principle be delimited in advance" (1995, 62).[22] Put this way, queer *is* the ethical aspiration of activism. This resonates with Muñoz's (2009, 11) suggestion that queerness exists only in the horizon and, referencing Badiou, as "the thing-that-is-not-yet-imagined" (21). This book is a mapping of queer horizons. How does "the thing-that-is-not-yet-imagined" become? How does the not-yet-imagined become a thing? And what are those moments in which the queer can be, and infinitely becomes, queer?

In the Field

There is no one setting from which to write an ethnography of lesbian activism in India: queerness has a way of moving about. Gay lovers escape oppressive regimes, lesbians run away from small towns, women leave their villages to become men, hijras move to the city, and nonresident Indians come looking for their roots, perhaps founding an NGO while they are at it. But this is not just an ethnography of the movement of people and things; it is also an ethnography of how queer people come to be, how they imagine, transform, and are transformed.[23] These are questions that require both physical location and conceptual mobility. My methodology was thus multisited. I accompanied activists as they traversed the network of their associations across India and also conducted short periods of research on my own in Bangalore, Bombay, and Pune. My place of everyday engagement, though, was Delhi.

Delhi sits like a third eye in India's north. It is a city of migrants and, in that sense, a city of hope. Laborers from neighboring states as well as from Nepal and Bangladesh come to work in construction, or in the informal service sector for the steadily expanding middle class. Young women and men come to study; others come to make it big in info-tech or manufacturing; politicians come to govern as they do; and gays and lesbians come for community, love, and work as well as for distance from those who don't understand.

In part because it is a city of hope, Delhi is also a city of frustration and misery. Delhi's population of approximately seventeen million ranks the city as the eighth largest in the world. Its location on the western bank of the stinking Yamuna River does not nourish its poorest millions. Electricity is also woefully scarce, even for the middle classes. Slum dwellers make up well over 15 percent of the population but are increasingly invisible as slums are demolished and pushed into the literal margins of the metropolis, leaving a city that is already exceptionally class-segregated by Indian standards even more so. Despite its absences in welfare, the state in Delhi is everywhere muscularly present, with government buildings dotting wide, beautiful roads in the center of the city, VIP caravans disrupting already impossible traffic, and roadblocks and baton-wielding officers in khaki a ubiquitous sight.

It is both the omnipresence and the absence of the state that has made Delhi a central site for Indian queer activism. Not only are national decisions made here, but the city's many sites of state power make for symbolically rich places of protest. India's first gay public demonstration, which I referenced in the opening of this book, was held in front of Delhi's police headquarters (see figure 3). India's first international queer demonstration also occurred in Delhi in 1992, when two hundred delegates walked out of the International AIDS Conference to protest the Indian government's stance against homosexuality. The first effort to decriminalize same-sex sex in India came in 1994, with a petition filed in the Delhi High Court; that same court was the first in India to decriminalize same-sex sex, in 2009. The presence of well-known women's groups in Delhi—created to respond to the absences and excesses of the state—has also been critical for the rise of lesbian politics in the country. Finally, it is Delhi's oddly pitched siren call to stars, migrants, intellectuals, and foreign travelers that has made it the center of Indian lesbian politics. India's first lesbian organization was started in Delhi by a globe-trotting scholar-activist and staffed by a white English lesbian, who then founded India's first lesbian help line with the aid of a woman who had migrated to Delhi from a small North Indian town. And India's spectacular "lesbian emergence" through the *Fire* affair was made possible through a nexus of state violence, transnational migrations, and the power of the glitterati (CALERI 1999a).

I lived and conducted fieldwork in this remarkable city between December 2001 and December 2003. My work began smoothly through a snowballing of acquaintances. As it happened, one of my graduate school professors in Ann Arbor had an Indian hairstylist, who had a lesbian sister in San Francisco, who was friends with a lesbian activist in Delhi. I'm quite sure that nearly everyone I worked with in India is linked to that first Delhi contact in 1999. Perhaps excepting the mediation of the Ann Arbor hairstylist, my circle of lesbian and gay acquaintances grew by simply following the regular movements of urban Indian queer life: I made friends and accompanied them to meetings, protests, friends' homes, support group meetings, or gay nights at a local club. I could soon move comfortably through this world on my own.

There were only two groups in Delhi—Sangini and PRISM—that I knew to be actively engaged with lesbian issues when I arrived, and so it was with them that I worked. The general rhythm of my data-collecting life was like this. All Saturdays of my first year were devoted to Sangini. I attended their

3. India's first known gay protest in 1992 outside of Delhi's police headquarters. The placard in the foreground reads: "Let homosexual people (*samlaingik log*) live with fulfillment (*chain se*)." Photograph by K. K. Laskar, courtesy of the Times Group.

three-hour weekly support group meetings in the afternoons, occasionally preceded by lunch at the home of Sangini's directors and followed by socializing there. For eight months between 2002 and 2003, I also volunteered weekly on Sangini's lesbian help line. Thursdays and Fridays were devoted to PRISM. I attended almost all of their Thursday night meetings and spent Fridays writing up meeting minutes and performing whatever other tasks I was assigned or had volunteered for the night before. I spent around five evenings per week with activist friends, just talking, having drinks, playing cards, or watching movies. The time that remained was my own: I spent all of my mornings writing field notes from the day before and most afternoons conducting interviews and doing archival work.

My primary method was participant observation. By participating in all those things that activists do—attending meetings, joining in protests, and spending hours at a computer jointly composing e-mail messages, press releases, funding proposals, and mission statements—I was almost always around and deeply engaged. By engaging in this "dailyness of life," as Virginia Woolf put it, I was able to absorb the minutiae of everyday life and the larger recurring themes and "critical nodes" (Mazzarella 2003, 32) of Indian queer activism. Among the nodes that I quickly recognized, for example, were that "leaving home" is a more salient rubric for Indian lesbians than "coming out"; that all activists debate means and ends and compromise; that queer activism is centrally about ethics. These recurring discursive themes shape the ideas that I present in this book, but it is the minutiae—of love, temperament, and daily habits—that gave me the familiarity with people to see and interpret those themes in the first place. This daily intimacy was thus also, unexpectedly, a method: a method for understanding the affect of politics (Gould 2009, 30).

I never used a voice recorder to record people in casual conversations or in regular meetings, whether support group or strategic. Most people, including myself, were either too hammy or too shy to remain casual when being recorded. And not only did the idea of recording seem intrusive in a support group, but a recent scandal with a researcher who had made secret recordings had everyone rightly suspicious of the devices. Instead, I kept a small notebook in my back pocket at all times, writing copiously in it everywhere I went. The notebook held the fragments and scraps from which I would construct my field notes the following morning. And it was through the writing and reading of my field notes that the critical nodes and contradictions emerged, which I then used to design semistructured interviews.

I conducted interviews with activists, support group members, and public figures in Delhi, Bombay, Pune, and Bangalore. With the people in Delhi with whom I spent months, I had the luxury of first recording oral life histories. These were rich with stories about families, realizing queerness, or first loves. My semistructured interviews were personalized for each interviewee and usually focused on organizational histories and involvement, forms of activism, dynamics between and within groups, and thoughts on gay and lesbian politics and support spaces. My interviews and recording of life histories usually took place in my interlocutors' workplaces, in my home or theirs, or in a café or restaurant, as they suggested.

While oral histories and interviews were certainly productive and strengthened my relationships with people—many of the conversations lasted for hours on end, one even from dinnertime to dawn—the bulk of my material and the spirit of this book emerge from the everyday, unscheduled interactions that define the ethnographic endeavor. It was in the simple and extraordinary practices of living life together—whether just watching television while piled in a bed, singing old love songs on a moonlit terrace, or riding through the empty streets of the city late on a summer night, shouting our conversations over the wind—that I often found myself most challenged, moved, or taught. My ability to experience such moments, and my inability to experience certain others, is about who I am, who they are, and the connections we forge between us.

To my surprise, neither did my Indian origin advantage me nor did my American birth seem to disadvantage me in the field. Queerness and gender were shown to matter infinitely more than nationality or social race in matters of access and trust. I was out in the field as a queer woman—the semiotics were such that this was never in any doubt. This minimum level of commonality was critical for the quality of relationships I could forge. While lesbians and gay men sometimes queried the motivations for and necessity of my research, they never doubted my solidarity and sympathy. The importance of identity in the queer landscape seemed to prequalify me for trust and often brought me close to people before I even had the chance to try.

That closeness, however, was a complicated thing. For an ethnographer of activism, the space between participant and observer is a particularly perilous place—the expectations for participation are high, as are the research consequences of not meeting them (see Merry 2005). For example, I once had to refuse to sign a protest letter; my efforts to remain in the good graces of the group being protested branded me a sellout in the eyes of some other groups. (Thankfully, this was largely temporary.) In PRISM, especially, I was expected because of my intimacy with people to give advice in times of uncertainty. When asked what I thought PRISM should do—refuse funding, for example, or boycott a meeting—I would not say, feeling that to give my opinion would be too close to creating my own information.[24] I did, however, participate energetically in every debate, knowing that I was subtly influencing discourse and decisions. I knew of no better way to both observe and participate, or to honor my friendships and our commonality.

Finally, on the subject of friendship. I refer to most of the activists in this book as "friend," simply because they were. My similitude with people based on shared sexual subjectivity, country, languages, and conviction meant that I had little desire, or ability, to compartmentalize my life into research and leisure. Many of these people were my whole life for two years. Thus, queer friendship and love are important and constitutive themes in this book about activism. It is through my experiences of friendship and intimacy that I came to see things about queer activism that I am certain I would not have seen had I only attended meetings and conducted interviews. The emergent structures of feeling in which new ways of living seem possible, and the radical ethical aspiration of activism to problematize, invent, and creatively practice those new possibilities, are entirely bound up in the security and hope we find in one another. An ethnography about queer activism is necessarily an ethnography about friendship, and its troubles.

On Troubles

I write in this book not only about my friends, but about people whose work I believe in. As a queer woman, these are also the people who have made my own life fuller, easier, and better. To write critically in such a context has been a source of trouble—for my conscience and, occasionally, my relationships.[25] One activist—perhaps my closest friend in the field, though even that doesn't seem to convey how deeply I feel about her—came to visit me in Ann Arbor just as I was finishing the dissertation that would become this book. She was curious, so I gave her the hundreds of pages that I had completed. To my surprise, she read it constantly and everywhere—as we drank martinis at Café Felix, as we sat on my front porch, as we lay in the grass at the Arboretum. I tried to be patient as she alternately grumbled under her breath, snorted with laughter, shot me annoyed or quizzical glances, and softened with emotion. The conversations that followed were hard and intense. She wondered, for example, why I hadn't shared more of my critiques with her at the time; I explained that so much of them had emerged only in the process of writing and with the seeming clarity of distance. But she begrudged me nothing and demanded no changes; the alterations I made after our conversations were mine alone, as I learned from her and others how to write about the people who have taught me what I know. The following summer I distributed my work to activists across India, some of whom organized workshops and reading groups full of enthusiastic exchange. These, too, constituted an education for me but also a confirmation: that critique is indeed a motor of ethical social action and of solidarity itself.

Although I have strived to be careful and accurate, and to honor my relationships of care and politics through a practice of critical solidarity (Chari and Donner 2010), my perspective, like anyone's, remains utterly partial. As I say again later on, I spent more time, and shared more deeply with some than with others. Often this was rooted in politics—I was drawn, for example, toward groups with strong feminist connections and, sometimes rather conflictingly, with feminists who sought radical, explicit queer transformations. An ethnographer with different priorities, passions, and education who sat through the same meetings I did at the same period in history would surely have tracked different debates and offered other conclusions.[26] But it is precisely the incompleteness—or, as Donna Haraway puts it, the "imperfection"—born of passionate partiality that allows us to "stitch" ourselves to another in relationships of intimacy and accountability (1988). As part of my queer and feminist methodology, I hope I have used this incompleteness as a source of reflection, a provocation to trouble our certainties and, thereby, reconfirm what we share.

A Note on Matters of Scope

The primary focus of this book is lesbian activism. But because of the dynamics of queer activism generally, and particularly in India, the book's narrative also centrally involves the gay men that lesbians are variably in alliance and competition with and, to a lesser extent, hijras and kothis. It is due to my focus on lesbian activism—not simply lesbian community or identity—that my analysis expands to include a range of queer people. But it is because of this same focus that my analysis is largely limited to lesbians who are middle-class, bi- or trilingual English speakers, and well educated. Although lesbians exist across the class spectrum, their activism is largely limited to people with means, and I explain the sociology and semiotics of this in chapter 1. My research lacks sustained attention to lesbianism in rural areas and urban slums in part because these sites have been marginalized from the lesbian politics I analyze here.[27] I also take responsibility for the limitations of my own scope.

My scope, already partial, was also shaped by place, as the structures and priorities of queer activism in India vary distinctly by city. If I had been based in Bombay, for example, I would have worked more with kothis. Queer alliances in Bombay are formed largely in relation to one personality, that of Ashok Row Kavi, the "father" of India's gay movement. Row Kavi has shown disdain for lesbians, believes kothis are false constructions, and has been repeatedly linked to pro-Hindu, anti-Muslim communal positions (L. Cohen 2005; see also chapter 5); thus lesbians, kothis, and anticommunal feminists in Bombay such as Awaaz-i-Niswan are unlikely but committed allies. If I had been based in Bangalore, I would have had fewer lesbians to work with and done much more research with hijras, gay men, and bisexuals. Queer organizing in Bangalore, as in Bombay, was initially built around one person: here, an activist named Manohar who founded his behemoth organization, Sangama, on a vision of sexual fluidity. A bisexual, he married a hijra employee, and their very queer, unlikely union symbolizes Sangama's—and Bangalore's—queer political ethos. Delhi, in part because of its sprawling and segregated geography, is not as defined by a cult of personality (but see chapter 1 for the story of one giant's influence). Delhi's queer organizations also tend to have shorter lives than their counterparts elsewhere, due perhaps to Delhi's transient population. The stories of these shifting but formative relationships animate this book's narrative about the history, ethics, and politics of lesbian activism in contemporary India.

A Map of the Book

The animating questions of this book are about the dynamics of struggle, so I have tried to write a book that is also dynamic. This book traces activism from its affective emergence through to its assumed resolution in the achievement of legal rights, reaching back for informative histories and flashing forward for glimpses of how certain struggles will work out. Each chapter is based on making sense of one political imperative—for example, community, identity, alliance, and visibility—and its relationship to the ethical work of queer activism. The order in which I present these imperatives itself contains an argument: that the value of activist engagement today replicates market value, in which worth is determined by an actor's ability to penetrate farther and larger realms of influence. I thus move from lesbian women's creation of local communities to the formation of institutions, the forging of alliances between lesbian and more established movements, the imperative of public visibility, and battle with the state. But this is not a scalar analysis. Part of what I demonstrate are the mutual imbrications of local and transnational, community and state, as they operate in activism (see Das Gupta 2006, 17–18). One chapter, ostensibly about the making of local community, is as much about transnationalism; another, about engagement with the state, is also about how affect and intimacies trouble legal activism.

I begin in chapter 1 with the interpellation of sexual subjects into community. Early in my fieldwork, I was granted access to hundreds of letters that same-sex desiring women wrote to one another in the early and mid-1990s. Through analysis of these letters, I trace the production of new hopes sparked by the nascent possibility of lesbian identification in India. While these women, linked only by a networking list, were constructing an imagined pan- and transnational Indian lesbian community, groups of lesbian women began locally trying to transform those imagined relations into "real," face-to-face communities. This chapter theorizes the dynamic between the hopes of possibility that were incited by the unexpected circulation of "lesbian" and the norms that shortly began to emerge around what "lesbian" could be.

Where chapter 2 begins, face-to-face lesbian communities in India were viable enough for competing philosophies of proper lesbian community to start emerging. Among the central contestations was whether new organizations should practice a Western lesbian identity politics or provide a supposedly more authentic framework for Indian same-sex desire. The striving for authentication, I show, was partly produced by foreign funders who encourage a diversity of fundable niches across the world. The primary site of analysis in chapter 2 is the Sangini support group and the life stories of two women who would become central to that organization. I argue that as limits to practice and desire are enforced through new forms of political belonging, life narratives present ideas of newfound freedom through those same limits as a way to negotiate subjection.

In chapter 3, I turn to alliance building. My theoretical focus is on the confrontation of queer ethics with a women's movement discourse of Third World women's virtue (Mindry 2001). I end this chapter on the fraught and crucial relationship of lesbians and feminists with the story of a public split in 2002 between a large women's NGO in Pune and its five lesbian employees. Through this story, I consider the affective consequences of the awkward confluences of NGO-ization and activism as ethics. Lesbian activism's dependence, both materially and symbolically, on the women's movement—which is now heavily comprised of NGOs—renders the politics of NGO-ization one of the most critical factors in the politics of queer activism in India today.

In chapter 4, I study lesbian women's conflicted alliances with public intellectuals and the liberal left more generally, in the context of the *Fire* protests. Close analysis of that critical event enables me to address a host of questions about publics, affect, and national discourse: What were the strategies and semiotic processes through which one counterpublic (the right-wing Shiv Sena) interpellated another (Indian lesbians), and to what effect? How did the spectacular context of that interpellation, which was violent and staged as a contest over national belonging, shape emergent lesbian discourse then and for years to come? And what role did the unique dynamics of the Indian public play in the claims and practices of newly public lesbian activists?

Chapter 5 focuses on two major goals of activism, queer and otherwise: the attainment of legal rights and the achievement of justice. I demonstrate how those goals are often at odds with each other as well as with the ethics of critique, invention, and creative relationality. The chapter centers on the judicial battle to decriminalize sodomy, set in motion most recently with the filing in 2001 of a public interest litigation by the Naz Foundation (India) Trust (hereafter, Naz or Naz Foundation) an HIV/AIDS NGO. That petition was successful, and the Delhi High Court decriminalized consensual same-sex sex in July 2009. This chapter is an ethnography of the hopes and conflicts among queer activists that followed the Naz filing and leading up to the historic decision. I focus particularly on battles about community authority; the place of law in social change; and the relationships among feminists, lesbians, and gay men. I also turn in this chapter to a coeval, but lesser-known legal battle among queer activists in India, this one a legislative effort to make sexual assault in India a gender-neutral crime. Most queer activists strongly opposed this effort, claiming that it would render gay people newly vulnerable to the law as perpetrators of assault rather than victims. Reading these two debates alongside each other demonstrates the tensions between law and justice, ethics and norms.

All of these chapters work together to analyze one primary kind of play—that of the ethical ideas and affective senses that animate queer activism in India with those norms and institutions in the postcolonial nation-state that necessitate, are necessitated by, and variously subsume a radical ethics of denormalization. Moments of fraught limitation do make up much of this narrative. But the spirit of this book is derived from those many moments of radical possibility, those affective moments in which we do not and cannot know in advance the limits of what might be.

chapter 1

RENDERING REAL THE IMAGINED

In the summer of 1999, a South Delhi disco called Soul Kitchen opened its doors to gays and lesbians of the city. This first ever "gay night" was, for queer people in Delhi, one of the most hotly anticipated nights in memory. As for me, then a novice fieldworker, the night held a pleasure even more distinct than that of participating in this historic public demonstration of gay abandon. It was on this night that I met the "mother" of Indian lesbian politics, Giti Thadani.

Thadani is the consummate cosmopolitan intellectual. She splits her time between Berlin and Delhi, is fluent in multiple languages, lectures across the world, and travels tirelessly in a search for "gynefocal" tradition and a Sapphic "symbolic continuum" (Thadani 1996, 9). Her presence at the disco that night surprised me. Thadani is notorious for her uncompromising disposition and evident bitterness, following years of isolation and struggle as India's first out lesbian woman. Because of her itinerant and purposely elusive ways, I was concerned that I would not soon, if ever, have the opportunity to meet her.

So when—through the ecstatic, bouncing bodies and the deafening thump of an American techno-pop hit—a friend pointed Thadani out to me, I couldn't help but look at her in awe. She sat alone and undisturbed in one of the booths that lined the side of the dance floor, the roving lights rhythmically half-illuminating her placid face. As I watched her watch the rest of us, I imagined her calmly surveying her own creation. There, just across the floor from her, were the directors of India's first lesbian help line and support group, Sangini, which had been organized as a distinct alternative to the lesbian collective that Thadani founded in 1991. To my right were members of PRISM, a group born, in turn, out of ideological and personal differences with Sangini. Between these known and watchful activists were two young women in the middle of the dance floor, dancing together in a manner utterly unburdened by care and history.

The story that I tell in this chapter is of how these contemporary lesbian communities—fractures and all—were made possible through the advent of the concept of Indian lesbian community in the early 1990s. I will argue that affect was both the necessitating condition for the emergence of this radical new world and also precisely that which had to be circumscribed—or disciplined into politically appropriate feeling—in order for this emergent world to present itself, both to itself and to the social world, as a community. I set this narrative primarily in Delhi because of Thadani's centrality in enabling an explicitly lesbian community in India to form. However, any effort to be located in one geographical site is necessarily limited and partial. One of the phenomena I shed light on is how the imagination and practices of lesbian community in India have been produced through a series of complex transnational mediations—mediations that, crucially, are then actively obscured through the moral politics of authenticity required to imbue a nascent community with a sense of coherence and political necessity.[1]

I begin this chapter by examining the first of two questions that drive this book: that of how categories of queer sexual alterity in India have been made to emerge, are called into being, and are variously adopted. In this specific case, how did women in India begin to think of themselves as lesbian, and what about the politics and poetics of this term's circulation lended themselves to passionate personal attachment (Butler 1997) and rendered it a powerful node around which a new imagined community could be formed? To be clear, informal groups of same-sex desiring activist women from India were already meeting by the mid-1980s; in fact, they began forging international commons well before national ones. For example, in 1985 Indian delegates attended a workshop for lesbians at the Nairobi Women's Conference (Fernandez 2002, 181). Five years later, seven Indian women activists from Bombay and Delhi attended a conference of the Asian Lesbian Network in Bangkok, where they met one another for the first time (182). However, informal groupings of same-sex desiring women in India at this time were constrained in two crucial ways: they were comprised primarily of activists, and—for reasons I will discuss in greater detail below—mostly resisted Western signifiers such as "lesbian" in the name of cultural authenticity and political expediency.

Thadani's founding of a Delhi-based lesbian network called Sakhi in 1991 democratized the possibility of lesbian community by taking it be-yond local activist groups to a pan- and transnational network of women who could communicate with one another about their desires through the relative anonymity of letters. Significantly, almost all of the letter writers contacted Sakhi after seeing the word "lesbian" in the network's ads, and they rapidly came to identify themselves, and their nascent network, as ex-plicitly lesbian, thus beginning to formulate an imagined Indian lesbian community where nothing of the sort had existed before.[2] Thadani pro-vided me with 236 of these letters, dating from 1991 to 1997. Through this extraordinary archive, I explore how nonactivist women from a range of so-cioeconomic classes, from Jammu and Kashmir to Kerala, came to think of themselves as lesbian and thus, as part of a larger web of belonging.[3]

This archive itself, as well as my use of it, is also worth reflecting on in terms of writing histories of sexuality. Ann Cvetkovich describes an "ar-chive of feelings" as cultural texts that serve as repositories of emotion in their content, production, and reception (2003, 7). She is particularly inter-ested in lesbian and gay archives, which, she argues, "must preserve and protect not just knowledge but feeling," because the history of queer life uniquely demands documentation of intimacy, sexuality, and love (241–42). I find the notion of an archive of feelings useful insofar as what I am tracing through these letters is a structure of feeling that was not yet avail-able to objectification (see Cvetkovich 2003, 48). But where I, and my ar-chive, depart from Cvetkovich is in her assumption of emotion's ever-presence in queer history. Cvetkovich sees affect's centrality in gay and lesbian archival practices as a corrective to institutional and cultural neglect (241). However, the narrative I present here shows quite a contrary motiva-tion and effect: it was precisely because of the institutional neglect of les-bian politics, and a desire to render that politics respectable, that Sakhi worked to devalue and limit the expression of feeling. The dampening of affect need not render this archive any less an "archive of feeling," but it might instead help to productively delimit what such an archive is: not an archive of emotion itself, but an archive of a *history* of emotion in its uneasy relationship to the political. An archive of feeling is constituted by what it contains, what it does not, and, as Anjali Arondekar (2009) critically reminds us, by the historian of sexuality's own impassioned presuppositions about what we must find in order to make sense of our queer present and presences. Reading Cvetkovich and Arondekar together, I take this archive of letters to provide insights into the production and circumscription of affect as well as into the archival dynamics of absence and presence (see also Dave 2011).

A central tenet of this narrative is that stories of invention are always simultaneously stories of loss. It is precisely this play between the radical ethic of forging new possibilities and the political imperative of containing those possibilities that best defines the consequences and felt experience of emergent social worlds. Thus, linked to the question of how a range of women in India came to adopt the particular sexual subjectivity of lesbian, and to formulate a sense of a larger imagined community, is the question of what potentiality had to be foreclosed—or what affective possibilities had to be normatively qualified—in order to produce out of the term "lesbian" not just a sense of immanent possibility, but an identity and a way of being in the world. I examine the sets of expectations that accompanied the adoption of a lesbian subjectivity and how those normative expectations circulated through popular media, the writing and reading of autobiographical letters, and the local, face-to-face meetings among lesbian women that emerged out of this network.

The second driving question of this chapter, then, is how to understand the relationship between the possibilities that "lesbian" was imagined to offer and the norms for proper behavior that would steadily come to define it. What I present in this chapter is a tracing of activism from its structure of feeling (R. Williams 1977)—the yet-embryonic moment of ethical possibility—to its circumscription, which crucially then serves as the condition for new affective possibilities. This movement from the imagined to the "real" is the story of political communities everywhere. It is also the story of lesbian community in contemporary India.

The Single Women

As I describe in chapter 3, same-sex desiring feminists in India have historically had a difficult task: to forge an affective community of women based on the commonality of their desires while being careful not to imperil

Indian feminism with the Western, bourgeois taint of lesbianism. Such cultural caution has been seen as necessary given that feminism and organized women's movements have themselves been dismissed by Indian nationalists as Western imports that undermine national unity (Kumar 1993, 87–88). Thus, Indian women's groups have historically distanced themselves from lesbian politics (N. Menon 2005, 39) in order to defend a hard-won image of being in step with national concerns.

Among the solutions offered for the dilemma between the centrality of lesbianism and the felt need to cloak it was the advent of the phrase "single women" (*ekal aurat*) by a group of Delhi-based activists associated with a women's NGO called Jagori.[4] The category of "single women" was meant partly to provide a community framework for women-loving women, but through a language that refused the Western politics of lesbian identity out of deference to non-English-speaking women in urban slums (*bastis*) and villages (Bacchetta 2002, 960). Several women in Delhi, most of them lesbian, met informally in one another's homes from 1987 to 1993 under the auspices of "single women's nights."[5]

In addition to this informal collective of "single women" in Delhi, another circle of same-sex desiring women known as the Delhi Group was founded in 1989 (Fernandez 2002, 182). All of them were feminist activists, and all had a commitment to understanding the macropolitical dimensions of compulsory heterosexuality (Bacchetta 2002, 959). Where the members diverged from one another was on the question of the macropolitics and semantics of lesbian sexuality in particular. Urban Indian feminists at this time were, as I have suggested, under pressure to prove their indigenous mettle—to show that their concerns were not Western and bourgeois, but had local relevance to a powerful construct known as the Indian grass roots (see Mindry 2001). Thus, groups like the Delhi Group collectively eschewed the signifier "lesbian" and instead spoke simply as "single women" or "women who love women." It is valid to ask how an English phrase such as "women who love women" could be any more palatable to poor, grass-roots Indian women than the term "lesbian." Indeed, this awkward commitment to euphemism tells us much more about the outward projection of Indian feminism's anxieties at the dawn of neoliberalism than it does about the linguistic and emotional capacities of the real Indian woman.

Lesbian Communication Is Needed

The Delhi Group's cautious linguistic occlusion of lesbian possibility was what Thadani and three others finally remonstrated with, breaking with the group to found India's first explicitly lesbian organization, Sakhi, in 1991 (Bacchetta 2002, 959–60). Thadani's commitment to advancing an Indian lesbian identity had begun in earnest in the early 1980s, when she embarked on an independently funded project to reveal India's rich *jami* (homo-sexual, or twin) traditions—traditions that, Thadani (1996) argues to the acute discomfort of today's activists, were violently obscured through Islamic and Victorian morality. (It is worth noting that academics and activists are not only uncomfortable with the possible anti-Muslim slant of her thesis; some also find her work historically inaccurate [see Bacchetta 2002, 965].) Thadani's methods of excavation included reinterpreting the Rig Veda (she reads and writes Sanksrit) to show the acceptance of erotic bonds between women and photographing lesbian erotic images in ancient temple carvings (showing, for example, how breasts were shaved down in modern times to transform same-sex couplings into hetero-sexual ones). In *Sakhiyani: Lesbian Desire in Ancient and Modern India* (1996), Thadani argues that characterizing these cosmogenies and images as "lesbian" is part of a crucial strategy to counter invisibility and isolation.

Accordingly, it was Thadani's hunch that Indian women from a range of social classes, educational backgrounds, religions, and marital statuses would find hope, solace, and freedoms in the offering of a lesbian identification. The four former members of the Delhi Group had Thadani's flat from which to operate, but few other resources. By way of a beginning, they printed some letterhead, opened a post office box, and announced their founding in a number of diasporic South Asian gay publications, as well as in India's own gay magazine, *Bombay Dost* (Bombay friend).[6]

Bombay Dost was founded by Ashok Row Kavi, Thadani's male counterpart in ingenuity, courage, and perceived madness, in 1990.[7] *Dost* made no claims to being a representative publication; it was a magazine founded by India's first publicly self-identified gay man, produced by a team of men, and read increasingly widely by a population of the same.[8] The subject matter of the magazine was also almost exclusively male-centered, aiming to promote a gay male sensibility and community. The magazine published articles about safer sex between men, battling body odor, and sustaining gay relationships in the face of marriage pressure. It had a ribald "Men Seeking Men" section, but no such page devoted to women.

Twenty-six-year-old Miss Kumar from a large city in Tamil Nadu described this void in a 1994 letter to Sakhi: "*Bombay Dost* is mainly for homosexual men and not lesbians. I need a magazine for *Lesbians. Lesbian communication* is needed."[9] And a Ms. Kapur from Bombay wrote to Sakhi in 1993: "Since I have not found any ad from Ladies seeking Lady Friends [in *Bombay Dost*], I am not able to put an ad on it."[10] Instead, she wrote to the South Asian Lesbian and Gay Association (SALGA) in New York, which, in turn, wrote back to her with Sakhi's Delhi address. Such were the convoluted, intercontinental maneuverings required for many a nonactivist lady seeking a lady friend in the early 1990s. (These maneuverings moved in all directions. As Monisha Das Gupta [2006, 159–60] recounts, SALGA was founded after an anonymous South Asian American saw an issue of a diasporic queer magazine, *Trikone*, published by a group with the same name; went to San Francisco; and met with a member of Trikone, who put him in touch with members of an unnamed gay group in Delhi. In 1990, they introduced the man to Thadani, who inspired him to start SALGA in New York.)

By the time Sakhi began advertising in *Bombay Dost*, it was available in bookstores and some newsstands in India's major cities and, judging from the addresses of its correspondents, had achieved an active readership in smaller cities as well. Judging, too, from the number of women who referred to *Bombay Dost* in their letters to Sakhi, same-sex desiring women in large cities and small towns were also turning to the magazine—seeing in the "gay" that boldly graced the publication some relationship to their own desires and, thus, the possibility of connection with other women. The brave actions that followed these moments of recognition—whether purchasing a gay-oriented magazine published at home or abroad, confessing same-sex desires to one's husband,[11] or writing to a lesbian resource center in hopes of meeting others like oneself—belied the convenient justification that so many gay men gave for the male-centrism of their politics: that lesbian women in India were too fearful and too hidden for political engagement.

The sexed disparity in queer organizing in India was and remains a large one. As I discuss in chapter 5, much of that disparity is attributable to the economics of HIV/AIDS. Men who have sex with men (hereafter, MSM) have been construed within a global discourse of risk and management as an "at-risk population," moving gay sex out of the realm of moral disagreement and toward the cold facts of immunology and risk management. Furthermore, the risk of gay sex is understood to travel to wives and children, especially in countries like India or Indonesia, where a vast majority of MSM are married. The attachment of gay sex to pandemic risk, matched with the concurrent liberalization of India's economy in the early 1990s, has made it possible for gay men to tap into a steady stream of funds from international agencies to form NGOs and create community spaces in order to mitigate risk (K. Misra 2003 and 2006). Lesbian women, understood globally as a practically no-risk demographic, have not had the profitable tragedy of HIV/AIDS on which to base claims of legitimacy.[12] Still, the disparity in the fortunes of lesbian and gay organizing in India cannot be reduced to the material question of who has more access to capital; there is also a more subtle logic at play. Under the guise of a liberal cultural and gendered sensitivity, it is often taken for granted that "the average Indian woman" does not have the wherewithal to even imagine herself outside her assigned roles, and certainly not to act in pursuit of such radical imaginings. This is a convenient fiction to justify exclusion that has been perpetuated by gay male activists, women's movement activists, and even cosmopolitan lesbian activists in India.

Thadani rejected the belief that Indian women would not or could not identify as lesbian. Her project, similar to Row Kavi's for gay men (L. Cohen 2005), was to provide Indian women with the possibility of lesbian identification and, thereby, direct access to a world of belonging. Thadani's aspiration was borne out in what was first a tentative trickle, and by mid-1994, a surge, of letters winding their hopeful paths into Sakhi's South Delhi mailbox (see figure 4). Sakhi's practice was to reply to each letter and, if the respondent believed the writer was a woman, to enclose a "networking list" consisting of mailing addresses that previous writers had agreed to share. Sakhi, after its initial rupture from the Delhi Group, was often just Thadani, with the fleeting assistance of lesbian women who stayed at Sakhi's guesthouse. A white Englishwoman by the name of Cath provided Sakhi with stability beginning in 1993. Cath had come to Delhi as a volunteer with Jagori, the same NGO that had brought the phrase *single women* into wide usage. Anxious to move beyond innuendo, Cath approached Thadani for work and was taken on to answer the eager, sometimes desperate, voices writing to Sakhi.[13]

4. Anonymous letter to Sakhi, beginning "Dear Sakhi, I feel to be different than others. I am told that you are our leader." Photograph by the author.

Among the early desperate voices was that of Anuja, who wrote from Allahabad in 1991: "We are very few lesbians [in Allahabad], and also we are not sure of each other, except a few. Please let me have some addresses of lesbian sisters. Well I am 35 years of age. I want to be an active lesbian member of your organization."[14] Ms. Nandita from Calcutta requested "names and addresses of other friends who are your members and who are also interested in the world of lesbianism/bi-sexualism." She closed her letter with "Yours-in-L/Bi."[15] And Ms. Bhan wrote in 1992: "I am a 21 year old lesbian of Jammu. I do not have any other companion except one here. I hope you will help me. . . . You are my only hope."[16] Yogini, a twenty-nine-year-old woman from Thane, Maharashtra, wrote to Sakhi in 1996: "Are most of the younger lesbians employed? In places where a lot of lesbians share apartments, do they remain steady to their loves, or do they change partners often? I am sorry that in my letter there are only questions. It is such a relief to write so openly to you."[17]

Anuja, Ms. Nandita, Ms. Bhan, and Yogini all underscore an important point: Indian women outside of elite, urban activist networks could and did consider themselves to *be* lesbian. Their concern was not with the genealogy of the identifier, or its nefarious links to global capitalism. Such concerns were, instead, more the province of urban-based feminist activists, who needed to manage the perceived risks of radical language within the limitations of their political field. The concern that the letter writers evince, rather, is with the possibility of belonging, and of reaching out beyond the confines of their loneliness. The recognition of themselves within the language that Sakhi offered was both catharsis and an impetus for action that they had not previously imagined possible. Thus, while it is important and necessary to critique the production of global hegemonies (how it comes to be, for example, that the proper way to be lesbian is to call one's self "lesbian"), it is just as crucial in the ethnographic practice of critical solidarity to pay attention to how, why, and to what effect people become passionately attached to the opportunities therein.

Mass Mediation

But how did these women—many married with children, living as "housewives," without female lovers, and with, at best, only a rudimentary and secondary engagement with English—come to know of the word "lesbian" so that they could become passionately attached to it at all? How and when did the term "lesbian" emerge in India as a possible category of self-definition? Many of those who wrote to Sakhi in the first half of the 1990s were actively seeking lesbian, gay, or otherwise queer media, suggesting that they already had a conception of themselves as lesbian or gay. What interests me here are the moments of such recognition—what were the means through which women came across the circulating term of "lesbian"; measured their experiences, desires, and pleasures against it; and recognized therein a cathartic moment, or a sense of being hailed?

Just as Tom Boellstorff (2005b) has described is the case in Indonesia, the primary means through which "lesbian" and "gay" have become widely accessible as terms for self-definition in India is through mass—and primarily print—media. The words "gay" and "homosexual" (as linked to Indians, living in India) began circulating in print media only in the mid-1980s. But the article that is most often anecdotally cited as marking a pivotal moment for an emergent "gay" subjectivity in India is Ashok Row Kavi's "coming out" interview, published in *Savvy* magazine in February 1986 (cited in Fernandez 2002, 195). This interview, accompanied by a photograph of Row Kavi, marked the first time that an Indian man publicly declared himself to be gay. In the stories that gay men have told me about coming out to themselves during this period, the sight of this interview is one of the most consistently cited moments of cathartic recognition, along with first contact with *Bombay Dost*.

The term "lesbian" was later to arrive than "gay" on the mass mediascape, but when it did first arrive in 1987, sensational accounts of lesbian marriages, suicides, and sex changes rapidly overtook the emerging fascination with male homosexuality. The first stories about lesbianism dealt with the marriage of two policewomen, Urmila Srivastava and Leela Namdeo, in Madhya Pradesh.[18] Urmila and Leela's fellow officers leaked word of their private ceremony, leading to the women being fired from their jobs and subjected to frenzied media attention. Leela—perpetually described as "sari-clad" in newspaper reports—was a widowed mother of three; Urmila —always "sporting" men's clothes—was promised at the age of three to a husband who turned out to be a drunk and a wastrel. Other constables noted that they "ate off the same *thali* [plate]" and "slept in the same bed," and were seen sobbing and consoling each other on occasion.[19] The tragedy of the women's personal lives was an oft-cited fact (see John and Nair 1998, 33–34). Well over a dozen articles appeared in national English-language periodicals in the weeks and months following the women's marriage. Most were vague in their calls to attention: "Bride Grooms Bride" read a headline in Savvy; "The Love That Dare Not Speak Its Name," announced *Sunday* magazine (Padmanabhan 1988); "Unbecoming Conduct," mockchastised the *Indian Post*.[20]

It is not surprising that lesbian women did not find in such pieces the "Aha!" moment (Boellstorff 2005b, 69) that so many gay men and women anecdotally report finding in early articles about gay men. Following sensational reports of this lesbian marriage between lonely, deserted cops came other articles in a similar vein. The *Sunday Mail* wrote in 1990 about "The Two That Got Away"—two young women from Bombay who absconded to Australia so that one of them could undergo a sex change operation, enabling them to live together as husband and wife. And in the same year the *Independent* published a tale from Gujarat fit for a Bollywood melodrama.[21] A young woman, Tarulata, underwent a sex change, becoming Tarun. As Tarun, he wed his lover two years later—a young woman named Lila. Lila's father, upon learning of Tarun's "true" identity as Tarulata, filed charges against Tarun and sought to have the marriage annulled. The father claimed that the marriage was illegitimate under the Hindu Marriage Act because Lila would never be able to bear children.[22]

Unlike the coverage of Row Kavi's courageous and unapologetic proclamation, these stories about lesbian women did not invite or inspire, but rather repelled. None of the women featured in these articles called themselves "lesbian." Leela and Urmila, for instance, angrily rejected the term in an interview, arguing that they had never heard of such a thing before (Saisuresh 1988). And these stories, which focused on "public opinion" and "expert" analysis of these same-sex desiring women, squarely associated the phenomenon of lesbianism with familial and social rejection (rather than noble resistance), with sorrow (rather than the "gay abandon" of male homosexuals),[23] and with isolation and abject loneliness (rather than the community of *dosti* [friendship] formed by India's gay men). The women who eventually began writing to Sakhi were, as their letters tell it, already well aware that their loves were socially impossible, or that they themselves were haunted by the demon of loneliness. Reading about the demonization of others like them was hardly cause for an "I have found it!" moment. This much they had already found.

The mass media stories that enabled women to consider themselves called, and called *to* some form of action, were those that, like the emerging stories about gay men, provided a sense of guidance and a vision of community. By 1988, the English media in India had begun covering stories about Indian gay life and activism in the diaspora. The *Illustrated Weekly of India* wrote in 1988 about the diasporic lesbian activist, Urvashi Vaid, and her popularity in the United States as well as about the advent of South Asian gay groups like Trikone in San Francisco, Khush in Toronto, and Shakti in London, all of which published newsletters that were offered free of charge to Indians residing in India (cited in Fernandez 2002, 196). Between 1991 and 1994, most of Sakhi's letter writers claimed to have learned of Sakhi from one of these newsletters or from *Bombay Dost*. It is important to keep in mind here that the form in which information about a lesbian world was initially circulating in India—in specialized magazines that required subscription, public purchase, or semipublic, furtive reading —would radically limit most women's access to this world, even if they did initially learn about these magazines through the more neutral medium of a widely read daily newspaper. It was thus the publication of an article aptly titled "Emerging from the Shadows"—and similar articles that it immediately preceded and followed—that would further democratize access to the inviting possibility of lesbian community.

"Emerging from the Shadows," by journalist Parvez Sharma, was a four-page article based on interviews with five of Sakhi's volunteers and

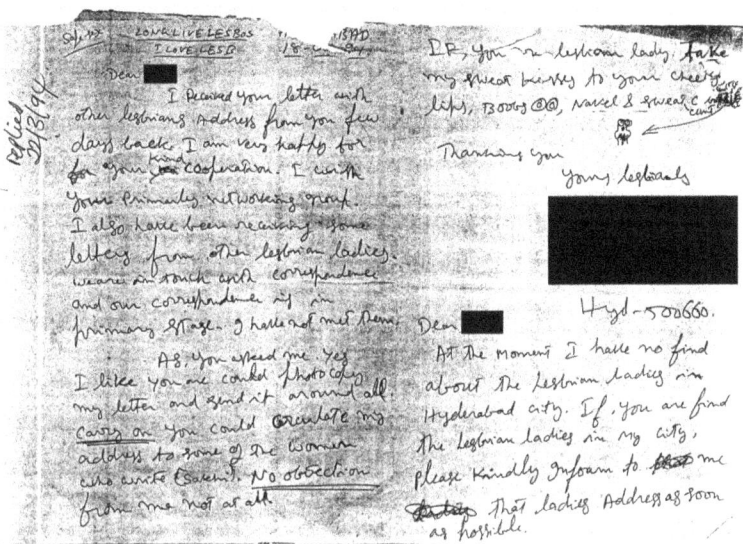

5. Longing in Hyderabad. The top left of the letter to Sakhi reads: "Safe Sex, Long Live Lesbos, I Love Lesb." The top right reads: "If you are lesbian lady, take my sweat [sic] kisses to your cheeks, lips, boobs, navel, & sweat [sic] cunt. Thanking you." Photograph by the author.

Thadani.[24] Significantly, a photograph of Thadani appeared in the article (the first time a lesbian followed Row Kavi's move). She stands on a terrace, hands on her hips, smiling shyly but proudly. She wears a T-shirt that she designed, bearing a lesbian temple image. In contrast to so many previous articles, Sharma remarks on the "infectious *joie-de-vivre* and indefatigable spirit" of the lesbians he meets through Sakhi. While Thadani philosophizes on the merits of nonpenetrative sex, the others discuss their lesbianism as a "political choice" and a source of happiness and strength.[25] One of the volunteers, Aparna, sends a message to lesbian readers: "My advice to young lesbians is not to crumble under pressure. . . . Believe in yourself— you are not a bad human being just because you have sex with a woman. Believe me, the rewards at the end have to be worth it."[26]

It appears that many women did believe Aparna and were enchanted by the idea of a lesbian *joie de vivre*, as the numbers of letters that came to Sakhi skyrocketed (see figure 5). In Sakhi's replies to letter writers, the volunteers apologized for monthlong delays, claiming that they were suddenly "swamped" and "overwhelmed." RS, in the north Indian city of Dehra Dun, was one of the aspiring new lesbians contributing to Sakhi's avalanche: "['Emerging from the Shadows'] revived my adolescent's passion for lesbianism. . . . I, being introvert and of secretive nature, unable to disclose this passion of mine even to my husband. I would like that you should also keep it absolutely secret. I am giving you the address of my friend. I can trust that she will not open my mail."[27] Ms. Sen of Calcutta also referred to the article, asking specifically to speak to Aparna by phone: "Since I am married to a respectable citizen of Calcutta, I need secrecy. Ms. Aparna can ring me up on any weekday evening. . . . I am 35 years old and have a daughter."[28]

The spike in number and intensity of the letters to Sakhi after the publication of "Emerging from the Shadows" spurred the group, now composed of Thadani and Cath with increasing assistance from a volunteer named Mita, to apply for funding in 1995. In its funding proposal to the Netherlands-based Mama Cash, Sakhi describes its many achievements to date, including opening a guesthouse in 1992 (which, as the proposal readily acknowledges, has been used primarily by foreign lesbian travelers); presenting a report on lesbian rights at the 1995 Beijing women's conference; and organizing a conference in New Delhi in 1994 called Alternative Sexualities, which attracted a number of high-profile foreign scholars.[29] The funding was granted, and this shift in Sakhi's fortunes—both literal and figurative—is important for understanding how lesbian community was being constituted. As Sakhi, in this moment of NGO-ization, increasingly articulated itself as a body with an explicit, fundable political mission—as one part in a struggle that would either be won or lost—a new division began to emerge between the politically competent and the politically incompetent, or the proper and less-than-proper lesbian subject.[30]

No Place for a Little Fun

To illustrate the emerging distinction between proper and improper lesbian subjects—a distinction that was based on the presence or absence of political competence—I turn to a writer I affectionately refer to in my field notes as Filthy Sumana of New Delhi. She sent forth the following olfactory musings and fervent demands in a 1995 letter to Sakhi:

> Especially my aunt had a highly erotic scent in armpits, pussy (just in the morning). My sister and my love, if you don't mind (till I find some

sort of partner), Can I have your scents. This is desperate request. I need your armpit hair, pubic hair, without washing. This will help me to fantasize while masturbating to reach orgasm. I am interested to correspond with lesbian from north India, who is dominating, healthy, sexy, . . . [illegible]. Can you put through some of them? Let me know where I can sex gadgets like dildos in India. I love to enjoy Indian sisters naked and in action. Are there any books/ films/ like that. If so, pl. let me know? I will definitely help to propagate / to help lesbian visibility in India.[31]

Sumana was far from alone in reaching out to Sakhi primarily for sex, and only secondarily (if at all) for friendship or participation in a political community. It is noteworthy that Sumana ends her missive with a promise to exchange political work for sexual pleasure. Several of the other writers who requested sexual partners or pornography made similar guarantees—at least after 1994, when Sakhi and Thadani's exploding publicity brought the notion of lesbian activism into the public imagination. (Another woman promised to open a "lesbian visibility showroom" in Orissa in exchange for pornographic videos from England.) These women were right to see their desires and priorities as of a somewhat lesser order, and as likely to be rejected. For no sooner had Sakhi begun to receive mass publicity and a modicum of political success than new divisions began to emerge between proper and improper subjects of the lesbian community. Tellingly, the volunteer answered Sumana's missive as follows (keeping in mind, of course, that Sumana asked for the volunteer's unwashed pubic hair): "Dear Sumana, Thank you for your letter. Unfortunately, we cannot provide the kind of services which you are requiring—we are a political organization. Sorry we cannot help in these matters, but we . . . can only offer the use of our resource centre in which we have collected articles on lesbian/gay life in India from a social/political perspective."[32]

So far I have been tracing the transformation in India from an absence of explicitly lesbian politics to the formation of a pan- and transnational imagined lesbian community through a series of mediations that were global in scale, both materially and imaginatively. Linked to that process of extraordinary invention were moments of necessary loss—the containment of a range of possibilities into new codes for right behavior. One such loss, the example I've used here, was a circumscription of the affective space of politics such that sex, pleasure, and desire—the very means through which most women came to their cathartic moments of lesbian recognition—were gradually deemed less than fit for this emergent, now politically aspiring, lesbian community. The nascent articulation of this politics in the language of a universal movement—seeking, as Sakhi puts it in the 1995 funding proposal, "to create a visible lesbian presence and an active lesbian voice"[33] —provides reason to look to those spaces of lesbian practice and desire that were increasingly incommensurate with this nascent articulation. What were those spaces of desire, pleasure, and practice that were neither silent nor visible, neither shrouded in shame nor proudly naked in the streets, neither not lesbian nor properly so?

The Anantha Health Club was one such space, and it takes my narrative to the southern state of Tamil Nadu in the summer of 1994. The guide is a letter writer called Miss V. Kumar. Miss Kumar began writing to Sakhi after finding its address in a copy of *Bombay Dost* that she had received from one of her (apparently, many) sex partners. Her first letter to Sakhi reads partially as follows:

> I am a 26 year old lady. . . . From my school days I am interested in homosex with classmates. During my college days in a ladies hostel . . . I find intimate friends with whom I have enjoyed homosex many times. But after graduation it is difficult to find lesbian friends. Recently I met a girl who is running a "Beauty Parlor" and a "Exercise class." She invites me to her club [the Anantha Health Club]. The ladies of various positions come for exercise. After exercise "massage" was offered. This resulted in total "nude" massage and finally homosex. The owner of the club . . . invited me for sex with her and finally we came to know of your address. . . . I am willing to spend any amount if you will write to me.[34]

Miss Kumar's story is on the fortunate side of familiar. Like many of Sakhi's letter writers, she was initiated into lesbian sex when young and unmarried, and within the relatively secure homosociality of the hostel. (The two other common sources of lesbian initiation are the aunt and the professor.) But unlike many of Sakhi's letter writers, Miss Kumar was able to locate a group of same-sex desiring and sexually practicing women after the common age of marriage, and after graduating out of the enforced mass homosociality of young womanhood. That access to collectivity is what is unusual about her case. But the simple ability to find and procure discrete acts of lesbian sex in unadvertised places in India is, as I learned, quite common indeed.

In the first year of my fieldwork, I was taking a walk through Central

Delhi with an older lesbian friend. Over lunch, we had discussed her work in progress—a collection of lesbian oral histories from rural India—as well as the role of foreigners in Indian lesbian activism. She expressed respect for the foreigners' dedication and fondness for them as individuals, but she shook her head sadly as she commented on their lack of cultural knowledge. As if on cue, I mentioned during our walk what I had learned of the Anantha Health Club. I told her with a barely suppressed pride, as if I had made an important discovery. She looked at me with some pity. "*Everyone* knows about beauty parlors," she said. "You're a foreigner too. You just don't have the cultural instinct, the *eye*, to know these things."

Chastised and challenged, I resolved to make the first beauty parlor appointment of my life: I would have my eyebrows threaded. The big day arrived. My eyebrows were neater when it was all finished, but to my surprise, I was not propositioned. I left the beauty parlor dejected, and called my friend. "You expect to go from eyebrows to *that*?" she exclaimed. I grudgingly accepted my error, but happily let this particular experiment slide. I trusted my friend's knowledge about sexual procurement; I would take her word for it.

A year later, in the middle of an extremely hot Delhi summer, my face broke out into a mess of sores. A doctor told me that it was the result of overeating mangoes. ("An unblemished face is an unmarried girl's most valuable possession," he said. "You must *stop eating mangoes!*") I was less concerned with the reason for these sores than with their disappearance, so, in my desperation, I decided to drop in to a neighborhood beauty parlor for a "facial consultation." I climbed the stairs to the second-floor shop and immediately realized that I was well out of my element. All five beauticians and all four South Delhi housewives turned to stare at the short-haired, jeans-clad boy-woman with a motorcycle helmet on her hip. "I would like a facial," I said meekly. The beauticians smiled at one another, while the housewives averted their eyes to keep from laughing. The one idle beautician stood and smiled broadly, then led me to a side room with a table and drew the curtain behind us. "Please remove your clothes and lie under this," she said, handing me a [thin sheet]. "I will be right back."

"I just want a facial," I said.

"We also offer massage."

"I only want a facial. Really."

She seemed exasperated. "Remove your clothes. I will be right back."

When she returned, I was fully clothed but lying on the table. She sighed loudly and began applying creams to my face. (She agreed, by the way, with the doctor's assessment about mangoes.) As she talked, she slipped a hand down the neck of my T-shirt. I leaped up, removing her arm. "I really don't want a massage." I thought I sounded firm, if not angry. She giggled and shook her head. Our miscommunications continued. I finally left, feeling shaken and a bit like a dunce.[35]

There was clearly a system of signs operating in that parlor that I was not able to fully interpret. Why I seemed like such an obvious customer for sex, I could not be certain. Perhaps it was my masculine accouterments; perhaps it was because I had stood with one leg cocked a certain way while I asked for a facial; perhaps it was because I looked like I had never seen a facial cream or an eyebrow threader in all my life, and thus had no other reason to be there. But by this time, I had seen, experienced, and heard enough to know at least this much: lesbian sexual encounters were there to be had, often in the most unexpected of places. If Sakhi's goal was to bring India a few steps closer to participation in a global march—a movement characterized by lesbian visibility, voice, and politics—they would have to contend with another set of realities: in the ostensibly heterosexual but homosocial spaces that women occupied in the everyday, lesbianism already thrived, and in ways that did not necessarily require insurrection. It was not always a lesbianism of monogamy, love, resistance to patriarchy, suicide pacts, or lifelong fidelity. In a world like the Anantha Health Club, lesbianism could be as simple as services to be provided, skills to be honed, and pleasures to be had.

Miss Kumar wrote to Sakhi again one and a half months later. In the intervening period, she had received Sakhi's networking list and had been in contact with a Tamil American called Maria, with whom she planned to make a trip to Delhi. She updated Sakhi on the goings-on at the club:

> *First* of all our health club members are interested in seeing the video film on lesbian themes. Most of our young girls who visit our "Anantha Health Club" are interested in nude dances, discotypes in "dimlight" with video film in T.V. Even Blue films[36] taken with *"ladies only."* Lesbian sex is very much welcome here. . . . Please send it by [courier] immediately. . . . Will you please let me know whether "lesbian sex" is offered in any "Beauty Parlour" anywhere in India. If so, please send the address to me. . . . Also we can learn the technique and provide the same here to other ladies. If ladies going from Delhi to South, we can take care

of them. Many married ladies come for seeing films and dances and nude bath, but they do so without the knowledge of their husbands. They enjoy homosex, but in secret. So please send the video cassette about "lesbianism." . . . It should contain actual sex relationships also.[37]

A month later, she added: "Do ladies stay together in hostels [at Sakhi] and have lesbian sex?[38] I hope Sakhi will take the lead and guide us. What about lesbian marriage and lesbian sex . . . [illegible] girls in Delhi? Are their numbers increasing? I am eager to know. Do foreign ladies come there and mingle with our ladies? Can you please send a educational note about 'lesbianism and female bisexuality?' "[39]

Miss Kumar offers us here a glimpse of a complex world—one that conforms neither to the most dire and pessimistic of proclamations ("There are and can be no lesbians in India") nor to the most hopeful and ambitious ("a future of lesbian visibility and voice"). Especially noteworthy here are the complicated relationships in the Anantha Health Club between abundance and lack, presence and absence, satisfaction and longing. To some extent, Miss Kumar paints for us a portrait of plenty: a group of women, recruiting and meeting regularly, watching blue films together, dancing nude under dim lights, and ending their evenings with sex. But shooting through this portrait of plenty are sensations of lack and declarations of need. The existence of Sakhi, and the mass media circulation of knowledge about lesbian lives domestically and abroad, led the Anantha Health Club members to aspire to ever more and, perhaps, to feel their isolation from a growing world that much more acutely. There is no sense from Miss Kumar's missives that the women feel, or have felt, insufficiently or improperly lesbian. They might be married, they might have their encounters in secret and under the pretense of exercise, but Miss Kumar identifies her group squarely as lesbian based on what she knows that word to signify. At the same time, it is clear from her letters that she understands "lesbian" to be potentially *more* than what they have (even though they are not less than what lesbian needs minimally to be).

What are those aspects of an emergent lesbian world that Miss Kumar and her fellow health club members aspire to? Above all they are information, education, and improvement. Though they are sufficiently capable of pleasuring one another, Miss Kumar believes that it is possible to subject their practices to the rules and technologies of an existing sexual discipline; indeed, she implores, to be "guided." "Techniques" can be learned, appropriated, and passed on through the media of film, books, newsletters, educational notes, and, of course, through "mingling" with the bodies of foreign (and presumably more knowledgeable) ladies. But this desire for sexual improvement and education—this desire to be something more and to offer something better—was tightly linked to yet another aspiration that Sakhi helped bring to same-sex desiring Indian women: the desire to roam and to make contact with what was only an emergent *imagined* lesbian community. Miss Kumar's letters are suffused with dreams of travel and transnational connection—sophisticated Delhi lesbians coming to Tamil Nadu, having first been transformed through a mingling with foreign ladies; lesbian marriages in the north; and the hope of meeting a Tamil American, traveling with her to Sakhi's promised land, and meeting there a lesbian Englishwoman.

Miss Kumar's sense of lack is not, however, limited to imagined possibilities; this lack would be materially borne out in the club's sudden demise, and in Miss Kumar's own forced relocation. She wrote in July 1994 that "the Anantha Health Club is in trouble. The owner of the building has left. Some of our girls are going for higher studies. But a new place will be found."[40] Miss Kumar did not write again for a year, and when she did, her world of plenty had been reduced to little: "Dear Sisters, I am urgently writing this letter. I have changed my residence to [a southern city]. But in my old address some letters are received and it creates a lot of problems for me. Because the people in their house open the letters and make a lot of fun and tease my family members. Please remove my name at once and save me from problem!"[41]

The worlds that many same-sex desiring women in India were creating, outside of the sort of urban activist networks in which Sakhi was enmeshed, tell us a great deal about the limits and possibilities of this moment in Indian lesbian community. The limits include Sakhi's inability and hesitation to reckon with women's sexual needs and desires—an ironic circumstance, given the fact that all of the women who wrote to Sakhi came to their lesbian "awakenings" through sexual encounter, fantasy, or both and continued to seek out touch, intimacy, and sex (though they did not always know where to find it). But the possibilities of this emergence were many and complex. Sakhi offered these women the promise of a larger world—an imagined community of disparate but soon to be mingling bodies, exchanging information, technologies, and touch. The promise was double-edged, offering both hope and producing previously unconsidered aspirations. But it is when we see evidence of the utter fragility of these semisecret worlds—their vulnerability to detection, hardship, social violence, or the simple passage of time—that we can perhaps understand the urgency, however flawed, of Sakhi's political project: to name, unify, and demand an insurrection.

It's Time for Us to Meet

As women in the letter-writing network became increasingly aware of the gifts that lay on all sides of them—increasingly aware, that is, of an imagined community of real, similarly desiring, similarly aspiring bodies—many women became ever more committed to transforming that imagined community into one that was real and face-to-face. The letters began to read with such lines as: "For how long will we remain shy? It's time for us to meet!" and "Enough of words now. Let me see you!"

One such face-to-face community forged from the network was Women to Women in Bombay in 1995. Lesley, an eighteen-year-old Catholic Indian woman from a posh western suburb of Bombay, was one of the founders, inspired to act after exchanging letters with Sakhi's Cath.[42] She introduced herself to Sakhi in a September 1994 letter: "I'm a . . . lesbian. I became aware of my sexuality when I was 12 years old because I fell in love for the first time at that age, with a woman in my building. I have never had a relationship with a man."[43] She said she had learned about Sakhi after her stepfather put her in touch with Row Kavi, and added that she "would like to help out . . . mainly by putting the point across to all gay women who care to hear, that we are *not* abnormal . . . and are as capable of giving love as any heterosexual on earth."

A Sakhi volunteer replied to this young firebrand, ecstatic: "Your letter really made an impression. Many women who write to Sakhi are married and living a 'hidden' sexuality—we are always thrilled to hear from women who have an enthusiasm for challenging the notions of lesbianism being so called 'abnormal,' 'unnatural.'"[44] (The claim that the volunteer makes here is an interesting one. As we have seen, most of the women who lived a sexuality that was "hidden" from their husbands and families did not do so because they thought of themselves as "abnormal" or "unnatural." This slippage, by which a failure to "come out" becomes equated with a psychosexual problem to be solved, is an example of a categorical imposition related to the internationalization of gay politics.)

The day that Lesley received Sakhi's letter and networking list in the mail would, she said, "go down red in my diary," and also because it marked her first conversation with Row Kavi.[45] She wrote to Sakhi, including a photograph of herself. She had short, dark hair, parted on the side, a bit of it flopping onto her forehead. Her babyish face, staring just to the right of the camera lens, bore a serious expression. She wore a pressed, white Oxford shirt and a slim black tie. Lesley described her motivation: "I decided that I'll come out fully in the open like Mr. Kavi and every time some things came in the way to make me stop. Like, my friends' reactions, their parents, my boss, my colleagues, etc. But I noticed a few 'Mrs.' [on the networking list] and just realized that if I don't speak out now and make it a little easier for us to be accepted, many more lesbians will also have to marry and be sad for the rest of their lives. . . . I'll find a way. Mr. Kavi will help me."[46]

And thus, out of the sorrow of a million "Mrs.," a lesbian activist was born. Partly with Sakhi's help, and after being inspired by hearing a Punjabi American talk about being a lesbian on All India Radio, Lesley made contact with an informal network of lesbian feminists in Bombay, who arranged a party to welcome her.[47] Within a mere three months of that contact, Lesley was writing to Sakhi as a representative of "Women to Women" —Bombay's first lesbian collective, founded in April 1995. She wrote: "The idea of forming this group came up at an informal discussion at Arti Rege's house. We then decided to throw a picnic as a sort of launch party, and also a get to know the group kind of thing. The picnic was quite a success. We are now planning the next one in July [1995]."[48]

Women to Women, like Sakhi, started as an explicitly lesbian community, eschewing the euphemisms that had defined earlier collectives, like the Delhi Group. Lesley began writing specifically to Cath about the group almost weekly, long letters brimming with stories and excitement about this new, visible lifeworld that they had created out of dreams.[49] But excitement soon gave way to disappointment and then anger, as conflicts emerged around the internal constitution and external boundaries of this new lifeworld.

One of the points of contention was a growing elitism within the group, not reducible to economic class. Lesley clues us in to the beginning of a friction along lines of access to discourse and political competence within Women to Women, writing to Cath about an "elitism that is creeping into the group, [as] a direct result of which some people are beginning to feel alienated."[50] Eight years later, in December 2003, I asked Lesley what she had meant in those early letters about the group's "elitism." Her answers centered on the ascendance of "dialogue" as the most salient marker of lesbian community belonging.[51] Chayanika Shah, another early member of Women to Women, makes a similar acknowledgment: "Some of these [closeted] women who came to [the group] were looking for . . . social spaces. . . . They were usually not interested in any kind of political action. Visibility, organizing, patriarchy, sexual politics, rights and fighting or struggling for them were alien concepts. . . . Those of us who identified as lesbian feminists were oscillating between wanting to connect with other women . . . and the utter exhaustion of being a support system to even a handful" (2005, 148–49). Shah's use of "other women" is telling in its indication of a tacit but clear chasm between classes of participants, between a political self and an apolitical other, between levels of perceived "competence."[52]

At this early stage in the emergence of a lesbian movement, then, proper lesbian subjectivity was continuing to be defined in the way that Sakhi had gradually set out, through a competence that was determined primarily by the ability to dialogue (and not desire) within the sphere of collectivity.[53] Engaging in political dialogue within a physical space of collective action requires access of two kinds: access to the cultural capital of political talk and access to practical freedoms of movement. The women whose letters I have quoted from were all—to varying degrees—women of means, as shown by their ability to read and write in English, however imperfectly. However, what emerges with the creation of face-to-face communities are demands on the quality and purpose of that language as well as the ability to physically enter into a circumscribed sphere in order to be subject to distinctions of competence and quality at all. The result of the two new bars to access in face-to-face collectives was that lesbian community, in its movement from imagined to real, increasingly comprised the same class of women who constituted local activist groups of same-sex desiring women before Sakhi's advent. In this Bombay collective's own self-description, they quickly became and remained an "urban, middle-class, upper middle-class group of well-educated, independent women" (Stree Sangam 2002, 147).

To make sense of the broadly middle-class and elite constitution of this, and most subsequent, lesbian collectives only requires following the interrelationship between the two heightened bars of access in face-to-face community: practical freedoms and political competence. To begin with the former, to travel through the city to engage in lengthy meetings requires both more time and relative freedom of mobility than does the writing of the occasional letter. Women with more time are women who do not have to spend their days engaged in work, whether outside or inside the home. Women with ease of movement (that is, movement not subject to interrogation or laden with great risk) tend to have more economic and practical freedoms. Women like Miss Kumar of the Anantha Health Club however, demonstrate the difficulty of arguing for any neat shift in lesbian community from women with little mobility and few means to women with much. Miss Kumar seems to have had fewer practical freedoms than the women of Lesley's group or Sakhi, as indicated by her need for anonymity, but she still managed to move relatively freely between her home and the health club. We can surmise that if the home in which Women to Women met was ten kilometers from Miss Kumar's home, she could have attended and attempted to commune. But then her participation would have been curtailed through the other major exclusionary practice—besides physical access—in the formation of new lesbian collectives: the shift in the basis of proper lesbian collective identity from a set of desires to competency in political talk. Miss Kumar might have found the road from dimlight dancing to compulsory political dialogue a long and demanding one.

Having drawn attention to the elite constitution of face-to-face lesbian collectives, I should distinguish my analysis from similar-sounding critiques made by women's movement activists and politicians on both the right and the left. I am not arguing that lesbianism is limited to a middleclass, Westernized elite; or that the ability to feel called by the term "lesbian" is limited to that stratum. Rather, I want to point out that the range of women who feel and have felt called by the term "lesbian" cannot always abide by the norms that variously emerge for what "lesbian" requires. Mine is simply an argument about the normalizing practices of community.

The exclusions based on political competence and practical freedoms in lesbian community that I have pointed out thus far were not, however, deliberately enforced. These exclusions were functions of a set of sociological realities concerning access to language and social space. There were certainly more deliberate acts of exclusion by which the concept of "lesbian" was sought to be imbued with some cultural character and local authenticity. At their first retreat, a majority of Women to Women's members decided to replace the English name with Stree Sangam (a confluence of women). And in place of "lesbian," the collective began shifting to the phrase "women who love women." Granted, the latter phrase is English, but unlike "lesbian," evokes no extranational genealogy of speciated perversity, no immediate accusation of bourgeois irrelevance.

Stree Sangam did more than strive for cultural commensurability on the level of the discursive. Many within the group advocated excluding nonresident Indians (NRIS) and otherwise foreign people from their community entirely.[54] Lesley wrote in January 1996: "As for this bullshit about excluding NRI or foreign women, that is all it will remain, just bullshit. . . . Though I *admit* that there is a problem about people aggressively taking up time and space for issues that are not of much import. . . . The others are arguing that 'Why should our time and space be given to outsiders?' Bloody rubbish! . . . We are having this retreat so that we can . . . put faces to the letters we all have been receiving all this time."[55] As Lesley noted, the impetus for this community was to enable women who were previously connected only through the visuality of script to actually see *one another*—to shift from an imagined community to the immediate materiality of face-to-face connection. It is important to note in Lesley's words the recurrence of the phrase "time and space," for it is precisely the introduction of "real" time and space into the lesbian imaginary that sparked a whole slew of new concerns about authenticity, power, and the right to share in a newly created spacetime.[56]

A world being created through the circulation of letters and a world being created through the rare mingling of rare bodies entail significantly different experiences of space and time. To put it simply, in the former, space and time are always excessive, and in the latter, space and time are always scarce. The spacetime of a community on the verge of being and seeing is uniquely felt: its time of communion has a beginning and an end; its space is hard-won and locally circumscribed. The scarcity of that spacetime infuses it with a value, and it is this economy that helps explain, at least in part, new efforts at actively policing borders and substance. Members of Stree Sangam had argued that NRIS and foreign women would "aggressively tak[e] up time and space" by discussing issues that were not relevant to Indian women. In an imagined world created through the circulation of letters, time and space are not valuable possessions to be guarded; they are only dreams that inspire efforts to seize. It was only the creation of "real" communities out of these ambitions that enabled lesbian women to begin to experience their space and time as tentatively shared, and scarce, resources that could be "taken up" or "wasted" at all.

This is not to say that overt practices of exclusion and selection (especially self-selection) were not at least attempted in the largely unseen world of the letter writers. Women like Lesley, Miss Kumar, and Ms. Bhan, as we saw, proclaimed their sexual identities in the first sentences of their first letters, understanding the unspoken protocol for collective inclusion. Or take Ms. Sunita of Calcutta, a thirty-five-year-old married woman with children who wrote Sakhi in 1994: "Well you must be having that million dollar question in your mind—'am I gay?' This is THE question. I am being asked so many times that I am getting a bit tired of it! Is it that important to know about my sexual orientation before you can become my friend?"[57]

Significantly, Ms. Sunita was introduced to this strict enforcement of identity as a prerequisite for communal inclusion not through the world of letter writing, but through her involvement with a face-to-face gay and lesbian organization in Calcutta known as the Counsel Club. Similarly, a Ms. K of Pune, who assured Sakhi that "you can be sure of security—I mean *I'm like you*" (emphasis added), came to her understanding of the sanctity of queer time and space through her previous involvement with lesbian groups in the United States and London.[58] But it was not just that lesbian women could begin to imagine spaces of their own that compelled a policing of community boundaries. We might look, too, to the dynamics within the spaces produced by the transition from imagined to real. How did the very visuality of the face-to-face collective encounter compel new practices of normalization?

I suggest that the answer lies in the use of the mirror as a metaphor for gay and lesbian identity and community. Kath Weston (1991, 138–45 and 162–64) has argued that society renders lesbian and gay relationships as less than by positing their basis in narcissistic similitude rather than the socially productive and reproductive difference that characterizes heterosexuality.[59] The assumed narcissism of a gay or lesbian relationship—that one loves an other only because the other is a reflection of the self—serves as partial grounds for the social and moral devaluation of queer relations. But the mirror is not just a useful trope for homophobes; lesbians use it, too, as a metaphor for love and community discovery.

A young woman from Pune, for example, wrote to Sakhi in 1995: "In my own life, I see and accept the fact that I love women like as if I was loving myself, a mirror image of myself."[60] Four years later, Ashwini Sukthankar edited a volume of Indian lesbian writing, titled *Facing the Mirror* (Sukthankar 1999). And a twenty-two-year-old woman named Prerna, describing to me how she felt when she first attended a lesbian support group, said: "It was like entering a room full of mirrors. Everyone there was just like me."[61] What I want to point out here is that modes and tropes of reflective visuality play central roles in the formation, or at least confirmation, of lesbian identity. Departing from Lacan's mirror-gazing subject, lesbian women will look at others like themselves in order to declare: "That is me."

The centrality of reflective visuality in the constitution of lesbian identity helps us to understand how and why the transition from imagined to face-to-face communities heralded new regimes of regulation. In the faceless and primarily imagined world of our letter writers, the ability to see other lesbian women meant little for the process of identity constitution: the circulation of narrative and proper subjective declarations ("I am a lesbian") was sufficient to produce a sense of identity and wider belonging, regardless of what the bodies that uttered those words might have looked like. It is not surprising that when somatic visuality was introduced into lesbian community, the bodies that produced the words "I am a lesbian" came under greater scrutiny. The fear expressed by those who assumed community authority was that women would match a lesbian declaration with the foreign body that produced it, finding recognition in the declaration but rejection in the body. Instead of peering into a mirror and thinking "That is me," they would peer into the face of a racial Other and think, "But that cannot be me." An imagined lesbian community, built on a faith in similitude, would be shattered by the shock of visible difference. Just as biological sex is overdetermined in the assumption of the mirror for queer self-recognition (Weston 1991), so are race and culture overdetermined in the assumption of the mirror for queer self-rejection.

I am arguing that increased surveillance of who could and could not be proper participants in lesbian community was rooted in two new phenomena produced through the attempted transition from imagined to real community: the forging of (scarce) space and time for lesbian interaction and the dynamics of visuality within those scarce scapes.[62] One of the classes of people newly deemed improper participants were foreign women. This was despite the fact that lesbian communities, and the identities they nurtured, were made possible only through a series of complex transnational mediations and movements: Thadani's Sakhi was built with the help of foreign money and transnationally circulated ideas; the person who sat, pen in hand, answering the prayers of women across India was a white English-woman named Cath; the founding of Stree Sangam was set into a motion when an Indian Christian named Lesley heard a Punjabi American talk about lesbianism on All India Radio and then contacted a group of women who had first met other Indian lesbians only in Bangkok. Similar, but prior, to the obfuscation of transnational mediation in defining Indian lesbian community was the circumscription of the affective space of politics such that sex, pleasure, and desire were deemed less than fit for an emergent, politically aspiring, lesbian community.

Such effacements of circuits of influence are not limited to lesbian communities, or to collectivization in India. Political communities always form with disparate needs, agents, and agendas. More importantly, they form by bringing together people who feel (and are educated to feel) under siege, inadequately recognized, and politically impotent. It is precisely through the process by which communities solidify, accrue social value, and inch toward recognition from their constituent outside, that the project of rendering community authentic and representable, rather than simply creating community at all, becomes prioritized. In other words, a community that was in the process of becoming seeks to become, at a certain point, a community that ontologically is. It is in this molarization that uncomfortable realities are obscured, differences are subsumed into enforced similitude, and ethical imaginings are made to be commensurate with representable truths. But if it is in the space of invention that the loss that is fixity is incurred, we might also, in honor of those who strive, see this in the reverse: that it is in the face of the lost that new ways of living, thinking, and being must be created. It is in this play between invention and limitation that brave new forms of social action reside, both relying upon and interrogating the suspect gift of our forged connections.

chapter 2

WITHIN LIMITS, FREEDOM

Interpellating the Lesbian Subject

Betu was born in Calcutta, the daughter of an army officer and a woman from a wealthy zamindar family.[1] The family of six settled in a small city in northern India, but Betu's father was almost always away. She spent most of her time alone, either hiding under the couch and away from the servants' eyes or in the market, avoiding schoolwork. Obedience was not her strong suit; people, she said, affectionately referred to her as a "devil." In one of our many interviews, Betu told me about her childhood attraction to women: "From the age of eight or nine, I was attracted to women. . . . Even if I couldn't touch her or be with her, I just liked being attracted, being in love with her. . . . I didn't think about sex for years. Then at the age of twelve or thirteen . . . I went to Haryana."

Haryana is a state just northwest of Delhi, and there Betu fell in love with an older cousin of about thirty. During the first evening of Betu's visit, as they watched television together, Betu's cousin stood and walked toward the bathroom. She asked Betu to come with her and help her with her bra strap. Betu told me: "I was very nervous! I never thought someone could talk to me like this. So I went into the bathroom with her, and it was really . . . you know that feeling? A sweet, sweet pain. [Later w]e went to a Radha-Krishna *mandir* [temple]. It was dark when we came out of the mandir, and suddenly she was holding my hand. I don't know how I managed to walk.

My whole body was weak. The way she was holding my hand. At night we were sleeping in the same room. I felt her touching me all over and I was acting as if I was sleeping."

She did not pretend to be asleep in order to will her cousin away, of course. She pretended again the second night and then the third, but on the fourth day, it was time for her cousin to leave: "We could never talk about it, we could never say anything. When she left, the look she gave me from the car, I remember—it was very painful. And I had that very different kind of pain in my heart. I had it for a month. But I couldn't do anything about it, I couldn't tell anybody. And it went *slowly-slowly* [*dheere dheere*] away. She got married, and that was my first experience."

Betu would fall in love several more times, with women her cousin's age as well as with schoolmates. They were all physical relationships, she said, but of simply kissing, hugging, and sleeping in the same bed. Often, she and a lover would go to the movies, and when the Bollywood actors would break into song, she would imagine themselves in the role of hero and heroine. At the end of the movie they would stay for a second show, so that they could hold hands in the dark for another three hours.

I have to admit that when I first interviewed Betu it was with definite assumptions, among which was that she would relate to me a seamless queer adult narrative beginning with, "From childhood I always knew I was different." And so I inquired: "Did you think it was strange that you were having these feelings?" She looked impatient: "I never used to . . . look, even now, I don't go too deep into things. If I'm enjoying, I'm enjoying. I never used to think, 'is this wrong, is this okay?' Something was giving me happiness; I was happy. Okay?"

It appears from my transcript that I wanted more. I asked if she had a coming out story. "*Nothing!*" she said. "I never thought I was a lesbian, if that's the question, and I didn't know this word. Number one, I was not into reading . . . so how was I to know it?" This last comment echoes Miss Kumar's letters in chapter 1, demonstrating again how lesbian identity is often seen as something that one should be educated into, even though the practices clearly exist before that education. As Betu's story unfolded, it would become clear that a formal lesbian education could emerge not only from books or videos, but through face-to-face encounters with women more "educated" than her.

At a support group meeting months before this interview with Betu, it dawned on me that coming out stories were much less salient narratives for ordering an Indian lesbian life than were stories about leaving home. A group member named Jasmin had told of leaving her family in northeast India. She knew only that she did not want to marry and that in order to avoid marriage, she would have to leave her family. So she took a job with an NGO, hoping to travel. It was at an NGO workshop in Delhi about HIV/AIDS that she first heard about lesbianism; that same day, she met her future partner. Though she has never come out to her parents, whom she trusts and loves, her relationship gave her the impetus she needed to leave home. Several others told similar stories that day, and none ever came out to their families. For them, it was the moment of leaving the natal home as unmarried women that marked their moment of rupture and arrival.[2] The rubrics of "coming" and "leaving" seem, on the face of it, quite opposed. The former connotes assertiveness, the latter capitulation; the former evokes a seizure of space, the latter a forfeit of it.[3] But the act of leaving for these women was one of courage and, indeed, of coming into, or arriving in, another world. In a society in which women are expected to live at home (or, at most, in a hostel) until marriage, the act of leaving home unmarried *is* a sort of coming out: a declaration that, for this young woman, things will be different.

Recalling this conversation, and hoping to ask Betu more resonant questions, I asked her if she had a story about leaving home. She smiled. Her story, which she clearly loved to tell, went like this. As a young adult, Betu was involved with a Christian woman named Martha, who lived several hours away in the charming northern city of Dehra Dun. They kept in touch through letters. Quite out of the blue for Betu, a suitor's relative appeared at her mother's door, asking that their children become engaged. Betu's mother demurred at first, thinking her daughter too young, but gave in after considering the rarity of good proposals. At this point in the story Betu lit up, leaning in to whisper, "I was so excited." I was confused: "What did you tell Martha?" "That's what I'm saying!" Betu exclaimed. "I never used to think about these things! Life was taking me. And I was excited about the new stuff. I didn't like the guy; I wasn't bothered about the guy. I was just excited about the new stuff."

She told Martha that she was engaged. Sure enough, and departing from the intensely dramatic script of lesbian lovers separated by arranged marriage, Martha was amused. Betu traveled to Dehra Dun to see Martha, and in the middle of the lovers' reunion, a friend of Betu's brother appeared on a motorcycle to take Betu back home. Upon her return she found two opened letters. One was from the boy's family, unexpectedly demanding a dowry. The other was from a hotel in Delhi, offering Betu a job that she had sought as a security guard. Her choice was an easy one. Two days later she left on a train for Delhi.

Martha moved to Delhi as well, and the couple lived together with two other unmarried women. One of her housemates came from a wealthy family, and her allowance enabled them all to live comfortably. When Betu's mother later threatened to cut her off if she continued "living with that Christian girl," Betu cut the tie herself in favor of this new family she had chosen. She did not consider her chosen life extraordinary. I know this because I insisted on asking, and her response was clear: "Nothing, *yaar* [friend, dude]! Nothing used to bother me. 'Oh, am I involved with this person, oh, she's a woman.' I didn't have to go out on the street and tell them what relationship we have. Because in India it's accepted, two women staying together. Because they think they're sharing a room for rent. Anything." Betu had several other lovers in Delhi, most of the relationships short-term, some on the sly. She didn't long for a community (she had one), and she didn't seek a name for her desires (she was able to fulfill them).

She only became aware that she was to have a type of sexual subjectivity when she was first branded with one by another person. A later roommate of Betu's became angry that Betu was always out with other female friends. Betu told me: "We were fighting, and she said, 'You're a lesbian.' And then I *slapped* her. I just slapped her. I didn't like her calling me this. I was somewhere denying."

"So you were familiar with this word," I said. "No," she replied, "but I knew that to be called lesbian was something bad. Cath was the first lesbian I met in my life. Only then I slowly- slowly became comfortable with that."

Cath is the Sakhi volunteer, introduced in chapter 1, who wrote to dozens of Indian women using the terminology that most of them would adopt. Betu met her one night at a club, an encounter of much consequence for her as well as for Indian lesbian politics:

> I had gone there, and there was a gay friend called Bobby. . . . I had gone with all my straight friends and it was raining and we were all high [tipsy]. Cath was there with this group of gay guys. She spotted me and said to them, "Look! That girl is a dyke." So Bobby looked at me and said . . . "I meet her every second day. I know her; she's not a dyke." Cath said, "I'm one hundred percent sure that she's a dyke. I want to meet her, and

you'll see." So next day Bobby calls me up and says somebody wants to meet me. I said, "Who is he?" Bobby said, "It's not *he*, Betu, it's *she*." [My roommate] told me it was true—that there was a foreigner who was staring at me the whole time, and she's the one who wants to meet me.

Betu and the foreigner eventually met and became involved. Cath lived in Thadani's building, where Sakhi was housed, and Betu began spending time there: "Lots of lesbians used to drop in. And they used to talk on this 'issue.' They would all say, 'Oh, we're working on lesbian this-thing and lesbian that-thing.'[4] And it was quite interesting to me! And slowly-slowly when Veronica [a childhood friend] came to Sakhi, that was the first time I came out to Veronica after all these years. I told her, 'I'm a lesbian.' And Veronica said, 'Even I am! I am a lesbian.'" Betu laughed, delighted.

Veronica is an Indian Christian. She and Betu attended grade school together, and their closeness is evident even in their appearance. Both are short in stature and small in frame, and both wear their black hair cropped short. Both dress in cotton pants and untucked, button-down shirts, though Veronica tends toward dramatic blacks. Their primary difference lies in attitude. Betu has an air of supreme confidence. Her eyes are mischievous, her gaze unsettlingly direct. Though she is objectively cute—built a bit like a teddy bear—her eyes seem to dare you to cross her. Veronica, on the other hand, wears her vulnerability on her sleeve. She is flirtatious but almost apologetically so, as if she is trying to overcome an old sadness and hopes you will play your part. She wears her hair like that of her icon, the Bollywood actor, Dev Anand, and struts about the support group reciting romantic dialogue from films to her amused crush—or crushes—of the moment.

Veronica, like Betu, had several love affairs with schoolmates. Her friends reacted to her romantic pursuits with support, rather than derision. Some helped her write love letters; another stole a sari from her sister's dowry for Veronica to give as a present to a girl she loved. Over the objections of her aunt, Veronica cut off her hair when she was young and wore only pants and shirts. Despite such transgressions, she said, "I never thought of myself as different. This was just how it was."[5] That was how it was, that is, until she experienced her first lesbian accusation. Consider the following conversation between Veronica and her cousin:

Cousin: You must be a lesbian.
Veronica: What is that?
Cousin: It's a woman who gets attracted to girls.

Veronica: Why do you think I'm attracted to girls? I play with boys.
Cousin: Exactly. You're like a boy, and boys are attracted to girls.

The cousin's comment reveals how the tight, predictive alignment of sex, gender, and sexuality can be made to accommodate disruption in the service of heteronormativity. Veronica's (female) sex failed to predict her (masculine) gender, but assertion of her (masculine) gender recuperated the initial disruption by predicting her essential heterosexuality ("boys are attracted to girls").[6] This exchange, however, did not constitute Veronica's cathartic moment of lesbian identification. The cousin's effort to subject Veronica to that identity failed because her call had no authority. Like Betu's accusing heterosexual roommate, Veronica's cousin made an assertion without formal authority as a lesbian and without an invitation to peer into a mirror and recognize that assertion's truth. To recall the letter writers in chapter 1, hardly any of them reported recognizing themselves as lesbians through an unauthorized accusation. Accusations can be, and usually are, denied. They might plant the seed for future knowledge, but they do not constitute the moment of "Aha!" A cathartic moment of recognition comes with a sense of being called to the truth of one's self. It requires assent, not coercion.

But how, then, is a lesbian successfully called to that identity? The points at which Betu's and Veronica's stories meet offer some insight. Veronica and Betu drifted in and out of each other's lives for some years. They were briefly estranged because they both desired the same woman (but could not speak about desiring her). Their reconciliation occurred around the time that Betu became involved with Cath and, by extension, with Sakhi. To Betu, Veronica suddenly began to make sense. So Betu asked Cath if she would be willing to "size Veronica up."

"Cath came to check me out and see if I am," Veronica told me. "She says that she took one look at me and decided '100 percent pukka [genuine] lesbian.'" Cath related her judgment to Betu and suggested that Veronica should be "brought out" by spending time at Sakhi. "Betu kept giving me all these hints," Veronica said. "'This girl so-and-so has fallen for you and wants to meet you.' But I was too shy to talk about these things."

Veronica might have been too shy to talk, but she overcame that limitation through her circulation of nonverbal signs. Veronica was a fan of the music of Milan Singh, a female who performed in the male persona of "Milan." Veronica brought one of Singh's cassettes to Sakhi and showed it to Cath: "Cath just showed it to Giti [Thadani]. Giti looked at the cassette, looked at Cath and said [about Milan], 'Definitely 100 percent dyke.' It was the first time I had heard this 'dyke.' I didn't know what it meant. I asked Betu, and she didn't want to tell me."

The next step in Veronica's subjectivization involved the mediation of film. Betu invited several lesbian women to her home to watch *Desert Hearts*, the classic and delightfully awful American lesbian film. "I felt so shy during the love scenes," Veronica said. "Betu and I couldn't look at each other. When we finally did, we both just *grinned!*" Shortly thereafter, a group of six lesbian women and Veronica met socially in Thadani's apartment. "They just took it for granted that I was a lesbian," Veronica told me. She continued, describing her moment of recognition: "They talked openly, and included me in a natural way. They all started talking openly about making love to women, and what they loved about it. Cath told a long story about Betu. That day I really felt it. Betu and I talked that day. She finally told me, 'I'm a lesbian.' And I told Betu, 'So am I. I'm a lesbian, too!' Betu felt a huge load off [her mind]! [Laughs.] She ran back into the room to tell everyone. [Laughs.] Cath laughed and everyone felt happy that I had opened up."

This sequence of events reveals much about the process of being called to a lesbian subjectivity within the context of emergent, face-to-face community. Veronica had never had a mirror before being "sized up" by Cath—she knew no one who called herself a lesbian, into whose face she could look for self-recognition. Cath had the authority to call Veronica to a lesbian identity, but she did not act as Althusser's cop (Althusser 1972 [1970], 174): she did not shout, "Hey, you!" Instead, she initiated and enforced a more subtle process by which Veronica would come to recognize herself in the other, rather than by force of the other.

Veronica's "sizing up" by educated authorities would rely on the successful recognition of signs. The first in this case (and many others) was the haircut—a ubiquitous sign that is taken to have a symbolic, but also indexical, relationship to lesbian desire. There was also trafficking in an iconic sign: Even after being sized up and brought into a lesbian community, Veronica still could not speak of her lesbian desire. But to signal her recognition of the terms of that sphere, she presented the authorities with a photograph of Milan Singh—a photograph that not only bore a resemblance to Veronica, but that further linked her to the image through her affective identification with it. The authorities did not have to point to Veronica and say, "Hey, dyke!" Instead, they "dyked" the image—an iconic sign that could now serve as the premise linking Veronica to the logical conclusion of herself ("This is a dyke. I am like this. I am a dyke.").

Next was the collective watching of *Desert Hearts*. The women on screen, despite their colors, accents, and nationalities, served as an almost (but not quite) mirror for Veronica's lesbian recognition. "Almost" because they were lesbians, watched by lesbians; "not quite" because they were a mirror once removed. Veronica's moment of recognition came only when her eyes met Betu's; it was the recognition of her similitude with Betu (and of Betu's identification with the actors) that served as the mediator between Veronica and the lesbian women on screen. Veronica's ultimate moment of lesbian self-recognition, though, was achieved later, in the community gathering in which communion was altogether assumed but not demanded; the exchange of stories about love, pleasure, and desire, not overtly determined by identity or reliant on rarefied knowledge; and finally, the reflective, seemingly immediate visuality so constitutive of lesbian identification. The process by which Veronica assumed a lesbian identity and, thus, inclusion into the community, relied on consent rather than coercion. But consent to subjection, in turn, depends on the acceptance of normative frameworks, the most central of which is freedom.

Freedom through Limits

Both Veronica and Betu describe the consequences of their respective discoveries as joyful ones. Veronica said to me: "It was the first time I could talk about my feelings. I couldn't really even talk to [her former lover]. But now I get this feeling like, 'Wow. I'm among my *own people*. Now I can talk and really be free.' I used to be scared to tell a woman what I thought. Maybe she would say I'm 'abnormal.' But if I get attracted to a woman here I could tell this woman, 'You know, I love you.' And she would *know what I mean*. I felt very free, Nais. Very free." Her sense of relief, like that expressed by the letter writers in chapter 1, is almost palpable, pointing to the comfort that identity and community enable. But along with expressions of comfort come uncomfortably adamant declarations of "freedom." In narrating the story of her life before becoming a lesbian, Veronica repeated phrases such as "nobody thought it was strange," "my life was never hard," and "I found girlfriends easily." In narrating her life to me after becoming a lesbian, however, she reconstrued that pre-lesbian past as one of fear and a lack of freedom. What can this tell us about the politics of memory in narratives of queer discovery?[7]

The freedom that Veronica experienced after her moment of recognition was, of course, real. As Judith Butler (1997) suggests, it is precisely the passionate attachments we have to our subjections that render those subjections so powerful. Butler argues that it is the loss of possibility we psychically experience when subjected to a particular way of being (for example, heterosexuality) that leads us to defend that way of being in order to justify the loss of all the now-impossible possibilities. Sexual identities, thus, are partly constituted through the melancholy of loss and limitation. Perhaps it is this melancholy of subjection that is negotiated by reframing subjection as freedom. This thesis is borne out doubly in Veronica's narrative: she speaks of her subjection to heteronormativity as a time of freedom when she spoke from the vantage point of that time ("I was free to do whatever I wanted, and nobody thought me strange"), just as she narrates her subjection to lesbian identity as freedom when speaking from the position of a lesbian ("I am now free").

Betu's story is similar:

I kept on meeting other lesbians through Cath. So many lesbians! It was an open field for me! [Laughs.] You get into that thing, you know? "Oh, now I can talk about things openly and approach women with the same sexuality" and all of that. So I was very, very happy. But now I feel—the biggest change in me is I don't flirt with straight women at all. I'm not interested in them. I can't think of them as attractive. That change is there in me since meeting Cath and this "lesbian" thing. It's not that I'm stopping myself. It's just not happening inside. I love lesbians.

Betu offers at least two insights into the relationship between the practice of new freedoms and the implementation of new forms of discipline. The first is tied to her unprovoked assertion: "It's not that I'm stopping myself." Like Veronica, Betu narratively reframes subjecting herself to the new limits imposed by identity and community as a source of freedom or, at least, the absence of imposed limits. The second point is related to the discourse of similitude as virtue and freedom. For Betu and Veronica, it was the sameness of the women they encountered that enabled their discursive and sexual freedoms. This is important, for once freedom becomes conceptually linked with and seen as dependent upon similitude, exclusionary and normalizing practices can be justified as simple acts of protecting the flourishing of life.

This investment in enforced sameness for lesbian community is not limited to sexual identity but, as I showed in chapter 1, extended to nationality and culture as well. Indeed, a growing perception of Sakhi as being too enamored of Western politics and Western lesbians led to a crucial redefinition of Indian female same-sex sexuality and its proper boundaries. Consider the following conversation between Betu and me:

Betu: Indian lesbians had a problem coming to Sakhi's space.

ND: Why?

Betu: I don't know. But foreign women came.

ND: Why did foreign women feel comfortable?

Betu: Because so many of them came! And NRIS also used to come. But I didn't see Indian women—women from Delhi—coming to interact there. But then I saw a photograph and I saw that they used to come. So I asked Cath, "Where are these people?" And she said they're here but they don't come. . . . They don't like this space anymore.

ND: So they had left the group?

Betu: That's what I'm telling you! There *was* no group! No help line, no space, no nothing. Just these [foreign] visitors. That's why we thought of Sangini.

Collectivity here becomes defined based on cultural and racial sameness in addition to a consensus on proper objects of desire. But it is not merely addition. The insistence on cultural sameness as a precondition for proper community would alter the very meaning of "lesbian" identity itself, producing and enforcing a division of political labor in which the Indian lesbian would be newly construed—in a departure from Stree Sangam's model —as outside of politics. The emerging shift that Betu gestures to in the conversation cited above is one in which foreigners were linked to politics, and Indians to something more pristine. But Indians need not forsake politics altogether. Authentic Indian community is posited as not quite ready yet for the identity politics associated with the West, thus internationalizing a division that had already opened up at the local level (see chapter 1) between the politically competent and the politically incompetent.

Sangini: The Founding of "Safe Space"

Sangini was founded in response to two feelings: that Sakhi was too foreign and not Indian enough, and that Sakhi had failed in its promise to be a safe space for newly minted lesbians. Cath felt strongly about both of these positions. While working as a volunteer for Thadani, Cath was also working for Jagori, the women's NGO known so far in this book as proponents of the category "single women" in place of "lesbian." Being associated with Thadani, Cath said, proved a great liability to her among the same-sex desiring feminists at Jagori, who resented Thadani's identity-political approach to sexuality. Cath's relationships with these feminists improved only with her own growing disenchantment with Sakhi's model of activism: "Come on. We sold handicrafts . . . and wrote letters. I knew this wasn't activism. We started organizing events [at Sakhi]—movie afternoons, gatherings, whatever. But Sakhi was *never* going to be the space we needed. People didn't feel *safe* going there. It wasn't a community space. It was a space for foreigners. . . . Sakhi couldn't change anybody's lives. The people who came there already had these things."[8]

I asked Cath how the idea for Sangini had come about. She smiled a smile tinged with nostalgia, and told me about falling in love with Betu:

> She gave me a major reason—not the only reason—to stay in India. It was a clash of worlds between us, though: my lesbian feminist one and her straight and closeted one. I was relegated to invisibility again in her world, and I resented it. I realized through this, though, that I had found a real lesbian community in India. . . . And I would look at Betu and see this amazing thing. All the dyke signifiers without calling herself one! It was such an *Indian* lesbianism, as opposed to Giti's. Betu's was *real*, it was *raw*. No ideology. We needed a space for women like that.[9]

So it was in an effort to create a space for the Indian real and its protection that Cath and Betu began dreaming of ways to bring Sangini into being. They had neither the capital nor the infrastructure to get the organization going on their own, but Cath did have contacts in the NGO world. She had been one of a group of eight women who organized a sexuality discussion group at Naz. Though the discussion group no longer existed, Cath still had a relationship with Naz, working in its Women's Sexual Health Program— a relatively small program compared with Naz's diversified Men's Sexual Health Division, which included help lines and three different evening support groups for gay men, kothis, and MSM—organized by language, identity, and social class. The men's help lines had received calls from women desperate to talk about their same-sex desires and relationships, much like *Bombay Dost* had been the recipient of women's letters. The men at Naz, like those at *Dost*, felt unqualified to address these women's concerns but had nowhere to send the callers. This is how the idea for a lesbian help line was born. Though a lesbian help line was seen as outside the scope of Naz's mission to prevent HIV/AIDS, its director agreed that Cath could run a lesbian help line out of Naz's office as a separate group.

On a Tuesday evening in October 1997, three counselors from Sangini, including Cath and Betu, waited patiently for their first caller in Naz's help-line room. They did have a first caller, but it was also their only caller that night.[10] In preparation for their work, the three counselors had undergone basic phone counseling training through Naz. They also sought to advertise Sangini's services, going to newspapers and women's glossy magazines such as *Femina* with short ads. Most newspapers rejected their ad outright, claiming to be "family papers." This was despite Sangini's effort to be culturally Indian and nonthreatening, never using the word "lesbian." The group's ads, in Hindi and English, were variations on the following: "*Kya aap aisi mahila hain, jo dusri mahelion ki taraf aakarshith hoti hai? Kya aap kisi mahila salaahakaar se baat karna chaahthi hain?*" (Are you the type of woman who is attracted to other women? Do you want to talk to a woman counselor?)[11] In addition to the newspaper ads that the group was able to run weekly in the English-language *Times of India* and the Hindi *Navbharat Times*, they also created small, brightly colored stickers that they placed in and around homosocial spaces such as women's restrooms and women's colleges (see figure 6).

The help line, from its single caller the first night, began receiving several calls each week. Sangini responded by adding a weekly Saturday support group in early 1998, which met in Naz's South Delhi office. Unlike the men's groups, which met in the evenings, the lesbian group met in the afternoons to facilitate safer travel for women coming to the group, and to give women a viable excuse to come. Although family members and neighbors would be suspicious about a woman traveling alone in the evening, Saturday afternoon is a perfectly reasonable time for a woman to, say, visit a relative or go shopping.[12]

I first attended a Sangini support group meeting a year and a half later, in the summer of 1999. *Fire* had already blazed through the city and the

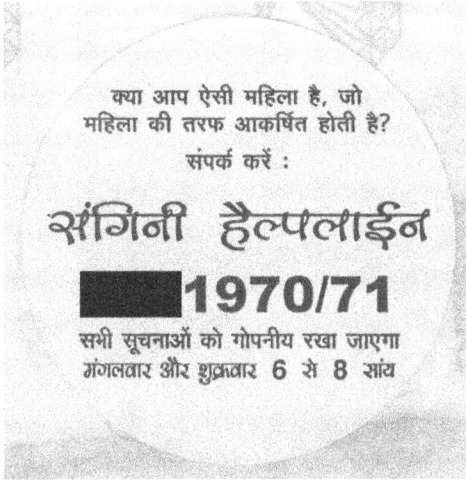

क्या आप ऐसी महिला है, जो
महिला की तरफ आकर्षित होती है?
संपर्क करें :

संगिनी हैल्पलाईन
■1970/71
सभी सूचनाओं को गोपनीय रखा जाएगा
मंगलवार और शुक्रवार 6 से 8 सांय

6. A sticker advertising the Sangini help line: "Are you the type of woman who is attracted to other women?" Photograph by the author.

nation, and the massive coverage of the events surrounding the film led to an increase in Sangini's help-line activity, to an average of nearly fifteen calls a week. Sangini had also received a grant from the Astrea Foundation, a New York–based feminist funding agency with a focus on international sexual minority issues. The funds were funneled to Sangini through Naz, the group's parent NGO.

The first meeting I attended was on an oppressively hot summer day. We met—as did all of Naz's support groups—in the main sitting room of Naz's office, which occupied the second floor of a four-story house. The first and third floors were occupied by Naz's director and her menagerie of pets, acquired over the course of her travels; the top floor was a terrace, where employees often had lunch. The support group space was set off from the rest of the office by the arrangement of furniture. Three couches and several wooden chairs made up a large square, in the middle of which were two tables. A television and VCR were nestled in one corner, and a whiteboard, used for word association exercises ("What comes to mind when you hear the word 'lesbian?'"), was hung on one of the walls. The posters on the walls left no doubt about the organization's mission—they showed a rainbow of well-built, robust-looking men accompanied by affirmative quotes about positive status, red ribbons, and artistic close-ups of prophylactics.

Our group of seven sat together in that room, sipping *nimbu paani* (lime juice) and conversing in English with a smattering of Hindi, primarily for comic effect. I was one of three NRIs in the group. Inspired by the other two, who were a butch-femme couple, we had a discussion about butch-femme relationships in which we were all encouraged to identify our gender and preferences. Mercifully for us all—the conversation was stilted—we soon disbanded for a break. It is often the case that breaks provide the best opportunity for honest discussion.

I joined several women on the back balcony—a narrow slab of a space, walled in by a latticed structure, with a view of a trash-strewn alley and other people's drying laundry. Four of us could fit there, shoulder-to-shoulder or nose-to-nose, smoking *bidis* (tobacco wrapped in tendu leaves) and cigarettes, gossiping, giving *galis* (playful insults), and flirting. After the others had skillfully flicked their cigarette butts into the alley and gone inside to escape the heat, I was alone with Betu.

"So, you want to do research on Sangini, huh?" she asked. With some embarrassment (I still felt uncomfortable in my anthropologist skin), I said yes. "You know," she said, "some other groups are talking shit about Sangini. They say Sangini is not into politics." I asked her why this was so, and she gave me a brief story about the aftermath of *Fire*.

I go into greater detail in chapter 4 about the role that *Fire* played in transforming the landscape of queer politics in India, but I'll summarize Betu's point here. Members of the right-wing political party, Shiv Sena protested *Fire* by rioting in Bombay and Delhi. In counterprotest, the Campaign for Lesbian Rights (CALERI) formed with the mission of attaining lesbian visibility. In their inaugural manifesto, they speak about eschewing euphemism and embracing the term "lesbian." Sangini initially participated in CALERI. But as CALERI's strict commitment to a politics of public visibility required increasing exposure, Sangini pulled itself and its members out of the campaign, citing the primacy of safety and anonymity for Indian women who desire the same sex. The historical moment of CALERI's emergence brought about a new subjectivity for the Indian female same-sex desirer—that of the visible activist who wears her identity on her body, staking her claim to rights in the public sphere. Sangini's inability to abide by this emerging norm marked the group's members as betrayers of a cause, and subjects without political competence. They were then largely dismissed by potential feminist or queer allies who saw Sangini as soft and inconsequential. This was the story, albeit in different words, that Betu related to me on the balcony. What she didn't say was that the members of the group felt the consequences of this division acutely. With Sangini outside the new circle of proper, modern lesbian subjectivity, the members thought of themselves as something less than public and less than political—self-conceptions, as I'll show, that shape what is possible to imagine.

The forced binary between the politically competent and incompetent, or between the public and the private, that Betu spoke to me about had its beginnings well before 1998. *Fire* and its aftermath only brought to light a division that had already been forged among lesbians and that was the very premise for the support group structure in the first place: the need for a safe space for the "raw," unpoliticized Indian woman who simply desires other women and has no ambitions for a politics around that desire.

When Sangini was founded in 1997 as first a help line and then a support group, the premise of the unpoliticized Indian lesbian subject was institutionalized, thus becoming a commodity of value in the emerging global activist marketplace.[13] Sangini's very language of "help" and "need" was bestowed upon it by its parent organization, Naz, which itself derived the language from an international discourse of development and nongovernmentally driven progress. In other words, the notion of Indian lesbians as a population in danger, and thus in need of safety and support rather than politics, was and is produced through the ostensibly benevolent humanitarian agendas of funding agencies.[14] The value of a grant, and the agency that provides it, is determined in part by the distance that the grantees can progress by virtue of that grant's receipt. By positing the Indian lesbian as beginning in a state of near impossibility, any development—indeed, the simple existence of a group against all odds—can be presented as an indicator of success and need.

In a globalized world of activism as a competitive marketplace, abstract development agendas and interpersonal rivalries over funding are the forces of politics—this is a descriptive claim, not a cynical position. The point for an anthropology of activism is to understand how these facts of politics differently constrain and enable the ethical practices that constitute activism—critique, invention, and creative relational practice. So, I want to try and describe how the support model was nothing short of a lifeline for many women, but also imaginatively limited what those lives might be.

The Help Line

In June 2002, the directors of Sangini invited me to train as a help-line counselor along with a longtime Sangini member, Roshni. Cath was our trainer. She had been a counselor on the Sangini help line from its first day and had since attended several NGO-sponsored seminars on the art and techniques of telephone counseling. We met once a week over two months in the upper-floor apartment of Naz's director. It was the height of Delhi's summer, and the monsoon was late in arriving. Daylong electricity outages exhausted the building's power generators. We held our sessions under a still fan and in near darkness, windows cracked open in prayer to a pregnant, sweltering sky that refused to grant a breeze. Sweating through our clothes and cranky as children, we often found it hard to sympathize with the callers Cath invented for our role-playing. "Go ahead and marry the bastard! Who cares?" we would shout into our pinky-and-thumb fake help-line phones. Cath was not amused.

On better days (which were most), we went through an official training manual on telephone counseling techniques. For each of the topics—"Confidentiality," "Counseling versus Advice-Giving," "Paraphrasing and Effective Questioning," "Clients Are Not Friends," and "Confronting Abusive Clients"—Roshni and I would perform relevant role-plays based on the stories Cath provided from past callers. My first role-play was on the topic of how to counsel (enable) without giving advice (directing). I was to play the counselor; Roshni was the caller. I picked up my imaginary phone, and she told me a past caller's story. The caller has been best friends for four years with the woman she loves. The caller self-identifies as a lesbian, but her best friend is straight. The caller is distraught and considering suicide because she cannot have this woman and doesn't have anyone to talk to. Afraid of giving advice, I ask her a series of inane questions about how this makes her feel—somehow ignoring the fact that she has told me she wants to commit suicide. When we were finished, Cath asked Roshni how she, as the client, would rate my performance. She looked at me with betrayed eyes and said softly, "That would have been the end of me!"

Over the next few weeks, we trained as if for some extreme sport. Every week, we confronted new situations, obstacles, and dilemmas, with an ever-smaller margin allowed for error. We were told, and began to feel, that people's lives—or, at least, their sense of belonging in an otherwise hostile world—could actually hinge on our words. To prepare, our role-plays ran the gamut of situations, rife with lessons and subtle traps: distraught parents demanding to know where their nineteen-year-old lesbian daughter and her lover have run away to (we are under no obligation to reveal, if we indeed know); or a woman whose lesbian relationship has been discovered by her husband and who needs help to run away (we arrange for her to stay at one of two lesbian-tolerant women's shelters in the city, something that had already happened six times before). At the end of two months, Roshni and I were appointed counselors.

I began that same week, on a Friday evening from six to eight. The help-line room at Naz is cozy and professional. A warm light glows over a long table with two phones, both of which sit on maroon mats in front of stationary office chairs. Bulletin boards adorn the wall above the phones, neatly displaying typed lists of gay-friendly NGOs, doctors, lawyers, suicide help lines, and shelters. All four walls are covered by posters about HIV/AIDS. The room doubles as a library for support group members of Sangini and Naz. Sangini's library, built primarily from donations by foreign visitors, displays the usual lesbian artifacts: Jeanette Winterson novels; Alison Bechdel's comic strip, Dykes to Watch Out For; and Annie Sprinkle's video workshop, Sluts and Goddesses. Folders and file boxes—containing newspaper clippings, reports, and past and current help-line logs—are neatly stacked atop every available surface.

As I waited for my first call—my fellow counselor was fielding a call from a support group member who felt she was being stalked by another— I browsed through some of the old help-line logs. All counselors are instructed to record the date, time, and sex of each caller as well as the reason for the call. Among the entries I read that day were: "M[ale]. Wants someone to clean his house," and "M[ale]. Wants a woman to look after his children, but not a lesbian." How a newspaper ad that asked "Are you a woman attracted to other women?" could call out to a man who wanted a heterosexual nanny was something that vexed us, but such clueless callers accounted for over 25 percent of the help line's calls and labor. In the year before I became a counselor, Sangini had received around seven hundred calls, of which 33 percent were prank and obscene calls; 15 percent were legitimate calls from men concerned about a lesbian sister, wife, or fiancée; and 26 percent were legitimate calls from women.[15]

The women who turned to the help line, like Sakhi's letter writers, had a variety of concerns. The major difference between the letter writers and the callers was that the latter were much less likely to refer to themselves as "lesbians." This was in part because Sangini chose not to use the word in its ads. That choice, a function both of the group's founding ideology and of the discursive censoring by the media in which they advertised, left women without a mirror, without the ability to recognize a lesbian self in the self-declaration of another in whom that self can be glimpsed. One young urban caller, for example, told me that she had sex only with women but was not a lesbian. "I've never heard of a *real* lesbian," she said. "Lesbians are only in fantasy, not in real life."

The "real life" of many of these women is indeed far removed from fantasy. There are certain verbal cues and performatives in the immediately dialogical medium of the telephone help line, unlike in the voiceless chasm of time separating the writer and reader of a letter, that permit a heightened awareness of another's pain. There were evenings, for instance, when the phone would ring at precisely six o'clock, just as the phones were placed on the hook for the evening's session. The caller would speak in a whisper, breathless and nervous. Her husband came home every evening around six, so she only had these few moments to talk. She would ask me about the lesbians who met there the previous Saturday, tell me a bit about her own life, and abruptly hang up when she heard her husband's motorcycle in the lane. One caller told me of an older brother who beat her in the kitchen with a cricket bat after finding her with a female friend, and then promised to kill her if he saw such a thing again. Another talked about her mother, who threatened to kill herself if the daughter did not marry. Some callers just cried. One woman, a college student, called every week, sometimes twice, to sit on the line with me in near silence. I wondered what these silent exchanges could possibly mean to her. But when I once told her that I would be away for three weeks, she responded with desperation and asked me to please not go.

Then there were callers who had nothing but pleasure on the brain, wanting information on sexual positions or pornography. Our official way of answering such queries was to explicitly reframe them as "sexual health" questions and then answer them as factually as possible. The audience for such a reframing is not the client herself, but a potential eavesdropper in the form of the state—a reasonable caution since Sangini shared a phone line with a high profile HIV/AIDS organization working with MSM.

Indian lesbians have been largely unrecognized as potentially criminal by the state, and as an at-risk population by transnational donors; consequently, they have not been constrained by concerns about organizational surveillance. The link between Sangini and Naz changed that. It's important to point out that the creation and perpetuation of the figure of the Indian lesbian in danger is not just the product of activist niche marketing but also of Sangini's formal relationship with a gay men's organization in the age of HIV/AIDS and the presence at the time of a Hindu fundamentalist state that kept a steady eye on cultural deviants.

The ease with which men could penetrate the sanctity of lesbian community through the anonymous medium of the help line was another factor in a growing discourse of lesbian danger and safety. Nearly half of the calls are from men. When the help line started in 1997, Sangini had a strict "no male callers" policy—regardless of a man's sexual orientation or reason for calling, the counselors would refuse to speak with him. Within a year, this policy was relaxed, as Cath realized how many women would be left unreached if Sangini was not willing to first go through a brother, father, or husband. Furthermore, as we were told during our training, changing a man's perception about lesbianism could have a positive impact on the lesbian woman he was calling about. There were several evenings in which we spoke only to men. Some were husbands, like a young man from Punjab who hoped we could assign his lesbian wife a partner from our "club." One of my most persistent callers was a husband from Rajasthan. Cath had recently chastised me for not being more assertive with male callers, so the next time this man called, I told him I would counsel him only if he put his wife in touch with us. He called back twenty minutes later and put his wife on the line. She spoke only in Hindi and then switched to English to make her request: "I am interesting in lesbian sex and sex partner." I told her (unwittingly echoing Sakhi from years earlier) that we could not offer such services; her husband came back on to beg until I finally hung up.

More problematic still were the male lesbian impersonators who called for information that, it was assumed, served as grist for their nocturnal fantasy lives. This was by far the biggest point of anxiety on every lesbian help line I came across. To deal with the concerns about inappropriate expenditures of time, energy, and seed, telephone counselors had developed a number of tests to confirm a caller's sex. The most foolproof was the menstruation test. If a counselor had reason to believe that a caller was a male lesbian impersonator, she would calmly answer one or two of his questions, regardless of how offensive, and then pose one of her own: "Tell me, when was the last time you got your period?" Almost every time, the caller, caught woefully off guard, would stammer and slam down the telephone. As a final step to confirm the authenticity of suspicious lesbians—male or female—callers were invited to a face-to-face session, and thus to cross the border between the anonymity of the help line and the verified community of the support group.

Meeting Face to Face

Veronica was knowingly guided through her process of lesbian recognition in carefully orchestrated face-to-face meetings. Sangini's later face-to-face sessions were a more formalized method of bringing people like Veronica closer to the truth of themselves and widening the circle of lesbian community and institutions. But the important difference between these two moments in Indian lesbian community—the informal moment of Sakhi and the formalized moment of the internationally funded lesbian help-line-cum-support group—is that formal face-to-face meetings were more about maintaining the integrity of the community border than allowing people to pass through it. In order to maintain the safety of the safe space (which necessitates a construction of danger outside of it), face-to-face meetings were a complex and crucial ritual of border control.

A counselor's invitation to a client for a face-to-face meeting served several purposes: to demonstrate to male lesbian impersonators that the counselor was onto them; to coax legitimate women-loving women into the support group; and to keep straight women out of it. The face-to-face sessions had to be held during regular working hours in the Naz office to ensure the safety of the counselor. In my experience as a counselor, a very small percentage of invitees actually appear—many of them were probably men, pranksters, or women who lost their nerve.

A support group meeting I attended on a Saturday in September 2002 gives a sense of how salient the face-to-face session is as a form of community control. Cath was unwell that day and stayed home. Betu and Sangini's third in charge, a young Austrian Indian woman named Maya, were facilitating the session in her stead. There were nine of us that day, mostly the usual crowd—Veronica, Franky (a swashbuckling butch dyke), Lila (a biology graduate student from Nagaland), and Monali (a young Delhi transplant from Calcutta who thought the group foolish but attended anyway). There was one unfamiliar person that day, a woman I'll call Rani.

Rani was in her late thirties or early forties. She carried a leather purse and the latest Nokia cellphone. She had clearly dressed up for the occasion, wearing trousers, a rayon shirt, an embroidered vest, flats, and an excess of jewelry and scent. We slouchy dykes looked at her with some curiosity; she seemed to us overly coiffed and refined. She glanced nervously around and, as we watched her, must have felt terribly self-conscious. No one was quite sure how to proceed until Betu took charge. Her questions began innocently enough, dealing with Rani's background, beliefs, and work. The fact that Rani answered only in Hindi didn't help her to bridge the gap of alterity. Due to the middle-class, urban constitution of the support group and the fact that so many members hail from outside of the Hindi-speaking northern belt of the country, English was the primary language of communication. On many levels, Rani hadn't a prayer.

Finally getting to the heart of matters, Betu asked her: "Do you get attracted to women?" "Yes," Rani answered with some hesitation, "but not in any wrong way." There was silence as this last phrase was digested, then pandemonium. "What did you understand about this group before coming here?" someone asked. Rani asked nervously if we could tell her what the group is for, but someone retorted, "We won't tell you! This is a safe space!" Another member was sent to call Cath and find out how Rani had found the support group. Cath, sincerely confused, said that she had judged Rani acceptable after a face-to-face interview. The group, however, did not, and Rani finally collected her things to leave. "I'm sorry," she said in parting, "I thought this is like a kitty party." On the balcony, we debriefed. "She's dangerous," Franky said, a cigarette dangling from her lip. "Is she a spy or something? Who sent her?" someone else wondered. There was a collective shrug and some muttering about infiltration.

My interest here is in the possessive passion that community provokes. As Miranda Joseph (2002) argues, the idea of emergent political community as a means for good has persisted despite decades of theorizing about the homogenization and reductionism inherent in the production of communal unity. Joseph attributes this persistence to two factors: affect, and the mutual imbrication of community and capital. I have, so far, concentrated on reasons for the former—that is, affective attachment to the signifiers of community and identity. Those reasons include the introduction of new spacetime to lesbian interaction; the role of reflective visuality in the constitution of lesbian identity and the attendant imperative of similitude; and, finally, the forging of a narrative of freedom within limits. I want to think more now about the mutual imbrication of community and capital.

One major strand of feminist critique of community is based on the propensity of minority activists to seal themselves off into carefully guarded groups in order to seize space that is rightfully theirs. An early example is Bernice Reagon's caution that the "barred rooms" we build and guard for a sense of security cannot be sustained, for the "door to the room will just be painted red and then when those who call the shots get ready to clean house, they have easy access to you" (1983, 353). What is interesting about what Shane Phelan later dubs the "red door problem" of lesbian identity (1989, 782)—the risk of being too easily identifiable—is precisely that it is thought of as a problem at a certain moment but later becomes one of community's most profitable assets. In this neoliberal moment, painting a "red door" for simplified recognition becomes the very object of activism. When activism is a marketplace of separate and identifiable niches, and when—for lesbians in the developing world—that niche is one of terror, the red door both identifies the product and signifies its state of danger. It is a combination of these factors—the explicit premise of danger and the need to carve out a marketable niche—that explains stories like that of the infiltrating house-wife. Support group members were never as invested in Sangini as they were when it was ostensibly in danger of being infiltrated by a member of the already safe class. This passion for external boundaries rather than internal bonds is a product of an activist marketplace in which the essence of lesbianism in India—and, more broadly, in the developing world—is danger; danger justifies defense and funding, and what must always be defended is an inviolable safe space.[16]

As was evident everywhere in this world that I occupied, many lesbians *do* live in fear of imminent harm, *do* suffer profound sorrows, *are* victims of violence, and *do* long for spaces of companionship and understanding. I am interested in how the political institutions that activists must engage draw attention away from precisely these sorts of painful realities—and sometimes other joyful ones—of day-to-day life. Activism, at its center, is ethical practice, concerned with problematizing norms and inventing new ways of being. So how does the project of dismantling fear become a politics of insisting on it? How does support become restraint? And how do practices of restraint, in turn, become the conditions of possibility for activist critique and invention? The remainder of this chapter explores these questions.

The Support Group

After calling the help line and passing the face-to-face interview, a potential support group member is given the day, time, and address for the weekly meeting, information that is otherwise kept confidential.[17] The meetings are loosely facilitated, usually by Cath, though Betu, Maya, and others occasionally facilitate meetings on a topic of their expertise—Maya would discuss flirting, Jasmin might speak on safer sex, and Sam would explore Sangini's policy on admitting transsexual women and men.[18] Periodically, Sangini invites foreigners and NRIS to lead discussions, as happened during a spring 2002 visit from members of the US-based Incite!—a collective of women of color, many of whom, especially those in leadership roles, are lesbians. They came to talk about violence between women. The support group members were cordial, gamely accepting requests to relate their coming out stories and to discuss their views on butch-femme relationships. That cordiality turned to boredom, however, as Incite! began discussing their work on lesbian same-sex violence. Sensing they had lost their audience, the visitors re-trained the spotlight on Sangini, asking about the organization's relationship to queer and feminist groups in India. We all turned expectantly to Cath, Betu, and Maya for an answer. Betu broke an awkward silence. "Nobody hates us," she said, "but they have a problem with us because we're not interested in 'politics.'" Cath was incensed and scolded Betu for her mischaracterization: "Our work is political, too. What's 'politics' anyway? Who gets to decide?"

Two days later I drove my motorbike to the South Delhi neighborhood where the three Sangini directors shared a large and beautiful apartment, decorated according to the rules of feng shui. Maya and I were meeting to discuss Sangini's website. As we sat at a Barista—India's Starbucks—I asked her what had happened at the meeting that weekend. Why had there been so little interest in Incite!'s presentation?[19] She answered my question this way: "Sangini is not a political group. Those women were only talking about politics and activism, more Western-type things. People here [at Sangini] have to work their *own* things out [touching her heart]. Those other things, like 'lesbian battering' or whatever, are too far in the future."[20] Clearly, the question of whether Sangini was sufficiently "political" was a source of tension among the leaders. But based on what I knew, I could not believe the claim that the support group members were too deeply mired in their own present realities to imagine and debate future worlds. A meeting the following weekend showed the gap between organizational discourse and the futural ethics of emergent worlds.

Earlier in 2002, Sangini had held an event for International Women's Day to better its relations with other women's groups. Cath had asked Purnima—a talented photographer and support group member in her early twenties—to take a series of photographs for the event, detailing Indian lesbian life. Five of us, including me, agreed to pose. We spent a week taking pictures at various sites around the city: eating and smoking at a lonely roadside *dhaba* late at night; climbing up onto cargo trucks; getting haircuts at a men's barbershop; eating *paan* and laughing, stain-toothed; riding motorcycles; fixing a car.[21]

In a Saturday meeting, Cath suggested that we discuss Purnima's photographs. We placed twenty of the prints around the room, took several minutes to view them, and began our discussion, in which everyone was to point out a favorite photo and explain why she liked it. One woman chose a photograph of Betu and Sam on either side of a paan seller, talking to him animatedly. She explained why: "They're happy. In all the other pictures, we're all trying to be so macho and serious, like we're always trying to be. Here, it's just two happy dykes." This articulation of the macho imperative sparked a lively argument. Lila, for example, asked, "Why can't our emblem be a lesbian changing diapers instead of standing on top of a freaking truck? Why do we keep showing these stereotypes of our community?" Cath pointed out that the women who agreed to model were all androgynous to butch. "How can we visibilize those who refuse visibility?" she asked. "Masculine women are a fact of our community," another agreed. "Like it or not, we can't be afraid to show it."

Their argument was, at heart, about the pressures of revelation—the burden of marginality that affects all those who struggle for recognition. The question is what can be shown and said in order to best reveal the best truths of ourselves to a public from whom we seek respect. The moral imperative is to be intelligible by showing the community at its most virtuous, paying respect to the normative order of things—being Indian, raising babies, or cutting vegetables while incidentally being that thing that makes one marginal. To ask for recognition requires discoursing on the plane of moral goodness. This imperative of (always unattainable) normative morality, however, is one of the burdens of marginality, applicable only to those who seek recognition rather than to those who already enjoy it. Not only this, but the imperative makes activism a series of moral calculations. The questions become: How must we show ourselves in order to be justly seen? Who and what of us must we conceal?

Veronica interrupted our argument to point out another print, a simple, striking image. Two women are sitting next to each other at a dhaba. They are caught in profile. One leans toward her plate, eating with her right hand. The other chews, casually satisfied, looking into the near distance. We all looked again at the photograph, some nodding slowly in agreement as they took it in. Cath asked Veronica what moved her about the image. "It's the ideal world," she said. "The kind of world I wish we had, where being lesbian only means being cool and sexy and being a person. We don't care who sees us or about doing any certain thing. We eat, live, and breathe. We don't even all have to know each other! We can just be like we want."

Veronica's musings unsettle the notion that members need only safety and not struggle, attention only to a troubled present and never to a seductive future. Veronica's imaginary is both beautiful and sad: it aches with ambivalent regret about the limits of her own world, poking fun at what has brought and kept all of them together: their shared marginality and agreed-upon actions, assented to in the name of community, or sometimes "family." To eventually "just be like we want" is Veronica's futural ethic, and hope is its emotional modality (Muñoz 2009, 97–98). She longs to be neither good nor bad, neither brave nor fearful. These dreams arise within and against a particular organizational context in which fear and innocence are central to the cultivation of Indian lesbian subjectivity.

On another afternoon at the support group, after eating *chhole bhatura* (spicy chick peas with puri) and opting not to finish watching *When Night Is Falling* on the VCR (too artsy and not enough "hot parts"), we sat around and waited for conversation to happen. Monali finally burst out, "Why do we have to sit around and talk all the time? Can't we go out and have some fun like the gay boys do?" The subject resonated with everyone—far more than the film did—and a woman called Amita looked around smugly and announced the remedy for our woes: "What we need is a lesbian cruising area!"

I expected reluctance, but there was only enthusiasm for this proposed seizure of public space. It became clear, though, that "cruising" meant something different for (most of these) women than for the gay men they took their example from.[22] I sometimes accompanied gay male friends cruising in India, just for kicks. A favorite site was a public park in Kerala, just off the grounds of a venerated temple. My companion for those forays was a young activist named Arjun, whose knowledge was so deep that he could have been a cartographer of public fucking in India. These walks were about nothing but sex. After a momentary exchange of glances with another man, he'd disappear behind a clump of trees. I'd see him again perhaps seven minutes later, running toward me from the distance with a huge smile on his face as he zipped up his pants. Sex is Arjun's god, and this form of secular worship is what makes him beautiful. He is full of life, coltish and exuberant. His every moment is devoted to making more plea-sure possible, activism and orgasm being tightly connected in his mind as worthy means of producing a better and more desirable world.

His unspoken philosophy of queer politics, shared by the activists he works with in the Gay Bombay support group, is one of radicalizing sex—making sex and pleasure the means to new freedoms rather than what need to be concealed in order to attain them (see Halperin 1995; Muñoz 2009, 30). This radicalization of sex is an easier proposition for gay men than for lesbian women, simply due to the socialization by which women are violently educated into concealing their pleasures and desires while men are violently educated into pursuing them. How is it, then, that the very formations—that is, queer life and politics—invented to critique such normative education and offer a new pedagogy wind up reinforcing that education? The answer lies in the developmental logic that values non-Western women as virtuous victims.

Tentatively shedding the weight of this logic, we planned our cruising area: it would be in a popular South Delhi shopping plaza that has a movie theater and restaurants; it would be held on Sunday afternoons in order to be accessible to women; and its purpose would be public visibility rather than finding and having sex. Someone suggested advertising the cruising area in a newspaper. This was called "unspontaneous" and "stupid." As suggestions flew, a senior member of the group intervened: "This sounds pretty dangerous, guys." We all fell silent and looked at one another. She continued: "What are you going to do if a woman does approach you and then you tell her all your information and find out she's been sent to talk to you by a man? Maybe a police officer?" Monali, defeated and walking off for a smoke, muttered that this is why she prefers the Delhi Dyke chatroom to the support group.

As I rode home that night I found myself thinking of an interview that Foucault gave to a French magazine three years before his death, in which he said that "homosexuality is not a form of desire but something desirable" (1994, 136). That optimistic claim was part of his advancement of an ethic of homosexual ascesis—not asceticism, which is moral renunciation of pleasure, but ascesis as that ethical work we perform on ourselves, through a multiplicity of relationships, to "make ourselves infinitely more susceptible to pleasure" and happiness (Foucault 1994, 13). Reflecting on this, I wondered about the roles of danger, safety, borders, and the renunciation of sex as an aspect of lesbian existence in the making of lesbian subjectivities. Rather than making queerness desirable we so often seemed to be stuck making lesbianism manageable. The other-oriented goal of recognition required sublimating the ethic of invention to the proper display of the collective. The consequence of this narrowing of possibility was to devalue joy as a central aspect of sexual freedom and to increasingly value adherence to normative ideals. The activists who must carry out this sublimation of affect to moral calculus are all too aware of its pains and consequences. That haunting awareness itself is part of the story of activism as ethical practice.

Where Life Is

One Saturday afternoon in 2002, at a weekly Sangini meeting, Cath revealed her growing discomfort with the support group model. The model, she suggested, "implies that lesbianism is a problem" and leads to a collapsing of sexuality with "oppression and sadness." She asked the members if they shared her feelings, and a few readily agreed. One said, "'support group' makes us sound needy, and I don't want to *feel* needy. What about 'club,' or 'drop-in space,' or 'community center'?" Maya quickly responded, "I hardly think 'club' is a good idea. When you try and put sexuality and fun together, people get scared, and they think all we do is have orgies!" Betu added, "We have to remember the *impression* that we are giving to society."

Two points are especially worth noting here. One is that Sangini's strategy for social inclusion—presenting lesbianism as apolitical and nonthreatening—comes with a new relationship to affect, turning from Sakhi's circumscription of affect to highlight sexuality as political to a different kind of circumscription of affect in which desire and joy are sublimated to fear in order to demonstrate a distance from the realm of politics. The other is that this concern about impression and proper display is directed solely at the constitutive outside of the group, rather than toward the people who are described, and ostensibly bettered, by it.

A few days later, I asked Maya about her reaction, and her response to me bespoke her, and Sangini's, larger philosophy: "There are two kinds of groups, Nais. There are 'the fighters' and there are 'the subversives.' We are the subversives. When I represent the group at a college or an NGO or a public place like Dilli Haat, [a crafts bazaar in South Delhi] I won't go up there in pants and shirt and say 'I'm a lesbian!' How can we do that? So I always wear *salwar kameez*. Already everyone thinks that lesbian is something foreign, or that all we think about is sex, so we have to be careful and show them that it's not. *That* is what is subversive, because we show what we have to show to get accepted, but we do what we want on the inside."[23]

Toward the end of my fieldwork, in December 2003, I made a point of getting in touch with people who had left that inside, and whom I had not seen since. I wanted to ask why they had left, and what their impressions of their time with Sangini were. Roshni, a slight thirty-four-year-old woman (the person I had trained with for the help line) was living in South Delhi with her partner and her partner's three siblings from a village in Northeast India. To a question I asked about Sangini she responded: "We have to have it [the group]; it's the only thing like it, so what would all those other women do? [Sangini] was important to *me* at one time, also. But now I have this life, this love, with Jasmin and it becomes less important. I don't know. I have a life now."[24] I might note here the similarities between Sakhi's and Sangini's paths, despite the radical difference in their founding orientations. In Sangini's efforts toward inclusion after its departure from Sakhi and then from CALERI it had to isolate itself from a range of possible forms: we are not political, we are not lesbian, we are in need of support, we threaten no harm. Integral to this process of isolation was forging a distinction between a true, hidden self and the necessary contrived self that presents itself for social recognition: in Maya's words, "We show what we have to show to get accepted, but we do what we want on the inside." The problem, of course, is that this separation is untenable. To prepare the external face for acceptance is also to subject the inside to practices of asceticism, renouncing pleasures that appear incompatible with social norms—pleasures that threaten to disrupt the always tenuous, ongoing process of collective objectification. Like Roshni, we might read these demands, inherent to strategies of inclusion, as a request for stasis, a call to defer life just until that moment when we are accepted. So it is not surprising that Roshni articulates her departure from Sangini as an assertion of life—or, perhaps, as made possible only by discovering life on the outside, in that interstitial space between inclusion in the body social and the concerted drive for it, where anything is possible except, of course, recognition.

In seeking better and more recognition, however, from other activists in India, Sangini hired an external reviewer. This person was a lesbian feminist in her late thirties named Vandana, the director of a prominent, respected, and well-funded NGO in Delhi. In our planning session for the review, Vandana first offered her personal assessment of Sangini's state. Her main critique was that feminists read Sangini's privileging of "support" as an inexcusable retreat from politics. But Vandana was not faulting Sangini for engaging in antipolitics, or suggesting that the group's members free themselves from antipolitical international development agendas. Rather, she felt that Sangini would do better with feminists by making lesbianism more a part of the development agenda and by learning to "market themselves beyond their single niche." Instead of understanding the imperative of marketability as an impediment to activism, Vandana spoke as a true free-market activist, seeing the transnational demand for ever more political niches as a horizon of perpetual self-invention.

Cath, for whom Sangini was a personal invention and her life's work, found all of this potentially useful, but academic. She asked Vandana, "Why don't *you* come to the group?" Vandana said simply, "Me? I'm free."

The Founding of PRISM

On June 22, 2001, dozens of activists gathered for the Sexuality Minority Rights and Human Rights symposium at the Indian Social Institute in Central Delhi. The symposium was organized around the launch of an Amnesty International Report on human rights abuses against gays and lesbians in Asia. It was here that queer activists discussed the need for a new direction in Indian queer politics, founding PRISM (J. Sharma and Nath 2005, 86).

One of these activists was Lesley, who—as I described in chapter 1—had written to Cath and helped found Women to Women (later called Stree Sangam). Lesley had left Bombay and moved to Delhi. A talented writer, she was freelancing for travel magazines around the time PRISM was founded. Lesley's charms lie in her leadership skills. Many meetings would be held with Lesley holding court, often in her bedroom, surrounded by playing cards and newspapers, directing us on strategy and encouraging us to be more intelligent. Lesley is emotion embodied; her temperament is mercurial. The one consistent in her personality is a profound intensity that manifests in periodic eruptions of urgent activity. Another activist at the symposium was Jaya, then Lesley's partner. Jaya was in her late thirties at the time, older than the rest of PRISM's founders, and from a well-to-do family. She is harder to befriend than Lesley is; her warmth is more reluctantly bestowed, but when she bestows it she does so completely. She appears as the steady balance to Lesley's emotion but is no less intense when it comes to her activism. She is the hard-working, dedicated cofounder of Nirantar, a respected NGO working on rural women's literacy and education. She was also relatively new to the world of gay activism, having only stumbled upon it the first time she saw—and fell in love with—Lesley, who was giving a talk on *Fire*. A third activist was Akshay, flamboyant and whip-smart, who hailed from Bangalore and moved to Delhi to work with the nonprofit Lawyers Collective.

Lesley, Jaya, and Akshay, along with two others at the symposium decided to form a new political advocacy collective around what they called "sexuality minority rights," but they did not immediately set it up. The breaking of the Lucknow affair on July 7, 2001, though, provided them with urgency to act. HIV/AIDS outreach workers in Lucknow had been arrested under the antisodomy statute and their NGOs raided by the police. The event shattered any complacency about the ability of queers and queer activists to meet and work without state retribution and inspired protests around the country. The events at Lucknow were for gay men (and thus for queer politics more generally) what *Fire* and the reactions to it were for lesbians: spectacular state violence that necessitated a radical alteration in the field of activism and resistance. Part of that change involved forming mightier collectives with broad-based alliances designed to withstand attacks by the state. One such collective was PRISM.

The group began meeting in August 2001, calling itself the Thursday Forum. Half of the participants were, or had been, involved with Sangini or Naz, and they met in the same support group room that Sangini uses, relying—like most fledgling sexuality groups in Delhi—on Naz's help. By September the forum had renamed itself PRISM, or People for the Rights of Indian Sexuality Minorities, and later left Naz for the office of the Lawyers Collective. ("We didn't want people to think we were one of [Naz's] support groups," Akshay explained to me.)

PRISM can be situated within and against previous models of queer organizing. Sakhi was premised on adherence to a Western model of lesbian identity politics, seeking to call women to their sexualities by linking them to the global signifier of "lesbian." As Sakhi sought its—and India's—place within a transnational politics and market of lesbian identification, Sakhi devalued desire and feeling and emphasized the importance of political competence and dialogue. Those who found themselves, or found others, to be disenfranchised by Sakhi's identity political model devised the idea for Sangini. Sangini's founders negotiated their marginalization from Sakhi by regulating the nonusage of the identifier "lesbian" in order to stake out a claim to a more authentic, more Indian sexual subjectivity for those women who needed a safe space of anonymity and social exploration, rather than a Westernized politics of identity. Sangini, excluded from the political subjectivities Sakhi was fashioning (and, later, from those of CALERI), sought its inclusion in society through the trope of innocence, replacing the lesbian as asexual activist with the Indian same-sex desiring (but not acting) woman as a thing of and in danger.

PRISM's emergence was the third movement in this story. Where Sangini largely defined itself by eschewing politics in favor of support and safety, PRISM defined itself as a political advocacy collective willing to take risks and to be public. Where Sangini turned to transnational donors, PRISM rejected funding in an attempt to be autonomous of market-driven agendas. Where Sangini's privileging of safety required the establishment of boundaries, PRISM thought itself open to everyone, regardless of sex, gender, and sexuality. Where Sangini was unable to forge alliances with other movements, the principle of coalitional politics was PRISM's bedrock.[25]

Lesley and Jaya were once members of Sangini and were among the organization's first help-line counselors—many of the earliest entries in the ledger are written in their hand. Their split with Sangini was antagonistic, based as much on political and philosophical differences as on alleged interpersonal misdeeds. The differences then became concretized into deliberate chasms between the groups. One PRISM activist who had previously been with Sangini described PRISM publicly as an example of "growth" over Sangini's support group model. Another described Sangini as "scared."[26] The activists who left Sangini and founded PRISM, much like Vandana and Roshni, identified Sangini as a space lacking in life, one demanding untenable sacrifices of politics and hope. And, much like Vandana and Roshni, the members of PRISM rejected the Sangini model, understanding themselves as more free.

As I argued through Betu's and Veronica's coming out stories, however, claims to new freedoms entail the imposition of new limits within which these freedoms can be realized and explored. The limit necessary for PRISM's freedom involved a return to Sakhi's model of circumscribing affect in order to highlight sexuality as first and foremost political. But unlike Sakhi, for whose leaders lesbian identity was laden with historical affect, PRISM would understand identity as stripped of affect and as a strategic calculus (rather than a source of endless personal narration, as Sangini would have it).[27]

PRISM's explicit grappling with these questions about identity politics began well after the group's formation. The impetus for the discussions was the Sexuality and Rights Institute (SRI), an international program for selected sexual rights activists from around the world. The program is designed to build leadership capacity, enable the sharing of strategies, and teach promising young activists how to effectively feed local struggles into a larger global movement for sexual rights. The participants also read heavily in poststructuralism, devouring Butler, Foucault, and Derrida. Several Indian queer and feminist activists had participated in the first SRI, held in Amsterdam—including Vandana (Sangini's evaluator) and Arjun (the sex radical). In 2002, the SRI was held in India for the first time, and both Jaya and Akshay were selected.

Life in PRISM was lonely with two of its core members away in Pune that March. I had become accustomed to a maniacal pace of activity. In only three months, for example, PRISM had become centrally involved in a national legal campaign against sexual assault; had helped organize a public meeting with an out gay justice of the Supreme Court of Australia, Justice Michael Kirby; and had produced a street play about queer issues that was performed in front of hundreds. PRISM had no paid members, and all that the group did was undertaken during evenings and weekends. Very often, those hours were long and full of camaraderie, highly caffeinated, with work stretching deep into the night in cramped and smoky rooms.

That intensity was revived with Jaya and Akshay's return from the SRI, when debates about the politics of identity consumed us all. Jaya and Akshay had decided in Pune that PRISM could no longer stand for People for the Rights of Indian Sexuality Minorities. First, "Indian" made too much of a claim to national belonging in a time of violent Hindu nationalist ascension. And second, "sexual minority" did not evince an adequate grasp of the intersectionality of sexual, gendered, racial, caste, and class oppressions.[28] As the advocates of an intersectional model saw it, PRISM's move had to be one from "an identity-based paradigm of sexual minorities to an intersectional framework, which sought to locate sexuality—in a dynamic and holistic way—in relation to other axes of social construction and control, such as gender, religion, and class" (J. Sharma and Nath 2005, 87). Rather than being solely for the protection of sexual minorities, PRISM should stand for an ethic of wider human connection through the call for ever more possibilities for pleasure. And so some of them suggested: People for the Right to Sexuality . . . and More!

In an effort to educate people about and forge a consensus on PRISM's position on identity politics, Jaya called a special meeting, for which nine of us gathered at Lawyers Collective on an April evening. The meeting revealed the degree of people's attachment to identity. "I don't understand why you want to do away with identity!" exclaimed a young journalist and activist who had joined PRISM relatively recently. She seemed pained by the very fact of the discussion: "Isn't this what we've all been fighting for? The right to call ourselves gay or bi, or whatever we choose?"

Akshay disagreed: "I think what we fight for is the right not to live in neat little boxes" (see Khanna 2005). (It is worth noting how a queer poststructuralist critique of identity sounds very similar to the critique of identity made by older, definitely not "queer" feminists like Abha Bhaiya: that identity imposes a definition on what should be fluid and dynamic [see Bhaiya 2007].) But Lesley agreed with the journalist, citing both her own coming out through Sakhi and Women to Women and her experiences on the Sangini help line. "Identity gives people something to believe in," she argued. "You remember what happened after *Fire*. All these women heard the word 'lesbian' for the first time, and the number of calls we got doubled or tripled. Don't tell me that's less important than all this 'intersectionality,' 'contextionality' talk."

Lesley's attachment to identity for the meaning it provides exemplifies Butler's summation of the identity politics dilemma: "The necessity to mobilize 'the necessary error of identity' will always be in tension with the democratic contestation of the term which works against its deployments" (1993, 229).[29] But in addition to critiquing the contestation of identity's seemingly necessary utility, Lesley also calls into question—with her sarcastic repetition of language inspired by SRI—the uneven access to elite discourse that seems to make such contestation possible, and that thus renders such contestation less than democratic.

The SRI graduates had a ready response, claiming that a rejection of identity-based politics is the way to democratize activism. "Our reliance on identity," one argued, "works to *obscure the differences among us*. When we make someone say, 'I'm a lesbian,' we ignore [the fact] that she might also be working class, Dalit, or Muslim." This speaker realized and played on identity's etymology. Collectivity based on identity presumes—in fact, requires—that we render ourselves identical (Joseph 2002, viii), as the members of Sakhi, Women to Women, and Sangini sought to do. This is not to argue that identity obscures difference; quite the contrary, the discursive work of identity is to produce differences that then serve as the phantasmic Self's constitutive Other. The point is that "the necessary error of identity" militates against exploring possibilities beyond the binary of sameness and difference—a militance that, however seemingly necessary, is also at odds with activism. The imperative to say "we are precisely this" prevents us from asking, "What else might we become?" Or, as Foucault has put it, "What can be played?" (1994, 140).

PRISM did decide to explore what else could be played. It was, as Akshay put it, "a refusal to live inside of limits and refusing to make others do so. It's realizing that [identity] just reinforces the same boundaries we're trying to deconstruct." However, the group didn't change its name to "People for the Right to Sexuality . . . and More!" or to "People for the Right to Sex . . . Mucho!," as was also drunkenly suggested. It became, simply, PRISM. In standing for nothing in particular, the people who made up PRISM hoped to stand for everything they believed in while rejecting the imperative of intelligibility. In the mission statement they later wrote, they described themselves as follows: "Our organizing is feminist, inclusive, non–identity based, and progressive. . . . We question . . . social concepts such as the primacy of monogamy, enforced heterosexuality and heteronormativity, the institution of marriage, and the concept of sexual identity and behavior as fixed . . . and unchanging."[30]

PRISM's shift away from identity politics had several consequences, of which I will emphasize two. First is the circumscription of the affective space of politics, which enables identity to be delinked from sentiment so that identity can be understood as only a selectively deployable political commodity. Second, the rejection of identity as the primary shaping mechanism of gay and lesbian life enables a search for and cultivation of alternative forms of empathy, connection, and care—in other words, an ethics of problematization, invention, and creative relational practice. The first consequence (the circumscription of affect) necessarily delimits, though certainly does not negate, the second (the cultivation of a critical ethic).

Steven Seidman argued that anti-identity politics is a necessary corrective for an "ethnic model" of gayness that destroyed the radical potential of early gay liberation movements by turning a liberatory ethos into a series of narrow, exclusionary practices. But a strong form of the poststructuralist critique of the subject transformed "anti-identity politics to a politics against identity *per se.*" Such rejection of identity displays "a kind of anarchist championing of a 'pure' freedom from all constraints and limits," demonstrating "the disciplining compulsory imperative to remain undifferentiated" (Seidman 1993, 133). PRISM's desire for "pure" freedom from lesser identity-political models of activism—such as Sangini's—required a disciplining of affect, a forceful delinking of politics from the ever-present longing to belong. In other words, a certain ethical orientation away from the imperatives of identity and toward multiplicity entailed its own form of closure.

In the first week of my fieldwork, I found myself alone with Jaya after a late lunch with her and Lesley. I asked her about PRISM's founding and the ways in which the group was distinct from CALERI and Sangini. She started to answer with reference to Sangini:

> I'll tell you what I miss about those days [at Sangini]. You'd go to one of these meetings . . . and we'd tell *stories.* We'd talk about our lives—all that stuff about coming out and marriage pressure [making a self-mocking face]. There's one afternoon I remember very fondly. Cath and Betu had invited a kothi [to speak]. And this kothi, he read a poem he had written on "why I wish I was a girl." There was not *one person* in that room who wasn't affected. Not one person in that room didn't have a tear in their eye when they heard this poem. And it really just brought all of us together. In PRISM, though, it's all about this law or that section, or that protest, or this strategy. It's all important, and that's why we do it. But it just can't bring people together in the same way. I feel sad about that. I miss it.[31]

Similarly, in a meeting held months later to write PRISM's revamped, nonidentitarian mission statement, Lesley spoke up. She had decided to take a break from PRISM since their identity discussion. She had one main regret to voice: "I feel that PRISM has become a group for *other* people.

You're all talking about serving as a 'resource group' or 'forging alliances' and 'making linkages.' Just because we don't think of ourselves as needy doesn't mean that we don't have needs. This group should also be about our *own* growth as people, our *own* learning. Or else, why are we doing it?" Both Jaya and Lesley argue, in different ways, that PRISM's insistence on a freedom from subjection to identity—even as that insistence was born of and enabled new ethical possibilities—has been translated into a retreat from the affective texture of activism. It is the functionality of sexual identity—its demotion from the truth of the self to the occasional, strategic tool—that they feel as a political and ethical loss.

What both of them are then asking is: "If not by norms, how else might we give shape to our lives? How else might we live?" It is precisely these questions that, to an outsider like me, seemed to serve as the ethical foundation of PRISM's political life. Politics was, for them, intrinsically about love, care, and connection; about using the fact of queer marginality as a reason to invent new ways to be. It was about having an open home, a bottomless fridge, a ready ear; it was taking in friends of a friend with no questions asked, providing them solace from whatever made them exiles. It was about creating strange family out of strangers, engaging every last person in the spirited debates that were the center of our lives.

These were the aspirations from which PRISM was born, and these were the practices that remained. What is interesting is not how the demands of political calculus turn radicals into sell-outs, but how the binary structures of political choice—as Sangini and PRISM know—can never do justice to everything we hope and need.

chapter 3

VIRTUOUS WOMEN, RADICAL ETHICS,

AND NEW REGIMES OF VALUE

On the eve of the Asia Social Forum I made my way out of the Hyderabad train station, looking for Jaya. I spotted her standing by an auto-rickshaw, and ran over and hugged her hello. Jaya was unusually quiet as we rode through the city, passing temples and mosques and speeding over newly constructed overpasses. I jabbered on about my trip and then finally asked her what was wrong. Jaya told me that just before coming to the station, she had met a well-known Indian feminist, A. Khan, in the hotel.[1] Jaya invited Khan to come to PRISM's seminar on queer sexuality. Khan replied condescendingly: "I don't think so, Jaya. See, it's all a matter of priorities. Women in this country are poor and starving. I don't see how we can talk about sexuality. The *janta* [common people] just aren't ready to hear about these things. This is not a priority for them."

I was far more surprised by Jaya's despondency than by Khan's comments. This particular refrain about the poor and hungry Third World janta not being ready to talk about sexuality was one that lesbian activists in India were well accustomed to hearing (J. Sharma and Nath 2005, 84). Still, Jaya could think of little else that evening besides Khan's rejection. As members of PRISM met that night to discuss their seminar, the conversation repeatedly circled back to how to address the relationship between sexuality and the Third World woman. How, they wondered, could PRISM make its politics seem more relevant to feminists like Khan? How could PRISM demonstrate its sensitivity to questions of poverty and culture? The answers to these questions were not easily come by, despite the number of times queer activists considered them. The everyday strategy of PRISM was to discuss the intersectionality of oppressions, particularly those of sexuality and class. Another, much more emotionally effective tactic was to evoke the tragedy of rural lesbian suicides, an approach that many queer activists use to show that lesbianism, and its violent oppression, is not a strictly urban or middle- and upper-class phenomenon (see J. Sharma and Nath 2005, 92; see also Dave 2011 and Vanita 2005).

I have two objectives in this chapter. First, I historicize and critically engage the conditions under which a moralistic discourse about the so-called real needs and capabilities of Third World women has emerged as a central preoccupation of Indian feminisms; and second, I analyze how ethical practices of critique, invention, and creative relational practice have fared in this normalizing terrain of proper and improper Third World activism.[2] In light of Khan's comments, I am interested in how it has become possible and necessary for Indian feminists to speak of priorities and to take certain forms of human limitation—poverty, in this case—as more authentic to, as separate from, as more dire than, and as more deserving of relief and attention than other forms of limitation. In other words, what are the grids of intelligibility through which poverty is understood as more authentic to, as separate from, as more dire than, and as more deserving of attention than the politics of sexuality?

To make sense of hierarchies of worthiness, I draw on Deborah Mindry's work on the South African grass roots and the moral politics of Third World women's virtue. Like Mindry, I am interested in how particular groups of women in the developing world become constituted as grass roots—a "morally pure terrain" of victimization and never aspiration and, thus, as a "naturalized object" of benevolent intervention (2001, 1202). In South Africa, "grass roots" consists of rural, poor, black women; in India, "grass roots" means the janta and women who dwell in bastis, or slums. The issue at hand is to examine the circuits of power and knowledge through which the notion of the economically suffering, virtuous Indian woman of the grass roots—she who is too mired in poverty to think of anything other than her family's most basic needs—has become a normalizing discourse that, instead of enabling new forms of social action, works to restrict what can be imagined and said. In sketching the history of India's women's movement,

I locate the roots of this moral politics in colonial-era discourse of Indian women as victims. Moving to and through the period of economic liberalization, I examine how this moral politics became increasingly class- rather than nation-specific.

The restructuring of India's economy in the early 1990s led to a crisis of legitimacy for the women's movement: as women's movement activists became better compensated and more cosmopolitan, their objects of intervention (that is, grass-roots women) became increasingly poor and increasingly bound to their "roots." This widening disjuncture between elite Indian activists and their grass-roots subjects has, I argue, been negotiated on the terrain of lesbian politics and of sexuality, more generally. In an effort to solidify their own cultural credentials, women's movement activists have painted lesbian politics as bourgeois and irrelevant. By protecting the poetics of poverty from the urban politics of radical sexuality, feminists like Khan demonstrate feminism's entanglement within a discourse of the virtue of victimization. It is through and against this set of political norms that lesbian activism has struggled for political identity and imagination.

It is worth stressing that the relationship between lesbian activism and India's women's movement is one of asymmetry—while heterosexual feminists like Khan see lesbian activism as a luxury, acceptance from the women's movement is a political necessity for lesbian activism. There are two reasons for this. First, in India, as is the case everywhere, lesbian activism grew out of an already established national women's movement (C. Shah 2005, 143–44; M. Sharma 2006, 8). The histories of feminism and lesbian politics are inextricably linked, and I detail those connections in this chapter. Second, lesbian activism depends on the women's movement because of priorities of scale. I have traced the processes by which an emergent lesbian politics gradually solidifies and widens its spheres of influence from imagined community to face-to-face community and then to funded and nonfunded organizations. This chapter traces lesbian activists' efforts to forge political alliances with other, more established progressive movements, both to receive material assistance and to demonstrate legitimacy. I am interested in the compulsory nature of these alliances and in how the conception of value in the political market—in which an activist's value is determined based on her ability to penetrate further and further fields of influence—has shaped notions of ethical value.

This chapter is organized around major moments in Indian lesbian history over three decades: the marriage of two policewomen in 1987, the expulsion of lesbian students in Kerala in 1992, a Marxist feminist's public attack on lesbianism in 1994, the effort of lesbian women to march as lesbians in a women's movement rally in 2000, and allegations of lesbian discrimination in a women's NGO in 2002. I precede my analysis of each of these lesbian-historical moments with an examination of critical events in Indian feminist history that are usually read by feminist scholars as if they had no bearing on broader questions of sexuality.[3] Through this examination, I trace how events in women's movement politics laid the foundation for how feminists could and could not respond to public controversies around lesbianism.

Organizational Forms of the Women's Movement

India's women's movement is no monolith. It takes unique forms in different cities (Ray 1999); different rural areas (Basu 1992); and, most important for my discussion, between affiliated and autonomous women's groups. Affiliated women's groups in India are the women's fronts of political—usually communist—parties, while autonomous groups are financially, organizationally, and ideologically independent of political parties. Internationally, affiliated women's groups, beholden to the agendas set by their (usually leftist) parties, are likely to focus on material inequality and the interests of women within the bounds of class interests. Autonomous groups, on the other hand, often focus on issues that are more threatening to the gendered order of things, such as domestic violence, marital rape, and reproductive autonomy (Ray 1999).

It thus makes sense that lesbian activists have made their deepest inroads through autonomous women's groups (in part by belonging to them) and that leftist groups have, by and large, been adamantly opposed to an explicit engagement with lesbian issues. However, the NGO-ization of activism has changed the very meaning of "autonomy." Even NGOs that are proudly free of political parties are still answerable to international donors and the Indian state. Consequently, the feminist NGO sector has a tense split identification between being autonomous and being establishment. The NGO-ization of feminism—and progressive, including queer, politics more generally—has had important consequences for the relationship between lesbian activism and the women's movement, and for the ethical possibilities of activism more generally.

India's women's movement began through the social reform efforts of the nineteenth century, which sought to respond to the British imperial claim that Indian women were in need of uplift and civilizing intervention. Indian male reformers agreed with the claim but argued that they, rather than colonialists, would be responsible for their women's uplift. There were two competing social reform approaches. The revivalist approach was to uplift Indian women through reminding Indians of women's hallowed position in Vedic texts and then focusing on reeducating respectable women—both Hindus and Muslims—who could demonstrate Indian cultural glory (Kasturi and Mazumdar 1994, xxxiv). The second approach, less wedded to a golden-age narrative, sought to abolish embarrassing antiwoman practices such as sati and child marriage through recourse to liberal democratic and rationalist values (Ray 1999, 183).[4]

Meanwhile, Indian women across class, caste, and region were playing their own roles, often militant, in the nationalist movement.[5] Much of the scholarship on Indian nationalism, however, suggests that male leaders of the movement largely orchestrated women's participation, or that the latter's contribution lay primarily in serving as guardians of culture in the private sphere (see Chatterjee 1990). Feminist historians have countered by showing how women organized themselves and staked their value far beyond the hearth and deep into international arenas (see C. Gupta 2001; Sarkar 1992 and 2001; Sinha 1995). But what feminist historians write against was anyway more of an ideal than reality, an idealized construction of the good Indian woman that a large number of elite women aspired to. These historically salient, dualistic models—liberal reform versus traditional revival, public versus private—are important for understanding the women's movement's future engagement with sexuality: Indian feminism has always had to contend with, and has thus been invested in, essentialist constructs of virtuous Indian womanhood.

The contemporary women's movement remains subject to such flattened representations, but this is largely on account now to a liberal, Western feminist discourse that posits the Third World woman as the First World's Other and as just the same: the pitiable victim in need of intervention (Kapur 2001; Mohanty 1991; Mohanty, Russo, and Torres 1991) but also the proto-feminist agent who desires freedom from patriarchy (Mahmood 2005). Although this presumptuous liberal discourse has been a frustration for Indian feminists, it has also been a boon, attracting resources and attention to women's organizations. These resources and that attention, though, fuel allegations on the home front that feminism is out of place in India—bourgeois, Western, and out of touch with the everyday needs of real Indian women. Privileging a construct of women as victims of poverty and circumstance, rather than as sexually desiring subjects, has enabled Indian feminism to mold itself to both Western and Indian perceptions.

Critical Events I: The Politics of Representation

THE MATHURA CAMPAIGN

In India, the decades following independence in 1947 saw a lull in the women's movement as the governing Congress Party enshrined the equal rights of men and women in the Constitution (Kumar 1993, 97), creating a sense of protection. Furthermore, without the common enemy of colonial power, the women's movement became fragmented and its activity dwindled (Kumar 1993, 97). In the early 1970s, however, international and national events converged to spark a resurgence of the women's movement and the beginning of its contemporary phase. A growing disillusionment with state policies led to a host of feminist actions across the country, such as the Shahada anti-liquor movement, a movement against price increases, and the rise of the Self-Employed Women's Association in Gujarat (John 2005). But when Prime Minister Indira Gandhi declared a state of emergency in mid-1975, political activity was pushed far underground. Life resumed in 1977, as did a women's movement that was increasingly suspicious of the state.

Rape and sexual violence became dominant themes for women's groups around the country because of several high-profile rape cases in the post-emergency period.[6] The Mathura case in 1979 was the most pivotal of these. Police officers abducted a teenage girl named Mathura, took her to the police station, and raped her. A lawsuit was later filed against the officers. The case went all the way to the Supreme Court, which acquitted the officers based on the unconscionable argument that Mathura, who had a boyfriend, was "loose" and therefore not capable of being raped. This led to outrage on a national scale. In Bombay, a group of feminists founded the Forum against Rape to spearhead the Mathura campaign. They persuaded other feminist groups that had been established after the Emergency to be part of a large, coordinated national protest on March 8, International Women's Day.

I want to note three main things about the Mathura campaign. First is the significance of a nationally coordinated, feminist-led campaign that marked a new phase of national collaboration (as well as a new phase of disappointments and disharmony). Second is the centrality of rape in this phase and, especially, the consequent focus on violence against women that is sexual in means and institutional in context. This focus has had far-reaching implications for how the contemporary women's movement variously has and has not engaged with lesbianism. For example, feminists constructed the realm of the sexual as an entry point for class, state, and gendered violence, not a taking-off point for a politics of pleasure, desire, or sexual agency.[7] In addition, the realm of the sexual was important to feminists insofar as it could highlight abuses of power between acknowledged classes of people: men over women, the state over its citizenry, landlords over laborers, and Hindus over Muslims. In other words, the sexual was a matter of politics only when it was both violent and collectivized. As we'll see, the women's movement has not seen lesbian politics as meeting these criteria. Rather, the women's movement has largely perceived lesbian sexuality as a matter of indulgence, not violence, and as private rather than social. Furthermore, to understand lesbian oppression as institutional and collectively executed would require recognition of a privileged class called heterosexuals. Such a concept within the women's movement is still in the making.

But the third point I want to draw attention to concerns an internal debate among feminist groups. The Mathura campaign introduced Indian feminists to an interrogation of the politics of representation. As Radha Kumar has described (1993, 129–30), several feminist groups attempted to meet Mathura before the planned protests. Two members of the Forum against Rape spoke with her, only to find out that she was apathetic about feminist campaigning on her behalf. Her apathy, says Kumar, "shamed" and troubled many of the activists. What if Mathura felt that publicity was only another insult? What if she had actually asked the activists to cease and desist—would the campaign have gone on regardless? Feminists were split. Some thought the campaign had gone beyond Mathura, while others felt that feminist ethics demanded Mathura's consent. The same issue would be revived later, when autonomous groups had to decide whether and how to speak for two women joined together in marriage.

The antirape campaign shaped the landscape of autonomous women's organizing in Delhi. A number of women activists from the campaign formed an umbrella group called Samta in the mid-1970s, which gave rise to the Indian women's journal *Manushi*. The group split, with *Manushi* and its editors going in one direction and the rest founding Stree Sangarsh (women's struggle) in 1979. Stree Sangarsh played a pivotal role in the Mathura campaign and also in antidowry agitations in the early 1980s. Their favored tactics of street theater and other public activism (Garlough 2008) gave way to a formal feminist collective called Saheli in 1981, which provided counseling and other resources for women in need. Saheli raised small donations and eventually rented a second-floor office under a highway overpass in South Delhi. Saheli and two other feminist groups, Jagori and Ankur, became central players in the autonomous women's movement in Delhi and remain so today.

This scene of Delhi women's activism in the early 1980s consisted of and brought together several women who were themselves partnered with other women. Despite their familiarity with, and involvement in, same-sex relationships, many of these women adamantly rejected lesbian politics in favor of what I call a poetics of silence (Bhaiya 2007).[8] One women's movement veteran, Abha, a founding member of Jagori and a former member of Saheli, speaks with nostalgia about the "beauty of silence" before the advent of lesbian politics: "[Lesbian sexuality] was never a big deal for me. . . . I myself was with women. I've known twenty-five years of these relationships, [in Delhi], Jaipur, Hyderabad, everywhere. I've known the beauty of them, the trust, the secrecy. Secrecy, contrary to what you people think, is not a bad thing. There is tremendous spiritual possibility in those bonds. The LGBT gain has been a loss in these ways."[9]

Abha speaks of lesbian relationships in the early days of the contemporary women's movement as far richer because there was no compulsion to speak of them publicly. These were relationships that were more in keeping with the rhythms of the women's movement at a seemingly more enchanted time—when friendships had no boundaries, when the spaces of work and home were one and the same. The imperative to name women's same-sex desire has, for her, struck a blow to the poetics of love: lesbian politics has turned a beautiful act of imagination into a disenchanted bore.

Abha proudly told me about the ways that Jagori initiated conversations about same-sex eroticism in rural settings.[10] A favorite activity in village-level training involved a woman rolling herself over a row of supine bodies. Quite amazingly, the facilitators would ask such questions as, "How did you feel when your breast and vulva rolled over another woman's body?" In the villages, Abha claimed, where women were not aware of lesbian politics, there was no discomfort around same-sex desire. She told me about two Rajasthani women who were married to the same man and in love with each other. The other women were so comfortable with the relationship that they openly admired the tattoo one had of the other's name.

Despite these romanticized narratives, there is plenty of tragic evidence showing that the absence of sexual identity politics in rural India does not imply an acceptance of same-sex sexual relationships. This is especially evident when female same-sex lovers attempt to resist the imperative of marriage. The discomfort that activists like Abha feel toward lesbian activists is certainly based more on protecting the women's movement than on preserving the pristine nature of same-sex love or denying the existence of violence against such lovers. Abha concedes this: "It has been my choice not to be public about myself. Early on, when the women's movement was at stake in such decisions . . . well, it wasn't like I didn't live my relationship or raise my voice. . . . It helped me to critique marriage . . . because nobody could write it off as, 'of course you're critiquing it, you're a lesbian!' Also, impacting 2,500 villages was far more important than entertaining the question, 'Is Abha a lesbian?'"

The tensions within the autonomous women's movement between personal identification and collective risk and responsibility came to a head in 1987 and early 1988, after the marriage of Urmila and Leela in Madhya Pradesh (see the introduction and chapter 1). I'll review a few key elements of their saga here. Fellow constables informed on Leela and Urmila after the women returned from a garland ceremony marking their marriage. Leela and Urmila were secluded while officers conducted an investigation. The women allege that they were kept without food for forty-eight hours and forced to sign papers they did not understand.[11] Some of the women's supporters speculated that Urmila was medically examined to ascertain her genital "normality."[12] Given the ambiguity around the legality of their marriage—the antisodomy statute says nothing about homosexual matrimony in particular, or about women at all—Urmila and Leela were dismissed for unauthorized absence from duty and forcibly escorted to the Bhopal train station.

When news of the marriage broke in February, women's groups in Bombay were the first to respond. All who responded were concerned about the unjust dismissal of the women and their allegations of abuse, but they did not agree on the meaning of the marriage itself. One group saw Leela and Urmila's union as a "result of marital harassment and incessant dowry demands,"[13] which fit neatly into the women's movement's campaigns against dowry and marital rape. It also fit with a popular tendency to see lesbian relationships through the prisms of violence and circumstance. However, Bombay's Forum against the Oppression of Women (FAOW, formerly the Forum against Rape) boldly declared the union between Urmila and Leela to be a lesbian marriage and a "viable alternative" to heterosexual matrimony.[14] FAOW recalls the affair as a watershed moment in their own thinking about lesbianism (FAOW 2002). The public form of the discrimination against the constables, coupled with the presence of lesbians within FAOW, compelled the collective to take its first public stand on behalf of lesbians.

In Delhi, intense debates ensued about whether to follow FAOW's lead. A group of about ten women, most from Jagori and romantically woman-identified, were troubled by FAOW's claim that Leela and Urmila's marriage was an "articulation of lesbian politics." Urvashi Butalia, a feminist activist, writer, and publisher, described these meetings to me.[15] The group, she said, focused on lessons learned from the Mathura campaign and debated the ethics of representing Leela and Urmila as "lesbians" given the police-women's own unequivocal rejection of this term of identification. Butalia told me:

> There was a concern that if these two women who had chosen to marry were not willing to recognize themselves as lesbians, what right did we have to walk in there and say, "Hey, you might not know it, but you are lesbians"?[16] It's [also] a question about the identity of the women's movement. Who are we? Are we a people who have an ideology and politics of our own? Or are we a service group who respond to the desires of others? . . . So in the end, what was decided about the MP [Madhya Pradesh] case was that a couple of women would go there and talk to the women themselves, and come back and we could discuss [what to do next]. Our responses were based on that. Anyone reading it from the outside might say that "the women's movement is scared of articulating the lesbian experience." If you see it from the inside, you might see it a bit differently. But sure, there was no doubt a kind of fear.

In the end, determining that neither they nor Urmila and Leela had any cause for an explicitly "lesbian rights" approach, one group—Jagori—decided to take a middle path. They wrote letters to political leaders in Madhya Pradesh labeling the marriage a protected, personal choice, calling for the women's reinstatement, and decrying the abuse of police power.

These important first steps on behalf of same-sex lovers set a precedent for how autonomous women's groups would engage lesbian issues. I have shown how, for many women's activists, rejecting the term "lesbian" was a carefully considered political and ethical choice. But simply rejecting the term and the struggles associated with it was no longer an option for the women's movement. Instead, women's groups would emphasize the private dimensions of lesbian sexuality and strategically frame lesbian issues in a language of (gender- and sexuality-neutral) human rights, such as the rights to livelihood, association, free speech, or—where lesbian suicide is concerned—to simply live. The effect was a double maneuver: women's groups could express ideological sympathy with the many lesbian women within their ranks, while also achieving a carefully calibrated distancing in which lesbian issues are framed as external to women's questions, so as to minimize the risk for—and the political responsibility of—the women's movement itself.

Single Women Speak

In chapter 1, I allude to Jagori's introduction of "single women" as a way to speak about and informally organize around lesbianism. The category of single women was also more than just an oblique way to address the concerns of lesbian women: it was an important category in its time for addressing the widespread discrimination that all unmarried women face at the hands of family, society, and the state. Until the advent of the category, the autonomous women's movement had primarily focused its energies on violence against women within the domain of conjugality.[17] But with Jagori's initiation in 1990 of a five-year single women project—culminating in a book and annual diaries featuring narratives by single women—feminists began examining the lives of unmarried women, many of whom were being cast out of their families for refusing to marry; being exploited by their families as unpaid domestic servants after their husbands divorced or abandoned them; being sexually harassed; or being unable to get a state-issued ration card in the absence of a husband, son, or other male guardian.[18]

Activists concerned with issues related to single women held intensive discussions at the local, regional, and national levels about who counted as single women (widows? prostitutes? nuns?). And by using the term "single women" instead of "unmarried women," these activists sought to focus affirmatively on women's autonomy from marriage, often by choice.[19] This further opened a space for speaking about sexual choice, and lesbian women made the most of that opening at the Fourth National Conference of Women's Movements (NCWM) in 1990.

The NCWM was first held in Bombay in 1980 as a way for autonomous women's groups to strategize about the antirape campaign.[20] The second NCWM was held five years later, also in Bombay, with the goal of critically discussing power politics and hierarchy in the women's movement. The third—held in Patna, Bihar, in 1987—was a site of much infighting, but the conference went on to hold a fourth meeting, which brought to light two major shifts in the women's movement.

The fourth NCWM was held in Calicut, Kerala, in 1990. From the outset, uncertainty was high about the rise and consequences of NGOs in the movement. The conference report noted:

> There was a change in the national situation. Various national, international and governmental agencies had formed organizations that employed women, as well as activists from the movement and these organizations were taking up issues concerning women in different forms. Besides autonomous groups and the women activists from struggle oriented mass organizations, these *Non-Governmental/Governmental Organizations* with developmental perspective participated in the conference. The conference was [now] called Conference of Women's Movements in India. There were large number[s] of women who came from these governmental/non-governmental development oriented organizations. (Fifth NCWM 1994, 4; emphasis added)

The ambivalence about NGOs and their place in the women's movement is striking. The writers of the report refuse to separate nongovernmental from governmental, and they pointedly delete "national" from the NCWM in reference to the movement's new international orientation. In conference sessions, divisions seemed to widen among autonomous groups, leftist organizations, and mass-organized struggles as they sought to make sense of the new activist landscape (3).

A second set of debates at the conference concerned single women. A couple from Jagori, Maya and Shanti, organized a separate evening session for single women. The two had long worked with single women, including same-sex couples in rural areas and urban slums. The gathering they organized was a small one—about fifteen people attended—in which lesbian women spoke about their relationships, their ostracization, and what set them apart from other single women. The organizers later described the gathering as being "in the wings and invisible" (Fifth NCWM, 49), but they were actually not invisible at all: several women in the larger conference accused the session's attendees of "creating differences" within the movement (ibid.). Nevertheless, lesbians carved out a critical niche at the NCWM, one that would expand to far greater consequence and controversy four years later, in the southern Indian town of Tirupati.

Narrative Interlude: The Transformation of Indian Activism

The period between the fourth and fifth NCWMs was one of dramatic change in India due to the effects of the New Economic Policy implemented under Prime Minister Narasimha Rao and Finance Minister Manmohan Singh. Starting in the 1950s, India, under the Congress Party, had favored a Nehruvian socialist model of development that protected trade, emphasized heavy investment in the public sector, and aimed at building national self-reliance. These economic strategies resulted in recurrent shortages of foreign exchange and made India's balance of payments ever vulnerable to sudden shifts in world prices. A drastic rise in oil prices in 1991 precipitated a balance of payment crisis and double-digit inflation, placing India at risk of defaulting on its debts. The New Economic Policy was passed in July 1991. Following World Bank and IMF recommendations for developing economies, the policy devalued the rupee, increased interest rates, reduced public investment in capital-intensive and high-tech activities, and decreased agricultural subsidies. The policy also called for privatizing national industries and withdrawing from investment in the public sector.

The effects of economic liberalization for women were wide ranging. The decrease in subsidies for small-scale farmers in favor of resource-intensive agriculture disproportionately affected women because roughly 15 percent more women than men earned their income from farming (Arora 1999). Extraordinary rates of inflation, a consequence of the devalued rupee, placed further burdens on women as basic daily necessities such as dal, rice, cooking oil, and grains took larger and larger chunks out of women's earnings (Arora 1999). This contributed to the feminization of poverty, as Indian women contribute an average of 95 percent of their incomes to the purchase of household goods, while men contribute only 40–50 percent of theirs (Lingam 2005). Furthermore, governments, which were generating less income due to their withdrawal from industries, reduced spending on health services and other public goods. In all, between 1990 and 1993, the percentage of the population living below the poverty line increased by 7 percent (Upadhyay 2000).

These changes had two major consequences for the women's movement and, by extension, for its engagement with sexuality. First, issues of class, labor, and poverty became increasingly urgent and threatened to exacerbate a divide between leftist women's groups (who saw themselves as guardians of the poor) and autonomous women's groups (which had long been critical of the Left's economic determinism). As I will show, the visible materiality of women's suffering under liberalization policies strengthened the resolve of leftist groups to resist issues perceived as Western or out of touch with India's poor. Sexuality would be just such an issue.

The second consequence was a restructuring of Indian social movements toward NGO-ization and transnationalization. Where the state withdrew its resources from health and education, NGOs emerged to fill its place. Dramatic social crises—including HIV/AIDS and women's poverty—coupled with friendlier policies toward international donors provided fertile ground for the flourishing of NGO activism and a new transnationalization of social action. However, this globalization of activism was not radically new. Social movement scholars have argued that the last two decades of the twentieth century saw a rapid growth in a "transnational public sphere" (Guidry, Kennedy, and Zald 2000) or "transnational advocacy networks" (Keck and Sikkinik 1998), in which activists forged important new spaces for international dialogue and solidarity. But India's women's movement had, from its inception, been an international one, created as it was in the cauldron of anticolonial nationalism (Forbes 1996; Kumar 1993).

There Are No Lesbians In India

Indian lesbian activism, too, had been truly international from its inception (see chapter 1) and, importantly, had been so well before a national movement existed. In fact, Indian lesbian activism had an inauspicious start at an international women's event in 1984. That year, feminist luminaries such as Adrienne Rich and Toni Morrison spoke alongside Urvashi Butalia, the publisher of Kali for Women, a feminist press, at the opening of a feminist bookstore in London. When an audience member asked the panelists to comment on lesbianism, Butalia frankly apologized, saying she was not familiar enough with the issue to respond. Giti Thadani picked up on Butalia's comment, and an international furor commenced. Over the next several years, magazines such as the U.S.-based *Trikone*, India's *Bombay Dost*, and a French magazine all carried Thadani's version of what Butalia was supposed to have said: "There are no lesbians in India."[21] This notorious misquote would long serve as a rallying cry for lesbians protesting their marginalization by the women's movement (see Sakhi 1994, quoted in S. Joseph 1996; Khayal and Heske 1986). More affirmatively, Indian lesbians began organizing themselves at international conferences. But while Indian lesbians were creating international spaces for protest and recognition, they continued struggling for a voice within the women's movement at home. Surprisingly, a group of high-school girls aided that effort.

The Martina Girls

In January 1992, national newspapers reported on the formation and forced dissolution in Kerala of a government high-school group known as the Martina Club (named in honor of the lesbian tennis great, Martina Navratilova). After three "Martinas" were found together in a classroom after hours, school authorities confiscated a notebook naming the other five members. All but one of the culprits were expelled. Reporters and the "expert" psychologists they turned to relished noting that all eight were "children of estranged lower middle class parents."[22] An "expert" psychologist reassured readers that "a passing phase" of adolescent lesbianism could be guarded against by not allowing girls to sleep or bathe together.[23]

Activists from Jagori saw both an opportunity and an imperative to respond. They sent one letter to the editor of the *Indian Express* and another one to the school's principal, signed by forty-four feminists in Delhi.[24] These letters were strident in their defense of the Martina Club. The aggressive response from autonomous feminists in Delhi on behalf of eight novice lesbians nearly 1,800 miles away can be understood through the fortuitous confluence of politically unambiguous issues for the women's movement in the era of economic liberalization. Jagori could champion what they called "lesbian sexual choice" in this case because the Martina girls were working- or lower-middle class, a space of moral certainty for feminist activism. Additionally, critiquing "expert" calls for further control over women's bodies was uncontentious. Finally, the vexing issue of "representation," highlighted during the Mathura campaign and resurrected in the case of Leela and Urmila, had already been resolved by the girls' self-identification. But for feminists to publicly state that "exploring our sexuality and our sexual orientation is an integral part of our educational process" was a radical and game-changing assertion. And the proper interplay of class, representational strategy, and control over women's bodies would continue to determine how women's groups would, and would not, articulate a public lesbian politics.

Critical Events II: Class and Sexuality

TIRUPATI

The already tense relationship among affiliated, autonomous, and rural-based women's groups over lesbianism came to a head at the fifth NCWM in January 1994 in Tirupati, a city in the south-central state of Andhra Pradesh. The roles of NGOs and international funding in the women's movement had become an increasing concern. The NCWM discouraged funded, affiliated, and mixed-sex groups from having organizing roles in the fifth conference, opting for leadership from groups that were "struggle-based."[25] Further, women's activists considered drafting a "Declaration of Autonomous Women's Groups" but, in the end, could not reach a consensus about what autonomy was, or even whether it mattered any more (Fifth NCWM 1994).

Times of uncertainty are ripe for radical change, and autonomous activists, seeking a clear identity, seized the opportunity to forge a lesbian politics. In addition to elevating the topic of "single women" to a place in the formal program, the conference included lesbians and bisexuals alongside Dalits, tribals, and poor women as people who are "further marginalized by other powerless facets of their identity" (Fifth NCWM 1994, 9). In addition, organizers created a separate official session on sexuality that lesbians and straight women participated in, discussing topics from bodies to masturbation and fantasies. Lesbian women contributed stories about their own relationships and how those had both enriched and complicated their lives. As it turned out, the session itself would have a dual effect as well.

During these conferences, every day ends with reports on that day's sessions. As the sexuality session's participants gave their written report and came to a line about "accepting lesbian sexuality," a group of angry activists noisily countered the proposal with a predrafted letter of protest (Fifth NCWM 1994, 58). In it, they declared lesbianism to be "unnatural and abnormal" (countering a Western scourge with Western sexological language) and a "deviant response to patriarchal society" (58). They concluded with a demand that the conference pass an antilesbian resolution. Everybody took a side. Several people present agreed with the antilesbian protestors, while several others defended lesbian women. One lesbian couple, feeling compelled to come out, stood together on stage. Other supporters joined them, holding hands in a quiet circle of defiance as protest swirled around them.

Such hostility justified the need for an exclusive lesbian space within the conference, and to meet this need, lesbians arranged a meeting for "women-centered women" the following night. Heterosexuals were asked not to come. The gathering was hastily planned to begin with, and its success was further imperiled when dissenters tore announcements about the meeting down from the walls. In spite of these problems, the meeting took place, and the twenty-five participants seemed to be aware that they were making women's movement history. On this night, they "simply listen[ed] to each other" and promised to meet again for more explicitly political purposes (Fifth NCWM 1994, 59).

This inaugural gathering of lesbians and bisexuals within the auspices of the national women's movement created a chasm between heterosexual and nonheterosexual feminists—a distinction that I do not believe had previously existed at the national movement level. Furthermore, the meeting also made it possible for divisions to emerge among same-sex desiring feminists. As I argued in chapter 1, the creation of face-to-face lesbian community sets in motion a series of exclusionary practices designed to protect the sanctity of this newfound space, the value of this newly forged time, and the visual homogeneity of these newly gathered bodies. The divisions that most commonly emerge are based on race and nationality, and between leaders and the led.

Cath was one of the lesbian delegates at the Tirupati conference. She had arrived in India two months earlier and was volunteering for Jagori and Sakhi. In one of our interviews, Cath talked about the significance—and personal disruption—of the lesbian gathering in Tirupati:

I had been here for two or three months and . . . well, there was this oppressive feeling of not being able to be out. So I was really excited that they were going to be having a lesbian meeting at this conference. It was an outdoor meeting. And I was literally walking up to this group of people who had gathered in a circle . . . and somebody . . . I won't mention names . . . somebody who you know said, "you know, we're very sorry but you can't attend this meeting." And I say, "Why?" [laughing]. I was really shocked! And this person says, "I hope you understand, but this meeting is only for Indian women. . . . There are women here who have never thought about these things before. And there are women who have never been exposed to anything like a lesbian identity." They were seeing me as somebody who was going to go in and talk about "lesbian identity" and "dyke" this and that. And that was really strange, considering the fact that I had been really background in the whole conference. I had purposely kept myself in the background. But this was *extremely, extremely* damaging to me. I was feeling so isolated because of the fact that I was a lesbian, and I didn't feel that the environment at Jagori was very accepting; it *wasn't* very accepting. And for the first time I was in a place where there was a lesbian group gathering. And obviously you feel *affinity*; you want to be a part of it because you feel, yeah, this will be a space where people will be bonding, where you'll have a sense of belonging, you know? And when this space was closed off. . . . I remember feeling really humiliated. I really felt like I wanted the ground to swallow me up. Some of the other women, they were wondering why I had left, because it wasn't a group decision. It was a decision that was taken by two or three women. This has been a repeated thing. It's been something that is really, really difficult for me.[26]

Both targeted and newly empowered by controversies within the women's movement, lesbian women's desire to create and protect a new community was strong. One way to protect the community at this political and economic moment in the women's movement was to assert itself as grass roots and indisputably Indian. Such assertions are less persuasive when made by white faces or in foreign accents. The policing of community borders and enforcement of a visual (and ostensibly cultural) homogeneity strove to render lesbian politics commensurate with the discursive demands of feminism and nation.[27]

What is important here is how an antilesbian position within the women's movement—one suspicious of the West and its globalizing preten-sions—did not suppress lesbian activism so much as it produced certain ways of operating within it. The point is not that lesbian women could not speak at all within the larger movement, but that in order to be heard, they had to speak in the language of local struggle and cultural protectionism, and about the virtue of being vulnerable victims rather than radical sub-jects. The consequences of exclusion went beyond humiliation and bruised egos. As I argued through the story of Sangini, these defensive maneuvers, precipitated by the women's movement's opposition to lesbian activism, fed an exaggerated sense of victimhood and fear. It was a discourse in which the Indian lesbian had to be protected not only from the state, but also from dangerous new language and ideas (such as "lesbian rights" or "dyke"). And if so many levels of protection were necessary, there would necessarily be some lesbians in particular who would have to do the pro-tecting. The early racial and national politics that emerged within lesbian activism during the conference at Tirupati, then, left a significant legacy for the politics of leadership and representation within lesbian rights strug-gles. Stree Sangam's early conflicts and retreats are part of this legacy.

The fifth NCWM ended on a continued note of rancor. On the final day, as a representative began reading resolutions on sexuality, a rumbling arose from the audience about a "takeover" by the "lesbian agenda."[28] Several prolesbian activists created a barrier around the speaker, but the protestors were not dissuaded from continuing their attack: they cut the electricity in the auditorium. In response, several lesbian delegates and their allies from autonomous groups like Saheli, Jagori, and FAOW boycotted the one re-maining event, an all-conference march. Only one thing emerges clearly from the chaos: the conference marked a critical point at which self-identified lesbian women, their supporters among autonomous groups, and their de-tractors among leftist and mass-based organizations were finally forced to declare their positions. The poetics of silence was being challenged by an emergent lesbian politics.

THE VIMLA FAROQUI EPISODE

The tension between feminism and lesbianism outgrew the women's movement and expanded onto the national public stage in 1994. Humsafar Trust, a gay organization in Bombay founded by Ashok Row Kavi, an-nounced that it was hosting a South Asian gay men's conference in Decem-ber. By October, the newspapers were filled with angry debate. One of the people most vehemently opposed to the conference was Vimla Faroqui, head of the biggest women's group in the country, the National Federation of Indian Women (NFIW), the women's wing of the Communist Party.

Faroqui wrote an open letter to Prime Minister Narasimha Rao, arguing that the conference would "surely start a move of sexual permissiveness among urban youth who have become vulnerable to the vulgarity of Western culture."[29] That Westernization, she added, was a direct fault of the Rao government's liberalizing policies. She said that the conference would constitute "an invasion of India by decadent western cultures and a *direct fallout of signing the* GATT [General Agreement on Tariffs and Trade, signed by India in early 1994]" (emphasis added). For good measure, she warned Rao about India's increasingly cozy relationship with the Clinton administration, which demonstrated "an immoral approach to sexual perversions." Faroqui might have been embarrassed about the company that she was now keeping. Joining her public protest was the vice president of the Hindu nationalist Bharatiya Janata Party, K. R. Malkani, who called homosexuality a "perverse behavior" to be looked upon "with horror." The rightwing political party Shiv Sena joined Faroqui, too.

Autonomous women's groups were now faced with a new configuration around the lesbian (and gay) question. The public stands that Delhi and Bombay feminists had taken thus far—in the cases of Leela and Urmila's marriage and the Martina expulsions—had not required them to confront other feminists, but this situation would. Furthermore, in the wake of the controversy over the GATT signing, a public alignment against NFIW and with lesbians and gays could further imperil the reputation of autonomous groups. In the face of these factors, Delhi groups chose to respond privately rather than publicly. Jagori took the lead, drafting a letter to fellow feminists that made two main arguments: against the Left's economic determinism, and for the "fundamental rights of homosexuals."[30]

If there was an upside to Faroqui's outburst, it was that her comments gave autonomous groups an excuse to express long-simmering frustrations with the Left's economic determinism. Jagori's letter said: "[Faroqui], as a member of NFIW, has been in the forefront of the women's movement and has contributed immensely to the struggle of working-class people. Therefore, her public statement against homosexuality becomes all the more disturbing. The ideologues of the left political formations need to acknowledge that class is not the only discriminatory factor in people's lives." In addition, the letter charged that Faroqui was neglecting working-class lesbians in aligning homosexuality only with the Westernized and middle-class. Urmila, Leela, and the Martina girls made frequent appearances in Jagori's argument.

In defending the middle-class gay activists, Jagori added the following lines: "The proposed conference is an assertion of the right of a discriminated group to come together and visibilize their oppression. . . . The right to form associations and the right to choose one's sexual and emotional partners are inalienable fundamental rights." The retreat to the comfort zone of fundamental rights was part of what I've argued is a larger strategy of the women's movement vis-à-vis lesbianism: to express camaraderie, but in a language that absolves feminists of an ethical imperative of self-critique. Arguing that lesbians deserved the right to organize and speak entailed no reflection on how feminists' own complicity with heterosexual conjugality necessitated lesbians to organize and speak in the first place. Loving women is not in and of itself a problem for lesbian women; the problem is the institution of heterosexuality and its hegemony.

It was toward such a critique of heterosexuality, and away from a "basic rights" model, that Saheli painstakingly moved. One factor that had long prevented Saheli from publicly engaging with the lesbian question was a lack of internal consensus. Radically egalitarian, Saheli would not assert collective positions if even one member was unconvinced.[31] As one long-time member of the group, Ranjana, put it in an interview with me, "If you can't convince the people you are closest to that something is right, how can you possibly convince anybody else?"[32] Saheli had not been able to agree on the place of lesbian politics in Indian feminism, but Saheli reopened the debate when they received Jagori's letter about Faroqui. They had agreed at the Tirupati conference, in the heat of the moment, to boycott the last day's march along with their autonomous allies. But, as Ranjana tells it, several of Saheli's members continued to struggle with that decision, still preoccupied with the question of whether lesbianism is "natural." Saheli's members dealt with their ambivalence by committing hours and days to debate. They eventually resolved not only to sign Jagori's letter, but to send a separate letter to NFIW in which they could reflect on their own intellectual journey. They turned their original question about lesbianism's "nature" around, challenging other feminists to say whether there is anything "natural" about heterosexuality. Drawing on their work with abused women, Saheli argued that the "paradigm of heterosexuality" was itself the source and justification for everything the women's movement so determinedly opposed: sati, dowry, abuse, rape, and women's lack of choice in their own lives. As a collective, Saheli—along with FAOW—was reaching a place where feminists took the realm of the intimate seriously: as a realm of violence and hurt, and also of radical, creative political possibility (see Geetha 1998).

Liberals and Radicals

The successive controversies of Tirupati and Faroqui were sparked by the demands of younger lesbian women for support from their straight or quiet allies. Increasingly, lip service to lesbian issues was not enough. A growing group of lesbian activists pushed their fellow feminists on precisely how, and on what grounds, they should articulate their support. The liberal language of fundamental rights that feminists used, for example, would become a political problem rather than a welcome gift.[33]

Lesbians' discontent with their women's groups rose as preparations began for the 1995 Beijing World Conference on Women, sponsored by the United Nations. As activists drafted their agendas for the meeting, a lesbian feminist from Jagori, Mita Radhakrishnan, sent an impassioned letter to local women's groups consisting of two main pleas.[34] First, she argued that Indian feminist delegates should insist that compulsory heterosexuality be a factor in all twelve of the "critical areas of concern" listed by the draft platform for action.[35] Her second call was specifically to other lesbians, urging them to use the opportunity of the global stage at Beijing to commit to radicalism. She wrote: "The 'human rights' approach to lesbian rights does not challenge heterosexual women enough. They can sit pretty and support the rights of a 'marginalized group' without ever having to question their own (hetero)sexuality. As lesbians, I feel we must NOT lose our radical liberatory role. Particularly as Third World lesbians, having to live with Structural Adjustment programs, increased religious fundamentalism (and having to face dismissal within the dominant women's movements) it's very important for us to draw connections between . . . those issues and our existence."[36]

Radhakrishnan was overly optimistic about the space that Beijing would afford an international radical lesbian politics.[37] The conference did provide opportunities for lesbian women to network, milling around inside the "lesbian tent" and exchanging ideas about articulating lesbian rights struggles in various parts of the world. In general, however, lesbian women's experience at Beijing mirrored that of lesbians in India: they were marginalized and disparaged, dismissed as sensational distractions from ostensibly more urgent (and supposedly separate) issues of poverty, labor, and violence.[38] Furthermore, Radhakrishnan's hope for a radical resistance to rights discourse was not quite realized. Pramada Menon, a lesbian activist who became head of an influential Delhi women's and development NGO, CREA, came to refer to herself as a "Beijing baby" precisely for how the conference influenced activists like her in the developing world to begin understanding their struggles and solidarities in terms of universal rights (see Merry 2006).[39]

Beijing shaped the directions of Indian lesbian activism. The first public campaign for lesbian rights in India was sparked by the slogan—born at Beijing—that lesbian rights are human rights. As lesbians from Bangkok, Nairobi, Shanghai, and New Delhi marched in Beijing under the cry of "lesbian rights," they achieved a sense of connection and collectivity and felt hopeful about circumventing the conservative cultural isolationism of the postcolonial nation-state. But Indian lesbians would find that the cultural conservatism of the state was championed as well in the front lines of the women's movement. Try as lesbians eventually did to usurp the primacy of the nation-state with a language of universal human rights, women's movement activists would use "culture" and "nation" as justifications for the continued deferment of lesbian politics.

They Are Still Not Ready

In the introduction I discussed the Campaign for Lesbian Rights (CALERI), which was founded in Delhi at the start of the *Fire* affair. On the eve of its founding, CALERI drew up a one-year mission statement with a mandate to render Indian lesbianism widely visible and to foster public and state recognition of the "rights of all lesbians to a life of dignity, acceptance, equality, and safety" (CALERI 1999b, 4). Representatives of thirty-one progressive organizations, including a number of autonomous women's groups, signed the mission statement and became members of the campaign. Under the surface unity, the women's groups that made up CALERI had plenty of disagreements on the language and importance of lesbian rights. I'll address some of those tensions in chapter 4, but here I'll present a story of some unexpected solidarity.

International Women's Day, March 8, is a huge event in India. The large affiliated women's groups—known somewhat ominously as the Seven Sisters—traditionally take the lead in organizing the massive annual rallies. In Delhi, the organizers transport busloads of women from outlying slums, villages, and neighboring states to participate alongside Delhi-based groups—including autonomous, affiliated, and NGOs. The scene is extraordinary, with a sea of heads, colors, and placards visible from any vantage point. Protest songs in Hindi ring loud, assertive, and off-key in the hot air of early summer. In 1999, the first full year of CALERI's campaign, the group brought a thousand fliers to the end point of the march, in Delhi's Jantar Mantar park. In *Lesbian Emergence*, an activist named J. B. tells of the female police officer who asked CALERI activists for several fliers folded in two and accepted them discreetly, with her head turned in another direction. All one thousand of the fliers were gone by the end of the rally, sheepishly requested, often in large quantities, by women speaking different languages and seemingly from a range of backgrounds (J. B. 1999, 73).

The 2000 march, however, was a more contentious affair.[40] The outrage at public right-wing violence against lesbians had died down, and CALERI didn't seem to see that lesbianism no longer enjoyed the wide, unproblematic, and temporary sympathy it had just after the *Fire* attacks. In the preparatory meetings for the march, CALERI asked that the official flier carry the group's full name, the Campaign for Lesbian Rights. Because the global theme for International Women's Day that year was violence against women, CALERI justified its inclusion in the flier on the ground that lesbians are victims of violence. Despite CALERI's efforts to be relevant, some NGOs and each one of the leftist groups rejected CALERI's proposal, arguing that "the *parchi* [flier] will go to the bastis where people are still not ready to talk of the issue."[41] CALERI tried again, asking if they could march with a single banner bearing the group's name. Again, they were rejected. Leftist groups and some NGOs feared that the media would home in on CALERI's banner, effectively obscuring all other issues. (There are parallels to this view everywhere, from the marginalization of drag queens and leather daddies at Pride parades to the treatment of hijras at gay press conferences.)[42] Several groups vowed to boycott the march if CALERI was allowed to carry a banner. CALERI quietly acquiesced.

Surprisingly, though, several of CALERI's feminist allies from autonomous groups and NGOs like Saheli, Ankur, Nirantar, and Jagori were less ready to capitulate to the Left's demands, and they boycotted the march. Jaya Srivastava, then director of Ankur (she has since retired), explained Ankur's decision:

It's a sad thing. . . . If you talk independently with these women [leaders of leftist women's groups], they're open-minded and liberal. But get caught up in the men of their parties . . . and their hands are just tied where lesbians are concerned! I said to Sheba [a leader of AIDWA, the All India Democratic Women's Association] that if the women's movement will not help lesbians, then who will? I said, "We won't march until you let CALERI hold their banner." We have a Dalit lesbian at Ankur who's been here for twenty years now. We know that this "[lesbians are] middle class" argument is stupid.[43]

Ranjana, from Saheli, agrees that it is not lesbophobia that animates leftist women's resistance to lesbian politics, but a desire to preserve the prestige and influence of their own organizations: "If you're in party structures, it's the larger interest of the party, and their vision of how social change will come, and the role that women will play in that change, that ultimately matters. We know that the people in AIDWA, most of them, did not mind having CALERI in it, but then they would have to deal with the larger party. In Saheli, we're not bound by the same restrictions. But the flip side is that we remain small. They are big and bad [laughing], and we are good and forever small."[44]

The sense that Saheli and other small groups had of their own ideological freedom and strength was tempered a bit by what followed. At a loss for how to spend March 8, the boycotters attended a program of the Delhi State Women's Commission. Ranjana ruefully recalled this event: "We were horrified! We decided to go against the Left, but then you go to a state-funded rally? The whole thing was *bankrupt*! Totally *bankrupt*! After this, we felt that maybe we should have just deferred to Left groups in the first place and joined them. Why not, then?"[45]

Feminist stalwarts like Kamla Bhasin had a similar question: why didn't those groups join the Left? Like Abha, Bhasin is an advocate for the poetics —not politics—of lesbian desire. Both she and Abha were once with Saheli but left that group in order to pursue paid feminist work—something Saheli did not allow. Bhasin worked on behalf of rural women for the United Nations. And as an advocate for rural women, she was contemptuous of lesbians who make a political issue of their sexuality. She told me one summer day in her South Delhi office: "I'll be *damned* if Brinda Karat is homophobic. They just can't take risks because they're working as part of the Communist Party. Look: class is *the* most important issue. If you don't have food on the table, you can't talk about anything else. . . . Is talking about lesbianism the most important thing when so many women can't even think about it? This is a class issue, and lesbian activists are on the wrong side of it."[46]

These false dichotomies—in which a woman can either love a woman or be poor, or a woman can either be a lesbian activist or support the poor—are strategic contrivances that maintain existing relations of power within the women's movement and stifle emergent critiques and practices. Some women have devoted their activism to bringing this inequality to light. One of them is Indiraben, a longtime women's rights activist and lesbian who started a group in Baroda, Gujarat, for working-class lesbians. I took a bus trip to meet her at her NGO one day while I was in Ahmedabad, visiting my extended family. I told her of my conversations with some women's activists in Delhi, including A. Khan. Indiraben put her fingertips together and looked at me intently. "These people," she said, "think that working-class lesbians are 'safe' because they think silence equals safety. Lesbians in the women's movement don't come out because of this [valorization of silence] exactly. This *saheli ka* concept [lesbians as only 'friends'] is no kind of concept. At any time you can be crushed, pressured, destroyed. Are you safe after someone finds you? Are you safe when your father forces you to marry? How can we talk about patriarchy on the one hand, and ask some women to live in silence on the other?"[47]

Moral Virtue, Radical Ethics

The women's movement's politics of class and nationality in a liberalizing economy worked to shape and delimit lesbian politics emerging within it. Moreover, the women's movement was itself thoroughly influenced by the emergence of lesbian politics and the imperative to respond to it. India's structural adjustment program of the early 1990s, and the transnationalization of social service provision that was part and parcel of it, brought the women's movement to a critical juncture. The increase in foreign funds for NGO building led to the production of an increasingly elite class of Indian feminists (described derisively as "full-time activists" by more staunchly autonomous groups) who flew overseas for conferences, traveled domestically by plane rather than train, held mass meetings during office hours rather than in evenings (leading to the marginalization of people with non-activist day jobs), and earned solidly middle-class salaries. Interestingly, this more evident elitism among NGOs came at the same time as—and through the same process by which—women's poverty was becoming a more visible and urgent concern for the women's movement. Indian women were becoming poorer and left with fewer safety nets, while women's activists were becoming more resource rich. This was a tension, I argue, that has since been negotiated on the terrain of lesbian politics, and of sexuality more generally.

Popular disquiet about the increasing influence of world bodies on India's economic priorities resonated with dissent concerning Western cultural influences. The women's movement, having negotiated accusations of being Western from its inception, sought to shore up its indigenous credentials by publicly distancing itself from the more radical, socially disruptive notions about gender, sexuality, and power emerging in lesbian politics. When women's activists did engage lesbian politics at all, they did so through the rubric of human rights, ignoring critiques of the structure of the family or of feminist complicity with heteronormativity. The effects of such normalizations—from radical structural disruption to political respectability—would influence the future dynamics of lesbian politics.

The discourse that has most centrally dictated the women's movement's engagement with lesbian politics and has, in turn, shaped the possibilities of lesbian activism in India is that of the moral virtue of poverty. The women's movement has had to take three conceptual steps regarding the poor: solidify the urban and rural poor as its base and reason for being; construct this base as authentically Indian; and performatively reproduce that authenticity by claiming to protect the poor from Western immoralities. The paradoxical result of this hyperbenevolence toward the poor was to represent them as lacking in complexity: the poor, because they are poor, can think only of what is materially necessary to survive. Oppression is the source of simplicity, and simplicity the source of virtue. The paternalistic linking of oppression with naïve virtue occurs at a global level as well, and on this level all Indian women in general (including feminists) are the virtuous oppressed vis-à-vis their Western counterparts. Indian women have been playing that role for Western feminists since colonial days, performing their oppression and virtue by focusing on sexual victimization. As activism becomes increasingly NGO-ized, the politics of virtue are intensified, as performances of grass-roots moral virtue are literally rewarded (Mindry 2001).

How and why does this matter so deeply for lesbian activists? Why was

Jaya so despondent when she heard A. Khan's critiques of lesbian activism, and so preoccupied with trying to respond to them? The norms of the women's movement matter for lesbians because their alliances with the movement are compulsory. Lesbian activists, a vast majority of whom do not have formal platforms of their own, rely on women's groups for organizational infrastructure and resources, a sense of wider belonging, and the legitimacy that such bonds afford. If the women's movement is invested in a moral politics of virtue, then lesbian activists learn to comply with it, too, managing their critiques, ideas, and practices within the limits that the women's movement supplies. These are processes, for lesbians and their feminist allies, that run deep with affect.

The Pune Controversy

OLAVA—the Organized Lesbian Alliance for Visibility and Action—was founded in Pune, Maharashtra, in 2000, with lesbian advocacy as its central mission.[48] The group was small, its membership ranging from as few as five to as many as fifteen people, almost all of whom were young feminists. Staunchly nonfunded, they relied on donations and, most importantly, the support of their greatest ally, Manisha Gupte and her women's NGO, MASUM.[49]

Gupte and her husband founded MASUM in 1987. It is a rural women's organization that works in drought-prone regions of Maharashtra on issues such as women's health, violence, and microcredit and savings. Based in Pune, MASUM has around a hundred employees, most of whom are fieldworkers. The organization is funded by both domestic and foreign agencies, and it is feminist and progressive.

In 1994, a bright, handsome young woman named Chatura heard Gupte speak at a local workshop. Extraordinarily for the time, Gupte spoke passionately about the right of women to love women. Chatura called Gupte that night to tell her how much the speech meant to her; it had been one of the signal moments of her life, she told Gupte. A relationship grew between activist and protégé, and five years later, the protégé helped found OLAVA.

Five of OLAVA's founding members were paid employees of MASUM, and the group had permission to use MASUM's resources to conduct business. Nonfunded but not quite autonomous, OLAVA gladly accepted the resources, legitimacy, and protection that MASUM provided it. But in the summer of 2002, OLAVA and MASUM found themselves trying to reconcile this easy mutuality with the realities of dependence and obligation. I base OLAVA's account of the conflict on a document its members published in 2003; my rendering of MASUM's perspective is based on personal communications between me and Manisha Gupte in 2011.[50] This is a story, somewhat painful, about conflict between allies and friends. But I agree with Monisha Das Gupta (2006, 8) in treating organizational conflict in activism not as a sign of failure that we should hide in the interest of unity, but as a sign of the critical vigor involved in any collective action rooted in the ethics of the possible.

LESBIAN RUNAWAYS FROM AMBALA

Two young women, both legally adults, ran away from their town of Ambala, in Haryana, after a marriage was arranged for one of them. In a bid to find them, one of the women's families researched lesbian groups (OLAVA was often in the news since its inception), called OLAVA's number, and traced the call-back they received to MASUM's office. Two male relatives asked the local police commissioner to summon MASUM's codirectors for a meeting. MASUM says that the directors stood firm, defended the two women's "right to self-determination," and refused to cooperate with the police beyond asking other women's groups if they knew whether the two runaways were safe. However, OLAVA avers that MASUM promised to find the two women and ordered OLAVA to help.

Another lesbian support group in the state—not OLAVA—had assisted the two women; that group told OLAVA that a brother and uncle had violently threatened the runaways. Knowing what they and every other lesbian group in the country knows about lesbian runaways, in-house imprisonments, forced marriages, and punitive beatings (see Fernandez and Gomathy 2005), OLAVA would have found it unconscionable to assist the police in returning these women as if they were property, to their families. Steeped in a post-Emergency feminist legacy of skepticism towards the state, MASUM would have found it unconscionable to cooperate with the police to return these women, as if they were property, to their families. Their miscommunication over the runaways makes sense only in the context of already existing tensions in MASUM between lesbians and straight women. In its document about their group's split from MASUM, OLAVA writes about conflicts over discussing lesbianism with rural women, lesbians wearing their hair short and smoking in the villages, as well as accusations that lesbian employees were using the office for (nonmonogamous) sexual encounters. In response, MASUM claims that the real issue was that many lesbian employees did not spend enough time in the villages to even know how easily rural women spoke of their same-sex relations (echoing Abha's points earlier in this chapter). Furthermore, MASUM did not take issue with nonmonogamous relationships; the group's concern, if any, was with the way that nonmonogamy served as a radical gloss on what seemed simply to be relations of exploitation and dishonesty among women, with consequences for everyone in the workplace.

All of these issues came to a head over money that was allegedly stolen from a lesbian employee's bag. Two lesbians accused three heterosexuals (MASUM points out that they were working class) of being the culprits, leading to a confrontation in the office that went on for hours. A MASUM codirector asked the two lesbian employees to apologize for their accusation. The members of OLAVA refused and instead held an officewide meeting to critique what they perceived as a growing homophobia in MASUM. The issues were never resolved, but the body count was high: two of the three women accused of theft resigned, as did four lesbian employees and their sympathizers; three other women received termination letters shortly thereafter.

The protestors and the terminated created a MASUM Ex-Employees Association (sometimes referred to as the Association of Aggrieved Women Ex-Employees of MASUM), and their first act was to send a letter to potential queer and women's movements allies.[51] Their central claim was that MASUM was in violation of labor practices and guilty of sexual discrimination. They argued that all of MASUM's lesbian, bisexual, and transgender employees had been fired or "purged"; that MASUM directors urged heterosexuals not to side with the "middle-class, lesbian agenda"; that MASUM actively "dissuaded [other women's groups] from giving OLAVA . . . meeting space, discouraged people from inviting OLAVA on their platforms," and "attempted to isolate and suffocate support for the group by misrepresenting the facts of the case." Overall, they rejected what they perceived as hypocrisy. Through this letter, OLAVA hoped to secure the support of India's other queer groups.[52]

ALLY RESPONSES: THE POLITICS OF NGO ACTIVISM

The first time I saw Chatura after OLAVA's split from MASUM was at a mutual friends' apartment in Bombay. She was on the living-room couch, surrounded by crumpled bedsheets in the late morning light. She had tried to find NGO work in Pune but had finally moved back to Bombay to live with her family. Her partner was still in Pune, also looking for work. Another lesbian former employee of MASUM had moved to Delhi to live with her parents while she searched for a job. My purpose in examining the fallout from this event is to study the language in which, and the emotions with which, the actors' conflicting positions were articulated—and not to evaluate the validity of those positions. I am interested in what those articulations reveal about the priorities and complicated consequences of activist engagement, an engagement that is centrally of sentiments. The fierce dispute between OLAVA and MASUM is not unique in the world of institutionalized activism, in which cleavages both political and personal drive and constrain solidarities. Recently, the Sangtin Writers and Richa Nagar have detailed an acrimonious and wrenching split between the pseudonymous NGO they call NSY and seven of its grass-roots-level employees (Sangtin Writers and Nagar 2006). That account leads them to a powerful critique of NGO-ization on the ground of disempowerment and increased hierarchization of feminist politics. While such critiques emerge from my narrative as well, the terrain here is too complex for villains and victims. The cautionary note I struck in the introduction is particularly relevant here. My perspective, like anyone's, is partial—I spent more time, and shared more deeply, with some people than with others. I acknowledge that the preponderance of OLAVA's perspective here, over that of MASUM and its allies, is a product of that partiality.

OLAVA first went public about its dispute with MASUM at a national workshop on sexuality and the women's movement in Hyderabad in April 2003. The three-day event was cosponsored by a Hyderabad women's group, Anveshi, with the aim of forging a new understanding between feminism and LGBT activists in the country. It was an important gesture on Anveshi's part, essentially organizing a teach-in for themselves and other straight feminists. We gathered around a large table and along the sides of the room. The debates were rather tepid on the first day, but on the second we began talking about NGOS.

The conversation began when a gay male academic and CALERI member, Ashley Tellis, told a story about NGOs taking the heart out of queer activism. As an out gay faculty member at a top Delhi college, Tellis had been subjected to obscene harassment from faculty members and students and eventually felt forced to resign. I had heard him tell this story in PRISM meetings, seeking both sympathy and action, and I was always surprised by everyone's apathy. People would look around uncomfortably, mumble words of shock and support, and, after an awkward silence, move on to the next—and usually more public—item on the agenda.[53] Tellis's story set the theme for what OLAVA would soon demonstrate: in the age of NGOs, it is the field of activism that matters more than the queer person himself.

Even before the Anveshi conference, Tellis had been a vocal critic of the role of NGOs in queer activism. He argues that NGOs have created in India altogether new sexual identity categories in order to carve a niche in a competitive funding field. His primary example is that of the kothi. Tellis and his fellow panelists variously argued that morning that NGOs produce and privilege certain categories of people, while further marginalizing others—such as lesbians—from circuits of capital.

Most of the queer activists in the room applauded the audacity of his critique, but not all agreed with his assessment of how NGOs affect queer politics. Some people argued that at least NGOs privilege select sites of queer activism (even if they themselves invent them), therefore enabling public conversation on previously unspeakable issues such as HIV and sexual risk. "Lip service to LGBT causes," one said, "is still a public commitment to speak." Another participant, Charu, a lesbian who had left an NGO job, argued against such a sympathetic interpretation. The perception that NGOs do good work, she said, is what allows them to elude criticism. But they should be criticized, she continued, for emphasizing service provision over structural transformation. We must ask, "What services, for *whom*, and who is excluded?" She continued, addressing Tellis's earlier comments: "I wouldn't say NGOs are *the* site of violence. *The* site of violence for LGBT people, especially lesbians, is the family. It is the family that sends people to mental health practitioners and forces their daughters to marry; NGOs just provide services. So they focus on things like making doctors more sensitive. But what do those doctors do? They 'sensitively' push women back into their families! The same ones who sent them to be 'cured' in the first place. These are not the services we need. These services are an outrage."

A women's activist agreed with Charu and added that one of the ways NGOs serve feminism is in alien and alienating terms: "In the women's movement, we had never talked about our bodies in parts before. Now we're all in fragments—everywhere is the poor wretched 'girl child,' the 'unborn female fetus.' Why? We're being distanced from mass resistance in India, by the market, by NGOs. This is the question for us today." Her invocation of the "wretched girl child" of NGO-speak elicited head-shaking and laughter (see also Sangtin Writers and Nagar 2006, 142). Charu continued, claiming that NGOS as a sector have little accountability. She cited labor practices within NGOS, such as long, unbounded workdays, low pay for fieldworkers, and a lack of structures for filing complaints against employers.

It was at this point that Zehra, an OLAVA member and former MASUM employee who would go on to conduct a research project on NGO abuses, spoke up. She said that LGBT activists should focus their critique of NGOS on two levels simultaneously: how NGOS manage the communities they work for, based on donors' priorities; and how NGOS treat their employees, many of whom are activists from those same communities. She continued: "Communities can't hold NGOS accountable because they often need those NGOS. Employees can't hold NGOS accountable because they need the work and the paycheck. And NGOS don't hold NGOS accountable because who can make them do so?"

The formal conversation ended on that note, but informal discussion continued late into the night. All of the twenty or so queer conference participants got together in a hotel room, drinking rum and Coke out of plastic cups, singing songs, and playing an ironic game of spin the bottle. After the rum ran out, we shifted our bleary attention to politics and what we wanted to accomplish with the women's activists that weekend. Chatura described her relationship with Manisha as a way to introduce the depth of these ties between young lesbian activists and feminist mentors. She and Zehra told their version of what happened at MASUM, and Zehra described the aftermath—OLAVA's near dissolution, the unemployment, the feelings of betrayal, and the difficulty of getting NGOS and even other queer groups to take their situation seriously. As the sun began to rise, people floated ideas such as city-level meetings between LGBT people and women's NGOS. We were, however, in the middle of just such a nationwide meeting that very night, and could do little else than feel guilty and impotent.

The debates that weekend in Hyderabad, as emotional and singular as they were, add texture to scholarly debates on the role of NGOS in activism and social movements. Some, if few, scholars have been relatively optimistic about NGOS, viewing them as well placed to advance humanitarian and democratic values by being less bureaucratic, more flexible, and more innovative than the state (for example Guidry, Kennedy, and Zald 2000; Nash 2005). A much broader swath inhabits a tense middle ground, ethnographically attuned to political possibilities that can emerge for local actors—even if prompted by distant institutional agendas—and to the awkward but very often necessary alignments between government and nongovernmental activism (for example, Baviskar 2004; K. Misra 2006; A. Sharma 2008). The work of these scholars, rather than seeing NGO-style practices of empowerment as either a panacea or as an impediment to social justice work, focuses—in line with Anna Tsing—on the productive friction of unlikely linkages, "the awkward, unequal, unstable, and creative qualities of interconnection" (2004, 4) that "proves key to emergent sources of fear and hope" (11). However, from the perspective of actors—like many of the lesbians at the Anveshi conference—this middle ground can be a thin and tenuous space, the friction searing rather than adding a spark.

Accordingly, much of the social science literature on NGOs in the global south—and specifically on NGOs in India—has been largely critical. Through attention to governmentality, scholars have emphasized the anti-politics (Ferguson 1990) of NGOs, showing how they effect a transfer of state responsibilities to local contexts (or privatize state responsibilities), engage local "participation" in those projects, and—through that rhetoric of participation—obscure the politics of governance at work at these microlevels (Cooke and Kothari 2001). Other scholars, expressing the views of many activists at the Anveshi conference, look to how the NGO sector literally governs, or structures, the field of what is politically possible—whether that sector is pushing specialized activism over collective forms of resistance (Sangtin Writers and Nagar 2006), emphasizing service provision over expanding the boundaries of what is thinkable, or parsing queer politics into new and separate identity categories that are perceived to be donor supported (Tellis 2003).

While most scholarly critiques of development have focused on the relationship of NGOs to their local (sometimes invented) constituents, some have also trained their critique on labor practices within NGOs. Sudha Vasan, for example, argues that "under the halo of 'non-profit,' the people who profit least are NGO employees" (2004, 2197). She claims that NGO workers in India, particularly low-level fieldworkers, work with little to no job security, no formal benefits, and no unions, and that women in particular are not afforded the same protections by these employers that government and other private employers are legally required to provide. This gap between image and reality is tied to two dominant discourses in the NGO sector: that NGOs do good works for local communities by doing battle with oppressive institutions, and that those good works would be in jeopardy if

NGOS had to spend what little funds they have on benefits and employee security—employees are pitted against the grass roots. Likewise, Harry Taylor (2001) concentrates on the gap between NGOS' claims of democratic functioning and the actual lack of access employees have to decision making. Taylor, Vasan, and other critics of NGO labor practices (see also Baviskar 2004; Lewis and Mosse 2006; and Sangtin Writers and Nagar 2006) all draw attention to one central point: within the liberalizing thrust of NGO-driven development projects lies an untenable contradiction: between democratic participation on the one hand, and the unyielding imperatives of a competitive marketplace on the other (Bob 2005; Karim 2008). As analysts have shown, it is not just local subalterns who are drawn into this characteristic instability of global capitalism, but employees and their activism as well.

Perhaps the element of activist practice that has been most radically reshaped by NGO-ization is the ethics of scale. As activism becomes more oriented toward and vulnerable to the market, an activist's value is increasingly determined by the size of her catch. Who does she reach? Who does she draw in? How *effective* is she? The activist is in competition for and with her field.

THE WOMAN AND THE FIELD

Following the Anveshi conference, PRISM debated what to do for OLAVA. Ultimately, they decided to do nothing, though they considered their inaction as being in the service of a larger good. At the heart of PRISM's philosophy, as I described in the last chapter, is the importance of building broad coalitions with other progressive groups in order to demonstrate an ethical commitment to social justice beyond sexual minorities and to show the composite nature of political struggle. After the success of their sexuality interventions at the Asia Social Forum, PRISM aimed to create an even larger coalition of progressive groups to articulate the interpenetration of economic and sexual marginalization at the 2004 World Social Forum (WSF) in Bombay. To create this queer presence at the forum, PRISM imagined an alliance of Indian groups called the Network for Sexual Rights (NSR). As excited as they were about this possibility, they were also wary of forging alliances with organizations that inevitably are or have been mired in ethical disputes. Sangama, for example, had recently been accused of discriminating against hijra sex workers in its organization.[54] One Delhi NGO, CREA—some of whose members were very close, politically and personally, to PRISM—had a unique problem: MASUM's Manisha Gupte sat on its board of directors. If CREA joined the NSR, OLAVA would not. If CREA was asked not to join in deference to OLAVA, PRISM would feel disloyal to CREA. So PRISM called a national meeting in late August 2003 to discuss the options.

On a dreary August morning, Jaya and I went to the Delhi railway station to pick up Shalini (from Bombay's Stree Sangam) and Chatura. Jaya was nervous; she wanted the alliance desperately but had little hope that the visitors would compromise on the Gupte issue. We collected them, weary from their overnight train trip; drove them home for chai; and then drove out again for the daylong meeting. It was held at Gautam's home, another PRISM member, who comes from a Kashmiri pandit family. We sat in ornate chairs of dark wood or on the thick Kashmiri rugs. Rich, milky tea with almonds and pistachios emerged from the kitchen on hand-decorated trays.

The luxuries around us did not defuse the tension in the room; if anything, they simply underscored the perceived differences between the Delhi queers and the Bombay women. "Bombay women" is an identifier (often spoken with a weary sigh by activists not from Bombay) based more on ideology than geography. There are lesbian activists in Bombay, like Geeta Kumana of the support group Aanchal, who are not considered "Bombay women," while most lesbian activists in Pune are. There are two characteristics that make someone a "Bombay woman": being a feminist lesbian and being an uncompromising purist. There are no substantive differences in the class backgrounds of the Delhi queers and the Bombay women (I might also note that the Delhi queers are not identified by gender as "Bombay women" are—I explain this in the introduction). But because the Stree Sangam and OLAVA activists came to, and developed, their lesbian politics through feminist work (Stree Sangam with FAOW and OLAVA with MASUM), the "Bombay women" are more sensitive to issues of class and to avoiding the appearance of being bourgeois. It was precisely the Delhi queers' seemingly ostentatious display of comfort and a willingness to compromise—the servants bringing chai, the desperation to ally with powerful NGOs—that exacerbated the divide between the corporate compromisers of Delhi versus the purists of "Bombay."

When PRISM finally broached the issue of the NSR, that divide seemed intractable. Gautam urged the Bombay visitors to see it as a "temporary, opportunistic coalition to get sexuality on the agenda at the WSF." Shalini and Chatura said that CREA's participation undermined any possible value of such visibility—a sexual rights platform created by people who supported discrimination against lesbians would be worthless. They asked CREA to rebuke Gupte publicly, and Pramada, CREA's director, forthrightly refused. After receiving the Ex-Employee Association document, CREA had taken the initiative to debate the issue collectively, and Pramada had decided that "these were internal, organizational dynamics." She said, "None of us can know what really happened there, so we can't call it 'homophobia.'" Another senior activist woman—a lesbian and labor activist—often intensely critical of NGO-ization, surprisingly defended CREA. She argued that the NGO had at least taken OLAVA's allegations seriously enough to discuss them as an organization. They at CREA had every right to remain loyal to Gupte, given that there were competing versions of what had transpired. Emboldened, a representative from CREA who often attended PRISM meetings stood up and asserted: "Our goal at CREA is to work with everyone who shares common issues. Our goal is to push the field. It's the field that matters in the long run." After four more hours of arguments and effort, we were left with nothing more concrete than irritation, distrust, and fatigue.

I left as I came, sympathizing with PRISM's intentions and frustrations, but annoyed by their inability to connect on an emotional level with what OLAVA was arguing. Richa, PRISM's youngest member, shared my ambivalence. She asked that night if the field of sexual rights really can be said to matter more than the people who, and even the ideas that, comprise it: "Is it not wrong? How can we talk about sexual rights if we don't stand up for five lesbians we know?" In earlier conversations with activists from Bangalore, we had all argued over this idea. Arvind, of Bangalore's Alternative Law Forum, had wondered if he could remain on Sangama's board after the allegations of discrimination against hijra sex workers there. In Bangalore, he said, they called these sorts of controversies "the petty politics of purism." "Such politics of nonalliance just aren't tenable," he argued. "Queer groups *have* to make alliances. That's what movements do." He espoused a different philosophy of queer politics at the NSR meeting, however, when he argued that "the queer movement should offer the world *new* ideological frameworks, *new* ways of seeing. Let's not just replicate the models of power and action we see around us." That both philosophies are his, and his with conviction, is a testament to how fraught the experience is of nurturing radical worlds.

Stree Sangam expressed this conflict in a letter to PRISM after the Delhi meeting. The group wrote that the NSR discussions had "[brought] to the fore some of the basic differences in our politics and standpoints. We feel that it will be difficult to work effectively as a network that will engage in political action and advocacy at the WSF, without sharing a common political understanding within."[55] They suggested instead a self-selected coalition of all LGBTKQH (lesbian, gay, bisexual, transgender, kothi, queer, hijra) groups in India that could join forces under the banner, only, of visibility. At least, they argued, we would not have to debate what we actually believe in when we talk about sexual rights.

This Is Your Field

I was in Bombay in late October of 2003, and arranged to meet Chatura at her new workplace for one last interview before I left for the States. She was working now for Humjinsi, a funded lesbian support and advocacy project of the India Centre for Human Rights and Law.[56] They were located on the fifth floor of a Jain school in a crowded, predominantly Muslim neighborhood of Bombay. I found her in her cubicle, figuring out which was hers based on the double Venus symbols and stickers with feminist slogans. We phoned in a lunch order to a nearby shop and, because the day was beautiful, sat at a table on the balcony overlooking the schoolyard.

We chatted lazily for a while and then fell quiet, contemplating the weather. Both of us were looking at the terrace of the building across the street, the water-stained walls, the sewage tanks, the scurrying rodents, and the electrical wires crisscrossing a blue sky full of cumulus clouds. When she spoke again, her remark was sudden and whimsical, addressing the fear of "losing one's way." I wasn't sure how, or whether, to ask, but I did: "Do you worry that will happen to you?" She answered without initially meeting my eyes:

> Ten years of working autonomously, and then I find myself with no money, nothing in the bank, no skills except in this sector. That autonomous work . . . it was something! There was a real energy we had. And now, to work for an NGO . . . it wasn't my choice. But it's *survival*, man. I don't want to be paid for my activism. Even if I'm not being constrained [by my employer], it just doesn't *feel* good. It makes you wonder. . . . You work autonomously, you're young, you say you don't want to work for money, that you'd rather struggle. You'd rather tough it out, you say,

because at least in that, you'll have some kind of *solidarity* [laughs]. But when it's all over, where are you left? No job. No money in the bank. And even that solidarity is gone. And it makes you question *everything* when all of the things you've criticized—your class, your privilege, a certain kind of professionalized activism—when it is all of these things that you have to return to. That it is all of this that you come back to, to *protect* you. It makes you wonder . . . what was any of this *for*? In the end, *what*?[57]

Chatura spoke as though I shared her criticisms of NGO activism and perhaps disapproved of her decision to work for Humjinsi. I did not, and I reminded her that my own research was funded by the U.S. Department of Education. We both laughed, and she said more about her wariness of doing activism through funded institutions: "Once we taste a bit of power, we forget what it's like to be on the ground. We forget what it's like to be where we once were, to be where we started from. And then we only keep wanting more—more influence, more recognition, more power."[58]

In PRISM, the voices against funded activism had echoed Chatura's critiques. Like her, they sought to protect the intangible spirit of autonomous collective work from the hierarchies that emerge when some activists are paid for their labor and others are not. They held this position, at least, until Charu (who spoke at the Anveshi meeting) introduced an ethical problem with PRISM's position. The "ethic" of unfunded activism, she said, privileges middle-class women with families, women who had other sources of financial stability. Working-class women who cannot afford to lose paid hours are then marginalized from activism, further consolidating the middle-class composition of women's movement leadership. It is not just the funding of activism that contributes to middle-class dominance in social movements, but the corresponding devaluing of volunteer labor. Furthermore, universally criticizing women who want or need to earn money for their labor can be both antifeminist and classist.

I told Chatura about PRISM's debates and asked her if receiving money for activist labor was, in itself, what she objected to. It was not: she had been a paid employee at MASUM. Furthermore, she understood that many women simply must work and choose the NGO sector as a way to connect income generation with activism. She simply insisted on recognizing that receiving money for one's activism, or being dependent on groups that do, requires acts of accommodation, both large and small, drawing ever more limits on the potential you began with. She cited Sangama's policies against hijra sex work and the privileging of the field over people in the NSR discussions. Her frustration crested here, as she recalled the comment about the field as priority: "'Our priority is the field,' they say! 'Our priority is the field!' I felt like lifting up my shirt, standing and saying, '*This! This* is the fucking field. *This* is your fucking field of sexuality!'" I stayed quiet, nodding in agreement and sympathy. She resumed talking several minutes later: "When you're young and you first hear about the women's movement, you just have such a fantasy of what it's like. Women who work together, sisterhood and all [laughs]. They take care of each other . . . but it's just not like that all of the time. We have our differences, our own needs. But yes, . . . we have to be able to care for one another, to relate on a human level, to try and really understand one another. I just sometimes wonder . . . what is any of this good for?"[59]

Maybe nothing, we reflected. But then again: everything.

chapter 4

PUBLIC "EMERGENCE"

Kruti is a twenty-three-year-old woman I met at Sangini. She lives with her natal family in a working-class neighborhood of North Delhi, and the first time I met her she told the group, with proud resolve, that she is a lesbian. She is quiet and self-contained, and seemingly slips back into the hetero-normativity of extended family life after each meeting. When I interviewed her some months later, I asked: "How did you come to think of yourself as a lesbian?" "*Fire*," she replied. I asked Kruti if she was referring to the movie itself. "No, no, not the movie," she answered with some impatience. "It was the placard: 'Indian and Lesbian'" (see figure 7). She paused for some time and then went on: "I picked up the newspaper in my family's house. It is hard to describe what happened. I felt like crying; I felt like kissing some-one. I felt like, I don't know—like jumping up and screaming at the top of my voice. But instead I just whispered it: 'Indian. And lesbian.'"[1]

Kruti's euphoria moved me. One way of reading her joy was to see it as emanating from the successful public resolution of two previously incom-mensurate identities: Indian and lesbian. Another reading, and the one I pursue in this chapter, is that the "Indian and Lesbian" sign sat precisely at the lip between a field of possibility and a moment of necessary resolution. Kruti's affective intensity arose not from commensuration ("this is now resolved") but from the public clash of the incommensurable (enabling the

7. Activists in Delhi on December 7, 1998. Images of the "Indian and Lesbian" sign were reproduced in dozens of newspapers the following morning. Photograph courtesy of *Outlook*.

question, "what will now be possible?"). As I will demonstrate, the "Indian and Lesbian" sign was crucial in rendering the Indian lesbian a subject of national politics. However, it was also a point at which potential would move toward its closure, with new criteria produced for the proper performance of both Indian and lesbian. I argue that the problematic of emergence is key to theorizing the pivot point in radical worlds between incommensurability and mandated commensuration; furthermore, I argue that what we learn from such theorizations of emergence are the affective consequences of transforming potentiality into normative criteria as social actors attempt, with passion and hope, to engage the world in radical, ethically new ways.

Anthropologists of non-Western queer sexuality have largely assumed that transforming incommensurability into normative criteria of belonging is the goal—that queer people in the non-West seek to communally make sense of their difference, and it is only activists, those influenced by Western politics, who make public demands out of these private struggles. This chapter, and this book, tell a different story. I show that incommensurability is an actively desired and desirable field of possibility for Indian lesbians, whether activists or not, by demonstrating the consequences of having to commensurate radical imaginings with social norms and political banalities. I make this argument about the desire for incommensurability through a focus on affect. Affect *is* incommensurability: the participation of that which is radical, unknown, and unfixed in the world of norms, much like "Indian and Lesbian" appeared upon Kruti's family's doorstep, or entered into her desires, or into national deliberation on a boisterous, candlelit night. I show the processes through which that incommensurability—an impetus to action and a moment of profound possibility—was made commensurate, bringing momentary closure to potential and normatively qualifying social intensity.

The public plays an important role in this chapter and, thus, in the narrative arc of this book. I have traced so far how value in activism replicates market value, in that worth is determined by activism's ability to penetrate ever wider circles of influence, from community to international donor networks, to larger social movements at home and abroad. Each realm entails newer challenges to activism as ethical practice, which is constituted by exercises of critique, invention, and creative relationality. The decisions to expand lesbian activism's scope and, thereby, to risk different forms and consequences of normalization can't be attributed to any one actor, group, or motivation. As I showed in the last chapter, building alliances with women's groups was both a desirable source of additional legitimacy for lesbians and a necessary means for survival. Lesbians' entrance into the national public was also a complex affair, but it was based even less on their own existing desire (here, to emerge publicly) and thus much more on necessity. Right-wing activists, I argue, sought to strengthen their political position at a turbulent time through a violent act of interpellation, compelling lesbian women to show themselves in the national public by denouncing them as antinational. It was in response to that act of interpellation that one activist, and then dozens more over the course of a single night, raised the "Indian and Lesbian" sign, a public-making text that introduced the incommensurability of "Indian" and "lesbian" as a problem to be solved.[2]

This might seem a counterintuitive claim. Didn't lesbians already know that they were other to the nation? Didn't Indians already know that lesbians did not properly belong? The answer to both of these questions is yes. But before this critical event of 1998, as I describe in chapter 1, lesbians and their politics inhabited what I'll refer to as a field of immanence, to borrow from Gilles Deleuze (2001). That field of immanence, exemplified by the letters women wrote to one another, was characterized by disparate communities of same-sex desiring women across India, women who called themselves "lesbians" or did not, sought formal recognition or did not, made their love secretly within the available fissures of heterosexuality or did not. With the remarkable exception of Thadani, lesbians did not address themselves directly to the nation or make available their transgressions. It was that stubbornly incoherent intensity that belonged to nothing but itself (that is, was only immanent) that was the problem the right-wing Shiv Sena party sought to solve by demanding lesbians' public emergence. That demand was met: the activists who hoisted the "Indian and Lesbian" placard declared their nascent movement a "Lesbian Emergence" (CALERI 1999a).

The public emergence of lesbianism through the critical event of the *Fire* affair raises the question of activism as ethics in dramatic ways. To refer again to Brian Massumi, "emergence" is a bifurcation point in which multiple, and normally mutually exclusive, potentials coexist, only one of which can be chosen (Massumi 2002, 32–33). An emergence of a new social form, then, is marked by a constitutive ambivalence: between a multiplication of existence, action, or expression (or ethics) enabled through the introduction of that radical new form, and a closure of potential through the commensuration of this new social life with existing norms and forms of life. I accept this theory of emergence but offer one critical caveat: the choice between potential and closure is ultimately a false one. Instead, we must see (and this chapter demonstrates) that closure is the very condition of possibility for social invention and the emergence of new potential.

The Fire *Affair*

On November 13, 1998, director Deepa Mehta's film, *Fire*, relatively unscathed after months at the Censor Board, was first screened in the major urban centers of India.[3] For nearly three weeks, the film was shown in packed cinema halls, many of which offered popular women-only screenings. People viewed the movie in quiet droves, lukewarm and unsensational reviews casually littered the English and vernacular press, and discussion of the film was had mostly in the circumscribed spaces of organizational meetings, hostels, and middle-class drawing rooms. What now stands out about this initial three-week period is only the pregnant silence.

On December 2, nearly three weeks later, the "Ire over *Fire*," as one headline had it, finally erupted. Approximately 200 activists from the Shiv Sena's women's wing, Mahila Aghadi Sena, stormed a Bombay theater during a matinee screening of the film. Shortly thereafter, another Mumbai theater was attacked, with windows shattered and posters of movie stills torn from the walls and torched. Theater managers evacuated their patrons and then surrendered their reels of the film to the government. The following day in Delhi, Shiv Sainiks attacked Central Delhi's historic Regal Cinema with similar audacity, ultimately leading to the suspension of *Fire* across the country, its resubmission to the Censor Board, and victorious claims from Hindu spokespeople about the obvious incommensurability of the film with "Indian culture," and of lesbians with the nation and history of India.

I should note here that the Shiv Sena is not isometric with either Hindu nationalism or with the state, which was at the time ruled by Hindu nationalists (Hansen 1999). The Shiv Sena is a political party that was founded in 1966 to claim the state of Maharashtra for Marathi-speaking people. Though its politics are primarily regional, the Shiv Sena expanded its agenda in the 1970s to Hindu nationalism generally, later uneasily aligning itself with India's Hindu nationalist Bharatiya Janata Party (BJP), which had swept into power the year of *Fire*'s release. The BJP's victory fanned nationalist sentiment across the country (as well as fear on the part of secularists) and legitimized the often violent tactics of other member groups of the Sangh Parivar (the representative association of Hindu nationalism), like the Shiv Sena. The *Fire* affair brought a brief but firm solidarity among this range of right-wing nationalist groups. Something on which they all agreed was the construction of what Paola Bacchetta calls a "xenophobic queerphobia," which posits queerness as originating outside the Hindu nation (1999, 143). For example, L. K. Advani, then the home minister in the BJP government, asked: "Why are such films made here? They can be made in the United States or other Western countries. A theme like lesbianism does not fit in the Indian atmosphere" (quoted in Naz 1999, 13). Pramod Navalkar, the minister of culture for Maharashtra, also supported the Shiv Sena, arguing that lesbianism is a "pseudo-feminist trend from the West and no part of Indian womanhood" (quoted in Sukthankar 2000). The Rashtriya Swayamsevak Sangh (RSS)—a volunteer organization of militant Hindu nationalists that is also part of the Sangh Parivar—declared that "the Shiv Sena chief may be accused of using force. . . . But the attack on the indigenous value-system by the ultra-westernized elite, who regard the nation as not more than a piece of land . . . is more appalling than the action of the Shiv Sainiks" (quoted in Bacchetta 1999, 153). The RSS added that the "ultra-westernized elite" "resort[s] to explicit lesbianism and perversities to disintegrate the family à la western society," all while failing to accept "male superiority as a natural course of things" (quoted in Bacchetta 1999, 153). In the strategic alignment among Hindu nationalist organizations around *Fire*, heteronormativity, queerphobia, male superiority, "Hindu values," and the very integrity of the state were brought into concert.

The film that provoked this strategic alignment revolves around the delicate and then impassioned romance that develops between two sisters-in-law, Radha and Sita. Radha is the resigned wife of a celibate husband, Ashok. Ashok spends most of his free time at the feet of his guru, or in bed with his wife to ascertain his resistance to sexual temptation. Ashok's younger brother is the pompous, self-absorbed, Jatin. Jatin is having an affair with a predator-beautician from Hong Kong who refuses to become a "baby-making machine" in Jatin's joint Indian family. Ashok, who has given up a life of the flesh after learning that his wife is infertile, still yearns for the idyllic family. He pressures Jatin to marry and procreate, even though Jatin has promised to be unfaithful to any future wife. That luckless woman is Sita, a frisky young bride with modern tendencies who tries on Jatin's oversize jeans, dances before a mirror to rock music, and brazenly critiques the "box called tradition." The two broken couples, along with the family servant, Mundu, work nights in the family take-out business located on the ground floor of their apartment building. While Radha and Sita take whiffs of the other's cardamom-sweetened breath, Mundu eyes them with growing awareness, Jatin sells porn videos to schoolboys, and Ashok maintains his blessed naïveté. One day, Radha catches the servant masturbating to the "Joy Suck Club" while supposedly caring for Ashok's mute mother, Biji. Radha gives Mundu a sound thrashing. Betrayed by Radha and enraged by her hypocrisy, Mundu summons Ashok from his guru's side and tells him to look into Radha's room. Ashok does, and finds his wife and his sister-in-law making love. Ashok and Radha have a confrontation in the kitchen. Radha tells her husband that she desires "Sita, her warmth, her body." Turning from him, her sari catches fire and she is engulfed in flames. Just as we think that she has lost this mythic Hindu test of purity, the trial by fire, we see her walking through the rain and toward Sita, who stands waiting among the pillars of the Sufi shrine of Nizamuddin.

What is interesting about the reception of this film is that the signifiers of a properly "lesbian" desire and its triumph are either everywhere or nowhere to be found. Instead of celebrating the film, many lesbian critics (for example, V. S. 1999) actually faulted *Fire* for a range of perceived misrepresentations: portraying lesbianism as resulting from confinement and heterosexual neglect; romanticizing silence and refusing a politics of visibility (see Gopinath 2005, 142 and 155); and exploiting Indian lesbians and their "anguish" within joint family structures for a Western audience (V. S. 1999, 7). Prominent feminists agreed, arguing that the film was less about lesbianism than about desperation. Mary John and Tejaswani Niranjana (1999, 582), for example, compared Radha and Sita to Urmila and Leela: both couples are understood to have fallen in love due to past suffering, current emotional destitution, and the "non-availability of men" within their purdah-like, homosocial seclusion (1999, 582).[4] The director herself downplayed the importance of lesbianism in the film, enjoining the public to see her film as something far more consequential than a "lesbian" one (Mehra 1998).

For right-wing protestors, however, *Fire* was about nothing if not lesbianism—and its immoral importation from a decadent and dangerous West. Such a reading was, as I pointed out above, fortuitous for the temporarily cohesive agenda of far-right groups, but it was also politically imperative. As Geeta Patel notes (2002, 224), in the two-week period between *Fire*'s release and the beginning of the riots, the BJP had suffered major electoral losses in three states and was facing a no-confidence vote. Furthermore, the price of staples was rising dramatically, leading to a swell of public outrage against the BJP government and, by extension, its Sangh Parivar allies such as the Shiv Sena, which was facing its own political and economic troubles in Maharashtra. A political cartoon in the *Hindustan Times*, for example, shows the Shiv Sena chief, Bal Thackeray, quivering and emaciated, trying to survive by warming his hands over a fire fueled by strips of film.[5] Geopolitically, the BJP government's nuclear tests of May 1998 (which had the ecstatic support of the RSS and Shiv Sena) were targets of international disapprobation and domestic protest—the latter particularly from the recently vanquished, but still powerful, Congress Party. The nationalist coalition's performative act of naming the foreign-born lesbian was not, then, simply about lesbians. Hindu nationalists in India have historically relied on the "queering" of Others to consolidate fear and respect: Muslims, Christians, and Westerners are oversexed; the Congress Party and secularists are eunuchs (see Bacchetta 1999, 155). The sudden possibility of "explicit lesbianism" in India, as the RSS put it, was a boon, adding to the list of queers, queers themselves, and their "direct attack on what Hindu culture stands for" (quoted in Bacchetta 1999, 160).

Nation and Sexuality before "Indian and Lesbian"

The *Fire* affair is but one rich episode in India's lengthy narrative of fanning nationalist sentiment through the production and management of female sexualities. Just in the last decade, Hindu nationalists have rioted over the celebration of Valentine's Day; young men and women kissing on park benches; the release of a film, *Girlfriends*, about a homicidal, psychotic lesbian; and the Indian actress, Shilpa Shetty, being publicly kissed and manhandled by a frenetic Richard Gere. But the violence surrounding *Fire* was also unique in its scale, the level of international attention it garnered, and its consequence. Why and how did one art-house film about two lonely women become the site of such furor?

Fire revealed, in spectacular fashion, to Indians and their global observers, what secrets and subversions lie not so dormant in the sacrosanct sphere of the Hindu domestic.[6] The stilling of women in conjugal spaces of the home (Patel 2004) and the careful regulation of their adherence to cultural law within it have been central to Indian national projects, both secular and religious.[7] But that stilling, as feminist historians of India have shown (C. Gupta 2001; Sinha 1995), is both a product and a source of cultural anxiety about female sexuality. The tethering of women to the homespace through obligatory conjugality would, for example, lead to fresh fears on the part of men and associated demands for increased control.

Charu Gupta, in her discussions on the deployment of sexuality in colonial India, writes of the anxiety in Hindu joint families about relationships between women and their brothers-in-law. Women, often left alone by husbands for work, were thought to be increasingly turning to their brothers-in-law for comfort and physicality; in response, books were written telling *bhabhis* (sisters-in-law) to avoid their *devars* (brothers-in-law), how to avoid them, and what the consequences would be if they did not (C. Gupta 2001, 155). A regional magazine published a series of cartoons warning against the intimacy of the devar-bhabhi relationship, and proverbs such as "A fool's wife is everybody's sister-in-law" gave voice to male fears about women's sexual desertion (151).

Fire unleashed the ghosts of the devar-bhabhi relationship, albeit with a special homoerotic twist. The devar-bhabhi relationship was threatening precisely because it revealed the imagined and felt inadequacies of the enforced Hindu conjugal order—the neglectful and distant husband; the lonely and wanting wife; and the absence of joy, fulfillment, and companionship. Sita is the devar to Radha's bhabhi—although, importantly, displaced into the female domain. Sita serves as a breath of fresh air, a conduit for sexual expression, and the articulation of all that is wrong and missing. Their union calls the nationalist bluff of the respectable and secure conjugal unit, no longer Other from the recreational, immoral, and unnatural forms of relation that were coming to define non-Hindu sexuality. Those who criticize Mehta for portraying lesbian desire as only a product of circumstance miss the historical continuity: Hindu female lust outside of matrimony has long been understood as a result of neglect and ineffective conjugal containment.

But efforts by Indian men—both Hindu and Muslim—to more effectively contain women within the private sphere were a liability for nationalist politics, and they would force a turn toward increased transparency of that sphere and increased mobility for the women who occupied it. A critical moment in the history and politics of modern Indian sexuality came in 1927 with the publication of Katherine Mayo's blistering polemic, *Mother India* (2000 [1927]; see also Sinha 1995). Mayo sought to undermine Indian nationalism by using graphic examples of violence against women and girls to show that Indian identity is founded on sexual pathology. One of her prime examples, also used by other British writers at the time, was the seclusion of women. Colonialists argued that Indian women were made to live lives of idleness, leading to sexual obsession, physical infirmity, and an altogether sickly race (Metcalf 1994; Mayo 2000 [1927]). Mayo and others were not only concerned with dysgenic heterosexuality, however; they also noted the likelihood of homosexuality within these spaces of sororal confinement. (Inderpal Grewal makes a similar point: European women travelers often remarked on the opaque domain of the Indian harem as a space of unfreedom in part because it was a breeding ground for homosexuality [1996, 50 and 82].)

The increasingly noisy discourse about the potential for homosexuality through the domestic confinement of women—this architectural logic—had two major consequences for constructions of Indian, and specifically Hindu, sexuality. First, it led to a redoubling of investment on the part of nationalists to require and maintain the transparency of the domestic space in order to survey the interactions within and emanating from it. And second, because female seclusion was more prominent among the upper classes, where respectability mattered most, allegations of homosexuality placed sexual perversion at the heart of the domestic sphere of elite Indian life, just as Hindu publicists were attempting to locate perversion elsewhere, in the lower classes, among Muslims, and in the West.[8] Such efforts were part of a project of asserting the superiority of a uniquely Indian sexual morality and spiritual and political integrity. Even if these efforts were not mainstream, they indicated, in Mrinalini Sinha's words, the "coming of age of a new nationalist perspective on Indian domestic and sexual norms" (Sinha 1995, 45–46)—an emerging bourgeois domesticity that, presaging the *Fire* affair, would be enforced through public controversies about obscenity.

Obscene

Sections 292, 293, and 294 of the Indian Penal Code (1872) define any visual or written material as obscene if it is "lascivious or appeals to the prurient interest or if its effect . . . [is] such as to tend to deprave and corrupt persons, who are likely . . . to read, see, or hear the matter contained or embodied in it."[9] Feminist commentators on colonial era obscenity campaigns often cite the importance of the case against the eighteenth-century Telugu poet and courtesan, Muddupalani (Gopinath 2005, 132–33; C. Gupta 2001, 31–32; Tharu and Lalita 1993, 241). Muddupalani's epic, *Radhika Santwanam*, celebrated the eroticism of Radha, the consort of Lord Krishna. When it was republished in 1911, the British banned the book on the ground of obscenity, but it had also come under attack from Indian social reformers as early as 1887 for its lewd details, indicating the collusion between empire and nation on sexual and moral interests (Tharu and Lalita 1993, 241). The case indicates, too, a larger shift in acceptable depictions of Radha, from the "erotic and sexually active *nayika* . . . of medieval poetry to the chaste and virtuous Hindu wife and mother" of anticolonial nationalism (C. Gupta 2001, 41). Mehta's decision to name her heroines Radha and Sita attempted to trouble this recent tradition of canonical chastity; her decision to rename Sita as "Nita" for the Hindi version was in realization of that tradition's ultimate inviolability.[10]

Tellingly, Shiv Sena chief Bal Thackeray demanded that Mehta's characters be given Muslim names—Shabana and Saira—suggesting that if the

film were about Muslim lesbians, it would no longer be obscene or problematic. Thackeray's eagerness to show Muslims as perverse also has historical precedents. Colonial era editors approved textbooks that detailed
Muslim royal orgies and newspaper articles describing the homosexual
practices of Muslim rulers (C. Gupta 2001, 244–45). The acceptance of
materials such as these, which would certainly have been considered obscene if they involved Hindus, bolstered two projects: the claim that India's
existing sexual ills (such as those described by Mayo) could be attributed to
the period of Mughal rule, and consolidating a uniquely Hindu moral and
sexual identity. The especially incendiary aspects of the *Fire* controversy are
situated within this communal history.

A related history relevant to the *Fire* affair, and one that brings together
these strands of religion, obscenity, and sexuality, is the case of Ismat Chughtai and her short story "Lihaaf" (1990 [1942]).[11] "Lihaaf" is a strange,
humorous, and often dark story, full of bestial and gastronomical meta-
phors for the things that women can do to each other under the ostensible
privacy of a quilt. The narrator of the story recalls her childhood, when she
is sent by her mother to live with her aunt, the refined Begum Jan, to learn
the ways of proper femininity. This plan, needless to say, was unsuccessful.

The begum's husband has a penchant for boys, whom he entertains at
home with little regard for the begum's needs or sentiments. The "perpetual itch" that the begum is thus afflicted with is scratched, and rubbed,
and massaged, and ever so very satisfied by the begum's new massage
woman, Rabbo. Rabbo is a working-class woman, far below the begum in
status, with dark skin and rough, masculine hands with which she works
her magic. She has no other duty at all but to service the begum, and she
does so with obvious aplomb. These massages are, of course, sometimes
just massages; but from what our narrator tells us of the movement of the
quilt, and the sounds that emanate from underneath it, they are also decidedly orgasmic. The sight of the quilt with the lovers underneath looks to the
narrator as if "an elephant was struggling beneath it" (Chughtai 1990
[1942], 13); the sounds they make are like the "sounds of a cat slobbering in
the saucer. . . . Smack, gush, slobber—someone was enjoying a feast" (1990
[1942], 18).

For reasons of space and academic training, I won't attempt a literary
critical reading of "Lihaaf" here. (For particularly illuminating readings,
see Ghosh 2000; Gopinath 2005; Patel 2004.) But to make sense of the
national, cultural, and sexual politics of the *Fire* affair, it is necessary to at

least note the convergences and divergences between the reception and production of these two notorious lesbian-themed works. First is the question of how "lesbian" "Lihaaf" is. Patel argues that the complicated play between seeing and yet not seeing Begum Jan and Rabbo in the act of making love shows that Chughtai "obviously refuses the performative theory of sexuality" (2004), in which performing certain acts transforms one into a certain kind of subject. Similarly, Gayatri Gopinath understands the quilt as a "surface area suspended between that which is hidden and that which is visible," thus "disrupting the discreteness of those categories altogether" (2005, 150). The fact that no one presents themselves, or names themselves, renders the act of sexual speciation impossible.

Indeed, Chughtai, like Mehta after her, adamantly rejected a "lesbian" label for her work. But she still received a summons from the Indian colonial government in 1944, charging her with obscenity.[12] The role of the quilt in her story, as a "surface area suspended" between visibility and invisibility, neither quite concealing nor fully revealing the truth of what lay beneath, was what ultimately saved Chughtai from a jail sentence. She says in an interview: "'Lihaaf' does not contain any [obscene] words. In those days the word 'lesbianism' was not in use. I did not know exactly what it was. The story is a child's description of something she cannot fully understand. It was based on my own experiences as a child. I knew no more than the child knew. The lawyer argued that only those who already had some knowledge could understand the story. I won the case" (Chughtai 1983, 5).

There is much that is interesting in this understanding of obscenity. First is the suggestion that a work cannot be obscene unless the act that constitutes it as such is even possible. Literary fantasies of things that are socially unintelligible (such as two women voraciously making love) are not, in this case, legally obscene. Another notable point is the lawyer's argument that "only those who already had some knowledge" of the acts beneath the quilt could understand those acts as obscene. It is a clever tactic, turning the tables and placing the court in the position of pervert. All the rest of us, presumably, who have no knowledge or ability to imagine that such movements and sounds could have meant that two women were voraciously making love are blessed with the innocence of the narrator child. Those others—those who have "some knowledge"—should be left to their just deserts.

Still, why was "Lihaaf" viewed as obscene in the first place? No sex was seen, no sins were named, no Hindu gods were invoked. The protagonists were Muslim. Patel argues that "Lihaaf" was singled out for censure because it "queried and queered the domestic arena" in fundamental ways (2004, 145). First, "Lihaaf" revealed and critiqued a nexus of desire and class—not only was the begum having a sexual relationship with a lower-class woman, but she was actually paying for the sexual services that her maidservant provided. Such was her desire that the begum would exchange money for pleasure. And second, the story told of the failed inculcation of "homeliness"—the young narrator, like all young women, was to be transformed into a respectable, marriageable woman through the practices of domesticated femininity. This transformation was thwarted by the unspeakable acts she (never quite) witnessed between women.

The "never quite" of the narrator's witnessing is, of course, critical here. Chughtai's story was amenable to an obscene reading, but the never-quite-visible, never-quite-named nature of the obscenity is what saved it. *Fire*, on the other hand, was in every way a visual medium, and it was received in that widest of Indian national social settings, the cinema house. The fact that experiencing *Fire* requires no reading literacy makes it available to a larger swath of society. Furthermore, the cinema house has long been a site for the mass inculcation of nationalist sentiment and cultural practices (Nandy 1999). Contemporary events highlighting the relationship between cinema and nationalism, such as the Maharashtra state government's edict that the national anthem be played before all film screenings or the obscenity scandals about *Bandit Queen* and *Ham Aapke Hai Kaun* (see Kapur 2001), indicate the state's policing of film and its reception by an ostensibly malleable public. *Fire*'s cinematic and symbolic depiction of lesbian desire within the home, and its more literal presentation within the nationalist laboratory that is the cinema house, lent itself to controversy even more widespread than those surrounding its literary precursors.[13]

Nonetheless, the continuities between *Fire* and its literary precursors in the colonial era seem much more remarkable than the discontinuities. In an independent India at the end of the twentieth century, *Fire* pushed the same buttons of cultural anxiety about the moral meaning of the nation. The controversy surrounding the film only demonstrates once again that the boundary between the domestic and the public has always been, and is necessarily, permeable and unstable. It is precisely the simultaneous instability and necessity of nationalist spatial logic that requires spectacular public events, like the critical event of the "Indian and Lesbian" protests, to continually recalibrate, redraw, and reinforce its fiction. In the context of the *Fire* affair—similar to previous contests over hidden homosexuality—it was not that lesbianism had already begun to pose a public, visible, political threat that compelled defenders of the nation to act. Rather, it was lesbianism's stubborn failure to cohere, its shapelessness, its uncanny ability to survive within the "cracks and fissures" (Gopinath 2005, 153) of Hindu national identity that necessitated a public lesbian disavowal—which, in this particular case, was the same as a public lesbian emergence.

I might stress again, returning to the letters I analyzed in chapter 1 and the histories and presents that I unfolded from there, that there existed at this time no such coherent group as the "Indian lesbian" that was eager to reveal itself, whole and finally commensurate, in the light of public recognition. Most lesbians were indifferent to the nation altogether, far more interested—like Miss Kumar of the health club—in commensurating local explorations with foreign expertise. Those same-sex desiring women who were increasingly invested in locating their sexualities within local cultural forms were largely antagonistic toward "lesbian" as their signifier, calling themselves "single women," a "confluence of women" (Stree Sangam), "women who love women," or *saheliya* (female friends), or simply using terms like *jaadu* (magic) to give shape to their experiences of unlikely and unsanctioned love (M. Sharma 2006). Many of these eager novices and "women who love women" preferred the cover provided by the public's relative ignorance of lesbian possibilities. Culturally enforced spaces of homosociality, they argued—much like the default purdah in which Radha and Sita existed—actually enable same-sex relationships to flourish undetected. Such was the argument of feminists like Abhabhaiya and Kamla and even, to some extent, the directors of Sangini. Against the Western queer narrative of silence as the handmaiden of death, this argument posits quite the opposite: that silence enables life, and naming is the kiss before death. The very plot of *Fire*, however, belied the safety of this space of nonrecognition.

The Shiv Sena's riotous actions against *Fire*, then, were not opposed to processes of democracy. Rather, they capture in ideal form the ambivalence of the postcolonial nation-state in a globalized world, where violent defenses of tradition must be reconciled with the more subtle hegemonies of liberal democracy (Povinelli 2002). As it happened, this process—meant to bring the disruptive intensity of lesbian desire into the arena of public discourse—produced a national, political lesbian emergence. Instead of being effected by a preexisting, organized movement of lesbian women from private to public, or an effervescent desire among lesbians to commensurate their sexual identity with a national one, the Indian lesbian's emergence was effected through a performative act of interpellation: the call to "Show yourself! Become what you are."

The Riotous Emergence of Incommensurability

With this imperative, "Indian" and "lesbian" were first introduced into the social world as incommensurate terms. It was a strategy to transform lesbianism into the commensurable—to normatively qualify the disruptive intensity of anonymous letters; quiet partnerships in open view; tender, queer passions in the heart of the domestic; and public cinematic spectacle. In this section, I discuss the public, semiotic process through which that incommensurability was made to emerge.

India's lesbian political emergence was two-pronged, beginning with an interpellation and carried forward by newly interpellated lesbian activists and their allies. On the side of the Hindu right, calling for the public materialization of lesbians from their state of subterranean intensity was a good in itself that also served other political and moral purposes. In bringing forward a perfect foil for ideal Hindu womanhood in globalizing times and distracting the public from the BJP's political crises, the right-wing riots also, as Patel (2002 and 2004) argues, had another symbolic effect: to assert Hindu ownership of what they considered Hindu land.

The end of November 1998 was notable for a surprise shift in electoral fortunes, but November's end in India has been notable every year since 1992 for resurrecting memories of a violent and critical national event: the destruction of the Babri Masjid (*masjid* means mosque) in Ayodha, on December 6 of that year, by Hindu fundamentalists.[14] On the eve of the *Fire* affair, a dispute eerily similar to that in Ayodhya broke out in the state of Karnataka when Hindu activists swore to destroy a Sufi shrine that they claimed was occupying sacred Hindu land. When the Indian Parliament's upper house, the Rajya Sabha, debated *Fire*'s significance and how to respond to the Shiv Sena's actions, one member of Parliament, Bharathi Ray, made the connection between religious and sexual violence: "The threat to the Sufi shrine in Karnataka and the threat to the movie are two sides of the same coin. Sir, both smack of intolerance. . . . This, sir, is a form of fascism" (quoted in Naz 1999, 10). Another member of Parliament, Pritish Nandy, might have agreed with Ray, but he urged Parliament to stay out of the fracas: "Let us not waste the valuable national time in either defending . . . lesbians or driving them underground" (quoted in Naz 1999, 10). (Nandy did, however, suggest that women's wings of political parties might find the issue more relevant.) Some lesbian activists later read Nandy's statement about the "wasting of national time" as demonstrating that sexuality in general, and lesbians in particular, are exiled from the spacetime of national production (CALERI 1999a, 10). Patel (2002), however, reads Nandy's words as a ruse, obscuring the fact that both lesbians and Hindus' religious Others are strategically moved into and out of the national frame in order to define what the nation is. The simultaneity of the *Fire* riots and threats against the Sufi shrine show Hindu national identity being formulated through conflicts over once sacred property: Hindu land and Hindu women.

When lesbian activists and their allies responded to the violence, their own actions were similarly diffuse and fraught. The lesbian-declared "emergence" was put into motion on the night of December 7, as thirty-two Delhi activist organizations joined the film's director, Deepa Mehta, for a peaceful, candlelight vigil outside Delhi's Regal Cinema. In newspaper photographs the following morning, one placard stood out from the rest. It read, simply and boldly, "Indian and Lesbian" (figure 7). Most other banners carried more conventional liberal protest slogans, railing against censorship or the violent, bullying tactics of cultural conservatives. "Indian and Lesbian" was not only a protest against the fundamentalist Right, but also against the liberal Left that chose to defend *Fire* on the ground of "freedom of expression" rather than lesbian rights.

At issue in the struggle between lesbians and the other activists (intellectuals, feminists, and artists) who rose to Mehta's defense are the subtle modes of censorship within a public sphere already weighted in favor of the elite.[15] If Mehta was anxious about the hijacking of her film by lesbian activists, the activists themselves were increasingly frustrated by the hijacking of their political concerns by liberals. Three days before the vigil, a group of prominent artists filed a petition in the Supreme Court for *Fire*'s re-release on the ground of freedom of expression.[16] Certainly, the intervention of India's glitterati gave the film legitimacy with the public. It also focused attention on the links between homophobia and anti-Muslim communalism. All but one of the artists who petitioned the Supreme Court was Muslim, and the Shiv Sena seemingly delighted in this fact. Shiv Sainiks held one of their signature protests, a *chaddi morcha* (underwear protest) outside the residence of one of the petitioning actors, Dilip Kumar (originally named Yusuf Khan), to publicly taunt him for his support of *Fire*; furthermore, a Shiv Sainik dismissed Kumar as a Pakistani in Parliament (Kumar is Indian). Kumar finally asked the Supreme Court, successfully, for protection from the scantily clad but indefatigable Sainiks. Dozens of other people, famous and otherwise, closed ranks behind Kumar and his fellow artists, shouting slogans outside the Regal Cinema about the right to expression. Thus the signal proclamation "Indian and Lesbian" not only heralded the completion of a clever act of interpellation, but it also demanded recognition of the sexed, unabstracted, and stigmatized lesbians in the activists' midst.

The power of that sign took even lesbian activists by surprise. Ashwini Sukthankar, seen holding the placard in many newspaper photos, ruminated: "'Indian and Lesbian.' Who would have thought that staking that saucy claim would result in such a furore?" (2000). S. L. seconded Sukthankar: "One brave act of holding up a poster that said 'Indian and Lesbian' had caused such a *hul-chul* [commotion]. . . . Why did the mere announcement of one's existence cause such a cacophony?" (S. L. 1999, 17). As the poster passed from hand to hand over the course of the protest and appeared the following morning plastered on the front pages of newspapers, both English and vernacular, it functioned almost as a signal from a lighthouse—a sign of arrival, or a long-awaited confirmation. But that confirmation was not of a long-sought commensuration (as I have argued, no such effort existed prior to this moment). Instead, it was of the existence of an intensity that, now publicly birthed, demanded to be recognized. That intensity lay not in the commensuration of "Indian and Lesbian," but rather in the space between those two terms, in the space of a problem that now had to be solved.

One response generated by the introduction of incommensurability came in the form of the Campaign for Lesbian Rights (CALERI) which coalesced as an answer to the anti-*Fire* riots. The summer following the riots, when I was in Delhi doing preliminary research, CALERI was deeply engaged in the process of writing a bilingual report on, and a manifesto inspired by, the *Fire* affair. Among their always heated debates was how to refer to exactly what it was that was set in motion on the night of December 7. Ultimately they would call that night, and their manifesto, "Lesbian Emergence" (CALERI 1999 a). It is worth thinking closely about the many layers of meaning, often conflicting, that "emergence" held for CALERI. I argue that the very way in which CALERI came into being—through the interpellative challenge to "show yourself"—produced a triumphalism of emergence that cast previous and existing ways of being lesbian as problems that could now be solved through lesbianism's public triumph. CALERI wrote:

> We are supposed to have been dwelling in comfortable silence for so many centuries. Silence about our existence, a conspiracy of silence. A social pact. Don't let us know! It does not matter that you must hide your love . . . as well as your heartbreak and loneliness in wells of silence. This silence is not spiritual . . . it is the poorest of defenses. It is a fundamental denial of the freedom of expression. It is to live a life filled with lies. *It is a daily slaughter of the soul.* On December 7, we were breaking that social contract. (S. L. 1999, 17–18, emphasis added)

In this declaration, CALERI describes lesbian lives before December 7 as marked by repression, even "slaughter of the soul." For CALERI to speak is for lesbians to emerge; to triumph over silence; to transcend interiority, confinement, and a state of existing but being not seen. Critically here, by evoking "emergence," CALERI announces the entry of an already existing social body into public recognition.

At the same time, CALERI's pronouncement of a lesbian emergence carries an alternative, if etymologically archaic, connotation: that of emergence as emergency. The title of CALERI's pamphlet is *"Khamosh! Emergency Jaari Hai: Lesbian Emergence,"* or "Silence! The Emergency Continues." Here, CALERI alludes to Prime Minister Indira Gandhi's suspension of democracy from 1975 to 1977.[17] For nineteen months, Gandhi ruled authoritatively, censoring the press, arresting hundreds of journalists and dissidents, and allowing her younger son and presumed heir to run a family planning initiative in which hundreds of thousands of Indians were sterilized, many under coercion.[18] Through CALERI's evocation of Emergency (the historical event), the group likens Gandhi's Emergency regime to life under Hindu nationalist governance, with the exercise of state power through the policing of sexed bodies and the censorship of free expression: "the state of Emergency," CALERI asserts, "is not over" (CALERI 1999b, 4).[19]

But the emergency that CALERI proclaims is not simply the one imposed by the state; CALERI is also proclaiming the emergency brought by a new social movement—the beginning of a state of affairs previously unforeseen and, thus, eluding any efforts at easy containment. Unlike the first notion

of emergence as a destined arrival (the suffering lesbian moving from silence to voice), the idea of emergence as activist emergency heralds the
unfolding of unanticipated and unpredictable possibilities. Through the
words "*Khamosh!* Emergency *Jaari Hai*: Lesbian Emergence," CALERI en-
acts a constitutive tension not only in queer politics, but in all social emergences: between the pronouncements "Pay attention, we are coming" and
"Pay attention, we know not *what* is coming."

The simultaneous existence and experience of these opposing proclamations—of immanent, unpredictable potential (the virtual) and clearly
delimited materiality (the actual)—are what render this moment of emergence "affective," in Massumi's (2002) terms. The case of India's lesbian
emergence, then, helps us to think about the critical role that the production of affect plays in the politics of public culture (Mazzarella 2008). Here,
this moment of affective intensity—a kind of triumphalism—was produced
through an act of interpellation in which, as in any efficacious political
speech, the addressee (here the Indian, but not properly Indian, lesbian)
was addressed as the stranger she was the moment before she realized, and
thus became, that addressee (Warner 2002, 57).[20] One key result of this
efficacious act of public speech was that those addressees recognized themselves affectively as subjects of contradictory potential, between immanence and qualification, thus pushing an existing intensity toward one
resolution or another. From that process emerged a certain form of public
Indian lesbian, for whom both anything was at that moment possible, but
something definitive had to happen. Given the terms through which the
lesbian emergence was set into motion, the struggle between the deeply
conflicting demands of unpredictable potentiality and commensuration
was already weighted in favor of containment.[21] In the two sections that
follow, I analyze how "lesbian" and "Indian" became delimited, and as
potentially commensurable terms.

Becoming "Lesbian"

Kruti answered the "Indian and Lesbian" placard's call as dozens of others
did, by placing an anonymous call to the Sangini help line whose number
she found located at the bottom of a news article on "women in love."[22]
Others, like those who would form CALERI, responded with the decision to
build a public campaign. After the candlelight vigil, around thirty-five peo-

ple met at Central Delhi's Indian Coffee House (the same place where CALERI would later draft its manifesto and, not coincidentally, where dissidents gathered during the Emergency). The group was not limited to lesbians. Many were feminists who identified as heterosexual, or were same-sex desiring but not lesbian-identified; some were straight artists, both men and women; and a few were men involved in ABVA, a radical collective organized around fighting AIDS and that had published India's first gay manifesto, *Less Than Gay*, in 1991 (ABVA stands for AIDS Bhedbhav Virodhi Andolan, or Anti-AIDS Discrimination Campaign). Like CALERI and Sakhi, ABVA was a transnational project; it was co-founded by a young gay man, Siddhartha Gautam, who first became involved in queer politics while a student at Yale. The lesbian constituents of CALERI, too, were almost all partially educated in the West (either before or after CALERI's founding) and had ties to diasporic Indian queers.[23]

Although all of CALERI's members were united in a desire to combat the Shiv Sena's violence and cultural terrorism, not all were in agreement about the language with which to undertake that task. Members of women's NGOs were as eager as artists and other progressives to shift the *Fire* debate away from lesbianism and toward liberal humanist values of artistic freedom. Many expressed opposition to the use of the word "lesbian" in the vigil and took a stand against its use in any future campaign that they were a part of. The political struggle at hand, they argued, was one of freedom of expression, not of sexual preference; furthermore, to use the word "lesbian"—so deeply associated with the West and elitist politics—would simply reinforce the Shiv Sena's claim that sex between women was foreign contagion (Saheli 1999, 26–30; see also Bachmann 2002, 241; John and Niranjana 1999). One member of Jagori, according to the CALERI report, said: "Lesbianism is incidental. What we are fighting for is the right to express ourselves" (quoted in S. L. 1999, 18). Activists from Jagori also contributed an essay, something of a dissent, to *Lesbian Emergence*, in which silence is personified and asks to be recognized as a source of good, beauty, and resistance (Jagori 1999).

Through and despite these protestations, a critical mass emerged, and the Campaign for Lesbian Rights was named into being. In its manifesto, CALERI explains its decision to work under the banners of "lesbian" and "rights":

> The group named itself the Campaign for Lesbian Rights. . . . It seemed important to foreground the priorities and the common agenda of the

group within the name, rather than use euphemisms for the word "lesbian," since our stated goal is one of gaining and promoting visibility and interacting openly with the public. We did consider arguments that the word "lesbian" is western and elitist, but we also felt that, in a campaign which is to take information to the people, we need to organize around a word whose meaning is unmistakable and direct. (CALERI 1999c, 24)

Using the word "lesbian," then, was directly linked to CALERI's mandate to promote visibility, to be open and seen within the optics of the nation. In order to "take" something "to the people," though, it had to construct and then take something that cohered—something that was rather than something that was only immanent. It was in this process of containing a wide range of practices and sensibilities within the coherent identity of "lesbian" in the effort of commensurating "lesbian" with "India"—a challenge made by the Shiv Sena and accepted by activist leaders—that new norms coalesced. As the protest played out, two particular norms for "lesbian" emerged: to be lesbian was to be of the nation, and to be public and marked rather than private and concealed (a norm that also necessitated certain social and economic freedoms). But to think back to the field of play before the *Fire* protests, lesbian practice and desire in India had been everything but these two criteria, being largely indifferent to the nation, and finding both their flourishing and oppression within spaces of nonrecognition. The founding of CALERI during this moment of public and spectacular crisis significantly raised the stakes of the fissures that had already emerged within Indian lesbian politics. The question of how to negotiate a rights-based activism when some lesbians could not afford visibility—nor, for that matter, afford access to the elite language of rights itself—initially emerged when Sangini broke from Sakhi. Women to Women had also struggled with the treatment of its constituents based on their level of politicization and political capability. Now on a national and global stage, those questions loomed larger. To whom did lesbian activists owe their labor? To the other, mostly self-supporting activists who desired unfettered access to the public domain as lesbians, or to those women whose tentative participation in groups like Sangini was based conditionally on the promise of their privacy and psychosexual anonymity?

Sangini was initially among the groups that would become CALERI, even signing a petition for *Fire*'s re-release (see Betu's story in chapter 2). But once CALERI began to require activities such as leafleting on college campuses, at shopping bazaars, and outside institutional sites such as the Supreme Court and Parliament, Sangini withdrew.[24] Sangini's leadership claimed to CALERI at the time, and to me later, that the group's mission was to provide a space for companionship and patience rather than one of ideology. Unlike the activists and artists who made up CALERI, Sangini's constituents tend to be financially dependent on their parents, or to be older and married with children—women who, though finding solace in an increasingly accessible lesbian subjective attachment, could not join CALERI's public emergence. The split between Sangini and CALERI still reverberates today in the severed relationships between leaders of these groups. From an analytic standpoint, it is also important to see that the split was not altogether new, but was another instantiation of that between Sangini and Sakhi, of a cleavage between the support group (comprised of those, like Betu, who are marked as outside of politics) versus the political advocacy group. But, as I show below, what was new in this later instantiation was the felt linkage of publicity and politics: those who were not public were not politically significant subjects—a formula, born of CALERI's lesbian emergence, that ironically reinforces the public–private divide upon which heteronormativity relies.

Even within CALERI, such distinctions emerged between proper and improper lesbian subjects. In a discussion after a day of leafleting, one woman revealed that she no longer felt comfortable handing out parchis on public streets: her "different" appearance had precipitated insulting comments and stares from passers-by, and she felt "threatened and intimidated" (V. T. 1999, 72). Other members of CALERI responded that "she should trust the rest of the group" and that "retiring from leafleting was not the political solution to the problem." Another argued that "we should be sensitive to each other's oppression, but not at the cost of the Campaign" (V. T. 1999, 72). I interviewed this activist, Vandana, three years later. She eventually left the campaign after the number of such incidences mounted and was more than happy to tell me about the group's "tyranny" about determining who was a "real" activist. Vandana (much like Chatura commenting on "the field" in the previous chapter) shook her head and repeated, "at the *cost* of the *Campaign!*" She finally shrugged: "We wouldn't want to be real people with real feelings and needs, now would we? No. Being a real person is not very radical at all."[25]

The symbolic cleavage between the political and the nonpolitical had real consequences, of course. In the two years that I spent with Sangini and since, I have been struck by the numerous and adamant declarations that "we are not a political group." Now banished from the sphere of what constitutes proper lesbian subjectivity, Sangini's members and directors sought to define themselves by regulating the nonusage of the "lesbian" signifier and thus cultivating an alternative commensuration of "lesbian" with "Indian." In this model, to be an "Indian lesbian" was precisely not to be whole and public, but to acknowledge the chasm between the two terms and gently manage that incommensurability as a space and means of private sexual and social discovery.

For example, at a meeting in November 2003 we were discussing the pros and cons of including the term "lesbian" as well as "women who love women" in the group's weekly newspaper advertisements. Many members thought that using "lesbian" would help Sangini attract more college students and cooler young women; however, Sangini's directors decided against the change. Maya explained the decision to me: "The average Indian woman fears this word 'lesbian.' First, these women just need to deal with the basic stuff. It does no good to scare them away with all of this heavy analysis and politics."[26]

A woman like Kruti is in a difficult position here. She is a closeted young woman, lives with her family, and is dependent on them for her material needs. Insofar as she cannot risk this safety for visibility, she does choose private support over public action. But it was the unjust linking of "lesbian" with either privacy and fear or publicity and courage that was a problem after *Fire*. Recall Kruti's moment of passionate attachment as she first read the phrase "Indian and Lesbian," whispering the words from her mouth like pearls. These words, painted together on a placard for all to see, at the precise moment between the introduction of their irreconcilable difference and the possibility of their profound and public resolution, held for Kruti a promise but not fear. These words, rather than coding action (now "publicity," now "privacy") constituted only action's potential, an affective moment in which the yet-unknown entered upon the world, rendering anything possible but *some*thing absolutely necessary.

It is this social paradox of emergence that renders this moment in lesbian politics both triumphant and melancholy for everyone the emergence implicates. To tie this to my larger disciplinary argument, it would be simple to claim that thus far in the narrative, the agendas of activists have been at odds with the everyday hopes of nonactivist queer people who only want to commensurate their sexuality with culture—to claim that CALERI un-wisely chose to impose a Westernized queer identity politics in India that then pushed Sangini to advocate for a fearful politics of cultural authenticity, both of which were betrayals of an everyday queer Indian like Kruti. But the point I want to emphasize is that before the critical event of the Shiv Sena riots, which issued forth the "Indian and Lesbian" emergence, no group—activist or nonactivist—was preoccupied with what "lesbian" must entail, what "Indian" must entail, or what it is to make those terms commensurate. Rather than being at odds, CALERI, Sangini, and Kruti all shared a sense of the enormous potential inherent in the introduction of "Indian and Lesbian" as incommensurable, a spectacular assertion that required acts of recognition and resolution. The only difference among the parties was in how that resolution was sought (but not in the fact of seeking resolution, which was inevitable). While CALERI devised criteria for "lesbian" that included publicity, political competence, and affinity with the nation, Sangini's criteria were fear, secrecy, and accommodation to cultural limitations. Neither was right or wrong; both were answers to a question—What is a lesbian in the context of India?—posed from elsewhere in order to contain. In the next section, I address how lesbian activists sought to resolve a corollary question: What is the lesbian's relationship to the nation?

Becoming "Indian"

Scholars have celebrated *Fire* for its "democratizing" impact, in that it served as the spark that catapulted lesbian rights agitators into the public sphere for the first time (see John and Niranjana 1999). This moment was truly extraordinary in the history of the Indian public, but it is also important to query such an easy equation between entrance into the public sphere of deliberation and the achievement of practical and discursive freedoms. As I have argued, the act of interpellation that brought the Indian lesbian into public view and offered her a public voice was a process that was not separate from liberal democracy and that still sought to violently recuperate the radical potential of an emergently disruptive world. As Dipesh Chakrabarty (2000) has argued, modern projects of citizenship and rights entail their violences, too.

In order to further understand how the interpellation of the Indian lesbian through the assertion of incommensurability was an effort to nor-

matively qualify disruptive social intensity, it is useful to consider the felicitous conditions (Austin 1976 [1962], 19) under which certain forms of
political speech are rendered intelligible and other forms rendered less
speakable. The force of a political proclamation, such as CALERI's, "I am an
Indian lesbian and I demand my rights," derives its efficacy not from its
own internal truth but from its ability to tap into an already existing regu-
latory regime of intelligibility. The placard "Indian and Lesbian" was an
effort at such intelligibility—and an efficacious one, judging by its wide
circulation. Such acts of speech show the struggle between the seemingly
multiple potentials inherent in a moment of social emergence and the
simultaneous introduction of commensuration. Most CALERI members
were eager to use the opportunity of an unforeseen event to effect a radical
new voice and refuse the earlier euphemisms of the *akeli aurat*, the *saheli*,
or the "woman who loves women." These euphemisms, as CALERI termed
them, were weak compromises (CALERI 1999c, 24). What CALERI soon
found, though, was that the emergence of a once-unthinkable new life into
the social world—a rights-bearing Indian lesbian—is also a necessarily
compromised formation: one that, in order to be seen and heard, assents to
the norms of identity and to the nation's affective primacy. In other words,
both CALERI and Sangini found that a radical emergence would demand
(not just simply allow) commensuration.

"Indian and Lesbian" was not the only sign attaching lesbians to India
on that night. Another that made its way onto the front pages read "Indian
Heritage," with images of temple architecture from the eleventh and
twelfth centuries featuring women in orgiastic positions with one another.
Another read "Indian Culture," boasting similar images from Hindu iconography of women delighting erotically with other women. One question
that emerges here is why CALERI, comprised of progressives who were opposed to Hindu nationalism, attached lesbianism to the nation and used
Hindu images, no less, to do so? Why, as some critics demanded, did they
not simply denounce the nation, its political possession by Hindu spokespeople, and the sexual inequality that the nation demands?

One response, as leftist activists in India know, is that even the most
progressive Indian politics has had to—and has sought to—demonstrate the
strength of its relation to "India." I discussed in chapter 3 how this demonstration has been important for feminists. This is an imperative born of
anti-imperialism and anti-Western capitalism, as well as from a related

belief that rights and equality are at home in India. The attachment of political claims to the nation, even by the Left, is an assertion that "one could be both 'Indian' and a 'citizen' at the same time" (Chakrabarty 1992, 8).

The efforts that lesbian women have made to attach their own political claims to "India"—an effort made by all Indian progressives—did not begin with the *Fire* affair. The *Fire* protests were only the most public and far-reaching articulation of a longer strategy that links same-sex desire to India through "historical symbolic recovery" (Bacchetta 2002, 969). For example, Giti Thadani's primary project, to recall from chapter 1, has been to document the presence and deliberate erasures of lesbianism within Indian traditions. (The images on the "Indian Heritage" poster were taken and first published by Thadani [1996].) Lesbians and feminists criticized Thadani for using Hindu iconography to represent India, much as feminists—both lesbian and straight—later criticized CALERI for using exclusively Hindu images to proclaim their Indianness. Some, like feminist legal scholar Ratna Kapur, asserted that CALERI's insistence on claiming national heritage at all, regardless of the iconography used, reinforced the Hindu Right's brand of cultural nationalism (Kapur 2002; see also Puar 1998). Although we need to take seriously the charge of conflating Hindu with India—for it is precisely that conflation that undergirds the violent politics of Hindutva—Kapur's critique needs to be unpacked in the ethnographic context of how emergent worlds come into being.

To say that any discursive turn to "India" reproduces the "India" of the Hindu Right is to hold a singular conception of the nation, and to surrender cultural production to those who have attempted to violently seize it. The "Indian and Lesbian" proclamation was optimistically agentive, a move in part to transform the nation by expanding the terms of its sexual citizenry. Furthermore, arguing that to use "India" is to fall into nationalist hands sounds very like the argument of some feminists that for CALERI to use "lesbian" was to fall into Hindu nationalist hands. "Indian and Lesbian" was to challenge existing limits—imposed by the Right, the Left, and the women's movement—to what could be spoken and imagined.

Bacchetta likewise argues that acts of reterritorialization—of insistence on the Indianness of lesbian existence—are efforts to confront lesbians' "multiple effacements" (2002, 969). Lesbians' sense of national exile is not based on a vague notion of being unrecognized or misunderstood: the exile is concrete. Queer people in India have had no legal rights to inheritance, adoption, custody, or marriage, all of which are basic rights of citizenship. The left-of-center Congress Party had long upheld the validity of the antisodomy statute, and the right-wing BJP and its allies were arguing that lesbians could not be Indian and thus did not have the rights of Indian citizens. "Indian and Lesbian," then, was also a way to confront this exile. Even while deploying already available tropes, lesbian activists were inventive. Commensuration—equating "lesbian" with "Indian" in a period of Hindu nationalist ascendance—was also an opening, offering the past up to queer reinterpretation.

At the same time, this story cautions against seeing lesbian claims to the nation as "mere"—or even deliberate—strategy. Lesbian claims to national belonging were, I argue, nothing less than inevitable at the time, if lesbians were going to make any claims at all. This recalls Hannah Arendt's principle of minority politics, that "one can resist only in terms of the identity that is under attack" (1968, 18). To resist interpellation might have made CALERI and its supporters "wonderfully superior to the world," but that would be an antipolitical superiority that belongs more to "cloud-cuckoo-land" than to the world of struggle and the desire for social recognition.

"Indian and Lesbian" is just as attributable to the orchestration of affect as it is to the felicitous conditions of national public speech. In interpellating the lesbian as specifically Other to the nation, right-wing activists introduced an incommensurability that did not previously exist, and in so doing, also introduced the possibility of commensurating queer desire with national belonging. The possibility that was made manifest and exquisitely succinct in a simple placard that read "Indian and Lesbian" was also the representation of a public moment of affective potentiality in which both anything could happen but something was necessary. That "something," in this case, was to newly grapple, publicly, with the meaning of home and the possibility of exile. The claim that lesbian activists made on the night of the candlelight vigil—that we are of this land—was not a mere strategic choice to be evaluated as politic or impolitic, effective or failed. That claim was inexorable, set in motion by the public production of an entirely new affect, produced precisely to render the claim, and lesbianism itself, assimilable to normative social domains of nation and identity. But, as with all instances of commensuration, the assimilation of Indian and lesbian would be the very condition of possibility for new social potential.

Conclusion: Publics, Containment, and Possibility

I have told of how members of one counterpublic (the Shiv Sena) interpellated another ([non-]Indian lesbians), which fully came into being around the text of a sign. Addressed as it was on the two common levels of public speech—of abstract citizenship and the affective level of national belonging or exile (Mazzarella 2008, 299–300)—this new lesbian counterpublic sought to address the national public, narrativizing itself as having always existed in a particular normative form that would enable it to acquire agency in relation to the state. But did this process of commensuration, of rendering unremarkable what was potentially extraordinary, amount to what Michael Warner warns of—that in addressing itself in normative form to the state, a counterpublic cedes hope of transforming the space of public life itself (2002, 89)? Warner's cautionary remark opens up two additional questions. First, to what extent, and how, did lesbian activists transform the space of public life through the *Fire* protests? And second—a question that has interested me throughout this book—how is the containment and limiting of possibilities not simply negative, but ethically productive?

Feminist philosopher Maria Pia Lara (1998) discusses the importance of narrative telling in the Mexican public sphere as a way for activists to imaginatively transform themselves and, more widely, to produce transformative conceptions of justice and the good. It is through the public telling of narratives—a linking of normative political claims and the aesthetic—that solidarity is created among previously antagonistic groups, and through which a "we" is continually expanded. The central point for Lara is that no party remains the same after a new group intervenes in the public sphere. In the case of the *Fire* affair, such illocutionary force was certainly to be found. The very construct of "India" was transformed such that watchful citizens could no longer be complacent with the illusion that "Indian" and "lesbian" are necessarily mutually exclusive categories. Furthermore, the idea that love and heterosexual conjugality are synonymous was soundly disrupted. Delhi's first Gay Pride parade, in 2008, was also made possible only because Indian lesbians had emerged as public, potentially rights-bearing subjects, captured in that particular normative form. Interestingly, on this more recent day of global celebration, hardly any placards or slogans made reference to India (although see figure 8); instead, they marked their joy in queerness; pride in bisexuality; or in the brotherhood of gay Muslims, Hindus, and Sikhs (see Katyal 2009).

8. With a nod to the origins of public lesbian activism in India, activists paint a "Proud Indian Lesbian" sign the day before the 2008 march. Photograph by Sonali Gulati.

Containment, as Massumi argues, is an effect of an interruption of a field of immanence by an operation of transcendence (2002, 79). Such an operation was precisely what the *Fire* affair was about, and the containment of a range of possibilities was indeed one of its effects. But the longer story I am telling indicates that in the course of social action, that which is contained circuits into immanence, into a field of possibility and becoming (79). Containment does momentarily halt variation, but it is precisely those points of momentous (and, in this chapter, public) closure that provide the limits against which previously unimaginable forms of possibility are continually invented and played.

chapter 5

TO BE LAWFUL, TO BE JUST

Whoever voluntarily has carnal intercourse against the order of nature with any man, woman, or animal, shall be punished with imprisonment for life, or with imprisonment of either description for a term which may extend to ten years, and shall also be liable to fine.

Explanation: Penetration is sufficient to constitute the carnal intercourse necessary to the offence described in this section.

—Section 377 of the Indian Penal Code

On July 2, 2009, the High Court of Delhi declared Section 377 unconstitutional.[1] In the courtroom, Jaya wept. Outside the court, journalists shouted; photographers craned for a better view; and queer people hugged each other and cheered, taking call after call on their cellphones as the once unimaginable news spread across the country (see figure 9).[2] Yes, by nightfall, as the celebrations turned into reflection, right-wing politicians were already promising to take the case to the Supreme Court, and swamis were reassuring the nation that yoga could be a cure for the "sickness" of homosexuality. But for a few days, none of this mattered. All was joy, disbelief, euphoria. All was solidarity. The story that this chapter tells is the remarkable one of how queer activists set on the path to this legal victory, many of

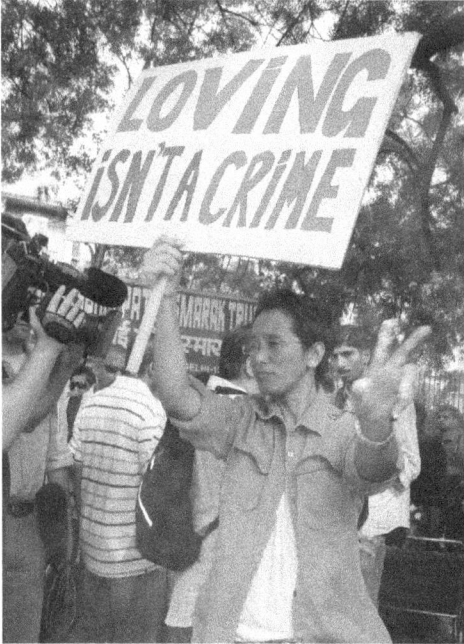

9. Activists celebrate the High Court decision on July 2, 2009. Image by Sonali Gulati from her film *I Am*.

them moving from firmly rejecting legal activism to crying with joy as Justice Ajit Shah read from the historic decision.

My narrative begins on a wintry Delhi evening in early December 2001, two nights into my fieldwork. I sat in Lesley and Jaya's living room with several of their friends, enjoying conversation after a take-out dinner of biryani. Among the group that night was Akshay, who was then employed by Lawyers Collective a nonprofit legal aid group, and who had been a founding member of PRISM. He lounged on the divan, regaling us with hilarious stories and spontaneously composed bawdy songs set to the sound of the bangles jangling on his otherwise rather manly (because extremely hairy) forearms.

But with one question, the atmosphere in the room suddenly changed. Akshay casually asked us, during a break from his impromptu performance, if we were aware that the Naz Foundation (India) trust (Naz) was preparing to submit a public interest litigation (PIL) in the Delhi High Court that week through Naz's legal counsel at Lawyers Collective.[3] Hearing only silence, and seeing the confused looks on the others' faces, he continued. You must know, he told us, that the petition would call for a reading down of Section 377. ("Reading down" means to limit the interpretation of the law rather than to strike the law down entirely.) What Naz and Lawyers Collective planned to achieve with this reading down, Akshay added, was nothing short of decriminalizing all same-sex sex that is adult, consensual, and had in the confines of "the private."

Perhaps in a less complicated world, such an announcement might have been met with elation. Lesley and Jaya might have been overjoyed that a powerful HIV/AIDS organization like Naz had marshaled its impressive resources to wage a legal battle on behalf of lesbians and gays across India. They might have hugged the messenger, congratulating him on his organization's role in staging this historic confrontation. Instead, there was only a stunned, angry silence that soon turned into a bitter exchange. Lesley, Jaya, and the others rebuked Akshay and Lawyers Collective for a host of related actions: not consulting with the larger community when planning Naz's legal action; betraying the majority of queer men by insisting on the designation of a respectable and mostly impossible zone of "private" sex, and betraying all women by further entrenching the public–private distinction; and, finally, assuming that legal change actually changes anything. Akshay, agitated but emboldened, finally spoke as plainly as possible, referring to the AIDS pandemic and Naz's primary argument about the negative impact of s.377 on HIV outreach work: "People are dying," he said. That simple fact rendered the litigation beyond politicking, beyond philosophizing. It was, he argued, "simply about the right to *live*."[4] How, he wondered, could anyone argue with that?

Activists *did* argue with that, and Naz and Lawyers Collective faced a barrage of criticism from movement representatives across India, many of whom boycotted the legal effort. The extent of the resistance was such that even the Indian government would chide Naz for failing to build a movement around its efforts. This chapter tracks these debates and the uncertain process of making a cross-gender, cross-class, national queer legal movement out of fractured pieces of ambition, hope, and dissent. If this process had been the only one involving litigation and justice in queer India, it would have been story enough. But one of the most interesting aspects of the s.377 controversy was its conflicted, if mostly unremarked, coincidence with a second legal debate that blurred the lines of strategic solidarity established in opposition to and support of the s.377 petition.

This second debate centered on a legislative effort spearheaded by a Delhi women's NGO, Sakshi. With international backing, Sakshi sought to change the sexual assault laws in India that are gender-specific (according to which only a man can commit sexual assault, and only against a woman), making them gender-neutral (so that the law would also recognize other forms of sexual assault, like that of a man by a man and of a woman by a woman). On the face of it, and certainly according to Sakshi, this seemed like legislation that queer groups could get behind. Technically, a gender-neutral sexual assault law would apply to the sexual abuse of a male child by a male adult—a crime that had heretofore been prosecuted under s.377 (which is why Naz and Lawyers Collective only sought to have the sodomy law "read down" to exclude consensual adult sex). A new, gender-neutral sexual assault law would provide one more justification for abandoning s.377 altogether. But on a more abstract level, gender neutrality could radically unsettle the heteronormative scaffolding of Indian law—the premise of women as universally victim and men as universally perpetrator, or the maxim that women have a vulnerable nature, men a powerful nature, and ever the twain shall meet, either in romance or in rape. Furthermore, a gender-neutral sexual assault law would, even if only symbolically, offer victims of same-sex assault a means of redress. But instead of supporting these shifts, the vast majority of queer groups banded together with autonomous women's groups to oppose a gender-neutral sexual assault law.

One of my objectives is to analyze the positions formed—and the ethical practices created, enacted, and even foreclosed—around these coeval debates. What reading these contests together shows is the uneven and always shifting terrain on which debates about the role of law in social change are contingently enacted. Along with a majority of other queer activists who were lesbians (and thus invisible to phallocentric sodomy law), nonelite men (for whom a private sphere is elusive), or feminists, Lesley and Jaya opposed Naz's efforts to amend s.377. The one factor that linked these groups and individuals together was a highly contextual sense of lack of vulnerability to the law, but only insofar as their lowly status (or the lowly status of their constituents) would persist regardless of what the law on sodomy said. For them, the law seemed meaningless to the already weak, serving as little more than a magic spell murmured by robed men over the cauldron of real inequities that constitute the social world. Among these activists who were antagonistic to legal efforts in the context of s.377, lesbians and feminists in particular (including those at PRISM) would come to feel deeply, and newly, vulnerable to the possible consequences of gender-neutral sexual assault laws. If gender neutrality were won, they protested, women could be accused of sexually assaulting men, or lesbians could be accused by third parties of sexually assaulting each other. Here their opposition to legal change was based on a radically different principle. Instead of continuing to proclaim that the law means nothing to us, they now argued that the law means everything—it is all-powerful, deeply consequential, and must protect the weak from the strong.

The question of the law–society nexus is a central preoccupation in the study and execution of social movements. Some scholars have argued, like Naz's detractors, that the law is irrelevant to social change and justice—that law is myth, magic, or meaningless. Many others argue that the law is not enough, that it can aid marginal actors somewhat, but that real change happens on the so-called ground. A small group of scholars and activists argue for progressive law as a real precursor to social justice.

As the political and ethical contests of Indian queer activists between 2001 and 2009 show, there is no one answer to the question, "How does law affect society?" One minor argument of this chapter is that an actor's position on this question depends on that actor's self-perceived vulnerability to a particular law at a particular moment. This contextual sense of vulnerability on the part of a vocal few, however, gives rise to a more sweeping philosophy about the law's efficacy, with consequences for their own ethical and political engagements as well as for the lives of those on the margins of political (and now legal) competence. But the major theme of the chapter harkens back to that of the previous one, in showing how certain forms of activism—here, legal activism and engagement with the state—are made to emerge. As was the case with lesbians and public visibility on the national stage, queer activists in India were largely reluctant to participate in, and even indifferent to, legal reform. Rather than eagerly organizing against the state, they were actively called to their action in the early years of this century by a confluence of the state and international donors and activists. This emergence of a queer engagement with the state, if much less spectacular and much more laborious than the emergence of a lesbian public, gave rise to new (and impossible) choices for queer activists that had not previously existed as such. As in chapter 4, those choices exist within a larger ethical contest, applicable to all activisms, between what could be and what must. The specific (impossible) choice here might be seen as that between justice and law.

Section 377 was introduced to the Indian Penal Code by the Indian Law Commission on October 6, 1860, with little debate. Based largely on anti-sodomy law in Britain, s.377 focuses on penetrative acts "against the order of nature."[5] The crime of sodomy itself is a statutory offense, but what constitutes sodomy is historically variable, determined through case law. Part of what that case law demonstrates is that the majority of cases prosecuted under s.377 have dealt with sodomy by an adult male on a child; that not a single case to reach a High Court has concerned female-with-female sex; and that a small fraction of the cases (six out of forty-six) have dealt with homosexual sodomy, half of which are concentrated between 1990 and the present.[6]

Given that the effects of s.377 have been more symbolic and discursive than punitive, certainly until the 1990s, it is not surprising that the first organized effort to repeal it was undertaken only in that decade. The effort was initiated by the AIDS Bhedbhav Virodhi Andolan (ABVA), a nonprofit, all-volunteer cadre of social activists that had worked, among other issues, on behalf of professional blood donors and the rights of prostitutes. The group had been cofounded by a gay man, Siddhartha Gautam, in 1989. Gautam had gone abroad to study at Yale, where he became involved in HIV/AIDS and gay rights activism. After returning to Delhi, he shared what he had learned about queer politics with a group of mostly heterosexual, but progressive, activists who would become ABVA. They published a groundbreaking pamphlet—equal parts manifesto and a report on discrimination—called *Less Than Gay* in 1991. Gautam died of Hodgkin's lymphoma at the age of twenty-eight, a few months after its publication. In his memory, in 1993 his sister and several others started a human rights film festival called Friends of Siddhartha, which, since its inception and until only recently, has been a significant annual event for queer Indians.

Even with its primary champion of gay rights gone, ABVA challenged s.377 in 1994. The effort was set in motion in February of that year, when a team of doctors conducted interviews with inmates of Delhi's Tihar Jail to assess the level of HIV transmission risk in the overcrowded prison. A sensational story in the *Pioneer* newspaper claimed that close to 90 percent of the hundreds of prisoners whom the medical team interviewed had engaged in homosexual sex.[7] With rumors that some prisoners had already tested positive for the virus, and with tuberculosis rates rising (a hint at rising HIV seropositivity), this confirmation of "rampant homosexuality" in the prison warned of a public health disaster.

The inspector general of Tihar Jail, the butch but straight, and popularly known Kiran Bedi, came down firmly against the suggestion—made by the World Health Organization and seconded by the team of Indian doctors—that prison officials supply condoms to the prisoners. Instead, Bedi said that Tihar was dealing with the homosexual menace by isolating queer offenders. Janak Raj Jai, a Gandhian socialist and dissident once jailed during the Emergency, then came on the scene, demanding an even firmer denouncement of condom distribution from the highest levels of government.[8] Jai filed a petition with the High Court of Delhi, arguing that condom distribution in Indian prisons would be tantamount to sanctioning antinational, immoral, criminal, and unconstitutional behavior. He used the very existence of s.377 to justify his arguments.[9]

It was in response to Jai's petition that ABVA filed its own on April 14, 1994.[10] The petition challenged the constitutionality of s.377 and called on the court to direct Tihar authorities to distribute condoms and cease mandatory testing of inmates and the segregation of HIV-positive prisoners. The first two-thirds of the petition focused on demonstrating that s.377 violates three fundamental rights: the right to equality (Article 14 of the Constitution), because it tends to discriminate against people solely on the basis of their sexual orientation; the right to life and liberty (Article 21) through that right's implication of a right to privacy; and the right to freedom of conscience (Article 25), because that freedom must be understood to include the right to have, and act on, a sexual orientation.[11] In addition, ABVA, in an uncharacteristic (homo)nationalist display (Puar 2007), relied on shaming strategies in its petition—pointing out that Britain and most of its former colonies had repealed their antisodomy statutes, leaving India in the backward company of Pakistan, Malaysia, and Singapore.

With no national movement for the repeal of s.377 in existence, ABVA's claims about the rights of queer people in India were brave, prescient, and forthright. Their petition stated, for instance, that "even outside the specific context in which this petition has been filed, it is essential that the Court declare 377 as *ultra vires* of the constitution in order to protect sexual minorities and to ensure that even outside prisons, there is no persecution of sex workers and persons who have a different sexual orientation."[12] As I've noted, a major impediment to recent efforts to build a movement around the repeal of s.377 is the absence of another law that deals with male-child sexual abuse. This absence, however, did not give ABVA pause—they asked for nothing short of a full repeal of the section, leaving the government to deal with any resulting lacunae in the law. As advocates for all victims of sexual moralizing—including sex workers, AIDS patients, and gays and lesbians—they demanded a complete undoing of s.377 and its suggestions of "unnatural sexuality." Realizing that such a repeal would be difficult to achieve (though still worth fighting for), they turned in the final third of their petition to the simple matter of Tihar Jail's inmates, making the case that condom distribution is a state responsibility, regardless of how the court decided on the question of s.377's constitutionality.

Bedi filed counteraffidavits to both Jai and ABVA, stressing that at no time had she, or would she, consider distributing condoms in the prison.[13] For one thing, she argued, referring to the overcrowded conditions there, "it is humanly impossible that people are indulging in homosexuality in the crowded areas where they are living."[14] (Is it the modesty of sodomites that she is overestimating here? Or the gymnastic virtuosity of their acts?) In her counteraffidavit to ABVA's petition, she added, famously, that "there is no justification . . . for supply of condoms in the prison. Supply of condoms will promote homosexuality" (2). Instead, she lays out suggestions to reduce homosexual behavior, including installing a "mobile position box system" and increasing bed checks.

But ABVA had reason for optimism. As a sign of how seriously the government was taking the issue, Attorney General Soli Sorabjee appeared in court, arguing for the admittance of ABVA's petition—a symbolic honor not bestowed on Naz. Coverage in the English-language newspapers was also overwhelmingly positive, and the public seemed willing to accept the idea that the antisodomy statute was not just about abstract notions of public morality, but also about life and death. But as is common in the Indian legal system—though far less common in the case of PIL (Desai and Muralidhar 2000)—the case languished in the court for years. With no computerized system in place, ABVA's lawyers and activists had to personally check the court docket on a weekly basis for years on end. An unfunded group with pro bono advocates, ABVA missed one critical scheduled appearance. The petition, neither decided nor formally disposed of, and with no supporting movement, lay buried for eight years in Delhi's highest court.

The Call to Action: Aversion Therapy and False Arrests

The efforts by ABVA to lift the weight of criminality off India's sexual minorities had surprisingly little consequence for gay activists at the time. Neither did it provide the center around which a queer legal reform movement would form, nor did it spark much debate around alternative legal approaches. Though gay and lesbian groups sprung up in great numbers between the two petitions about s.377 (filed in 1994 and 2001), law reform was not central to any group's agenda. Lesbian groups, for the most part, sought to forge alliances with and gain support from women's organizations, and to establish support groups, help lines, and an infrastructure for domestic crisis intervention. Predominantly men's groups such as Delhi's Humrahi, Bombay's Humsafar Trust and Udaan, Calutta's Counsel Club and Integration, and Bangalore's Sangama prospered through the funding, international attention, and legal noninterference necessitated by the HIV/AIDS crisis. Through HIV prevention efforts, these groups reached out to kothis, MSM, and gay men, forming viable social communities despite the existence of s.377. To lesbian collectives, the state seemed politically out of reach; to the organizations serving gay men, kothis, and MSM, HIV provided a reason to feel beyond the punitive practices of the state.

However, two events in 2001 threw light on the relevance of s.377 to the lives of sexual minorities in India. In the spring of 2001, a young gay man from Delhi approached the Milan Project, a subgroup of Naz, with allegations against a psychiatrist at the All India Institute of Medical Sciences.[15] He had been seeing this psychiatrist for nearly four years, during which time the doctor had given him unidentified drugs and aggressively trained him to avoid same-sex fantasies and make women the object of his desire.[16] The Milan Project filed a formal complaint with the National Human Rights Commission (NHRC) in May 2001, arguing that such aversion therapy constitutes a violation of human rights.[17] The group asked that the NHRC direct the Indian Psychiatric Society to follow the lead of the World Health Organization and the American Psychological Association and declassify homosexuality as a mental illness. It was this classification, they believed, that served to justify aversion therapy, a set of practices that—according to much queer anecdotal evidence in India—often includes electric shock treatment (Narrain and Chandran 2005, 62–65). The NHRC replied a month later. According to a report in the *Pioneer*, the commission wrote that "sexual minority rights did not fall under the purview of human rights" and, therefore, it would "not take cognizance of the case."[18] Another NHRC source asked the *Pioneer*'s reporter: "Homosexuality is an offence under the [Indian Penal Code], isn't it? So, do you want us to take cognizance of something that is an offence?"

The NHRC case demonstrates that s.377 is more than just punitive. As Arvind Narrain (2004) has written, we cannot understand its impact on gay lives and politics merely through its enforcement or nonenforcement in the courts. What gay activists were made to understand through NHRC's haughty rejection is that s.377 not only limits what two men can do; it also limits what can be said and what political possibilities can be imagined. Realizing this, gay activists began to speak. With stories and posts about the incident mounting on the LGBT-India e-list, activists sent letters to the NHRC and a host of international human rights organizations, yielding yet more electronic furor and a global action alert from the International Gay and Lesbian Human Rights Commission.

It was only a matter of days before this attention was diverted elsewhere, to the North Indian city of Lucknow.[19] On the night of July 6, three men were arrested for having sex in a local park. One of these men said that he had only been on duty as an outreach worker for the Bharosa Trust, an NGO focusing on HIV/AIDS. The next morning, police raided and sealed Bharosa's office and that of NFI, an NGO based in the United Kingdom that provides training to organizations focusing on HIV/AIDS and MSM throughout South Asia, including to Bharosa.[20] The police confiscated safer-sex aids such as condoms, lubricants, instructional videos, and—much to their delight and that of a giddy press—a variety of dildos (which were probably used to demonstrate condom application, but few were interested in such banal explanations). The police also arrested two members of Bharosa and two members of NFI, who became known in activist circles as the Lucknow Four.

To peruse the media reports from the next several days is to remember just how dense a node homosexuality is for contests over class, culture, and nation. In the numerous references to the "gay clubs" and "male sex worker rackets" that were "unearthed" from "under the guise of AIDS NGOs," descriptions abound of the perverse items seized from the otherwise "modern," "luxurious," and "palatial" offices of Bharosa and NFI. The ostensibly remarkable amenities included air-conditioning units, refrigerators, and televisions, all utterly commonplace in the middle-class urban NGO world but serving a crucial purpose here. Much of the publicity about the Lucknow raids tried to forge a divide between the wealthy, foreign-funded "ring-leaders" of these NGOs (and the high-level politicians they allegedly sexually serviced) and the poor local boys whom they were exploiting—an exploitation made possible only through an initial exploitation of India's dramatic HIV/AIDS crisis.

The focus on this ostentatious display of AIDS monies, then, was tightly bound up with a nationalist discourse against foreign intervention. An article in the *Times of India* in the week following the arrests revealed that the National Intelligence Bureau had been tracking foreign-funded HIV/AIDS NGOs in seven Indian cities since 1998.[21] The bureau's purpose was twofold: to survey the role of these NGOs in supporting the rise of gay "cultures" and movements across India and to track the related influence of Pakistani nationals and their money as they slipped in under the guise of HIV service provision. Indeed, as Lawrence Cohen (2005) points out, the Lucknow arrests were all the more symbolically dense because the director of NFI, Shivananda Khan, is a Muslim based in the United Kingdom who had long been a special target of the bureau's investigations.[22]

Within this nexus of sexual perversity, cultural contagion, and national insecurity, s.377, a historical manifestation of these same anxieties,[23] was deployed more as a symbol of state power to police morality than as a legally legitimate charge. Lucknow's superintendent of police repeatedly told the press that he had charged the accused under s.377 to "stop the vice of homosexuality" and to rid Lucknow of the spread of gay culture. In service of this project, the Lucknow Four were kept in jail for forty-seven days and reportedly beaten, harassed, and unsuccessfully pressured to sign a confession stating that they were running a "gay sex racket" (Bondopadhyay 2002, 52). Ultimately, prosecutors were unable to marshal evidence of actual unnatural acts sponsored by the organizations or engaged in by these men, and all charges were dropped before the case could appear in the Allahabad High Court in Lucknow. What did succeed, however, was the inculcation of queer fear and demonstrations of the effective exercise of state moral discipline.

As was the case with the *Fire* affair, though, a muscular act of nationalist violence, drawing simultaneously on legal and illegal techniques, called queer people out from spaces of quiet intensity (in this case, not the purdah of middle-class female domesticity, but the shadows of urban parks and the sanctum of NGOs) and toward a form of previously unknown action. Activists held protests across the country, from Delhi to Bombay and Bangalore, the discourse of which centered on a new prioritization of law reform through queer activist engagement with the state. However, as memories of Lucknow faded, this consensus proved fragile when Naz formally submitted its petition in December 2001, using Lucknow as its righteous justification but simultaneously introducing new fissures in the world of Indian queer activism.

Between Justice and Law

The disagreement among Akshay, Lesley, and Jaya on the eve of this new legal battle made it clear to me just how tenuous the lines of solidarity among queer activists were. The main fault line was the introduction of an impossible choice for queer activism—that between law and justice. The smaller but often more deeply felt divisions concerned the meaning of queer community and the value of consensus; hierarchies of gender, money, power, and legitimacy within the movement; and the goals, visions, and ethics animating queer politics. One important document, and the conditions of its production, reveal these points of contention most clearly.

On December 7, 2001, Naz submitted its civil writ petition to the Delhi High Court.[24] They were represented by Lawyers Collective, which had been founded in the mid-1980s by a women's rights lawyer, Indira Jaisingh, and her partner, an attorney, Anand Grover. A nonprofit, nongovernmental legal aid collective with a focus on women's and human rights law, the group had successfully represented the first person known in India to be HIV-positive, Dominic D'Souza, calling for an end to his solitary confinement under the Goa Public Health (Amendment) Act of 1986. Ten years later, Lawyers Collective pursued a case to the Supreme Court, *Mr. X v Hospital Z* (1996), in an unsuccessful effort to establish the right of Mr. X, an HIV-positive man, to marry an HIV-negative woman. Although up to this point Lawyers Collective's engagement with HIV law and the rights of people with HIV/AIDS had been scattered and unsystematic, the group received a grant from the European Union in 1998 to develop a legal aid and policymaking program specifically around HIV/AIDS. Its HIV/AIDS unit, dedicated to the memory of D'Souza, was established that same year. The collective later received a grant from the Swedish International Development Association to further the unit's work.[25]

In 2000, well before the NHRC controversy and the case of the Lucknow

Four, Naz's director, Anjali Gopalan, and the director of Naz's Milan Project, Shaleen Rakesh, approached Lawyers Collective with the idea of filing a new PIL concerning s.377. The collective agreed to represent them, and the groups jointly decided on the following argument: s.377 is unconstitutional, and the very existence of an antisodomy statute drove homoerotically inclined men further underground, and thus beyond the reach of HIV/AIDS NGO workers.

Over the course of my fieldwork, I met and talked often with Aditya Bondopadhyay, Vivek Divan, and Alok Gupta, all of whom had worked with Lawyers Collective. They praised the group and Grover, the main attorney who worked on the petition. All of them noted that Grover was deeply invested in consulting with NGOs and other activists as he drafted the petition. History made it clear that such consultation was wise. In the 1996 right to marry case, even though Lawyers Collective was representing one client (Mr. X) adversarially against another party and not filing a PIL, the collective had faced criticism from HIV/AIDS groups. Those groups argued that the legal and social climate was not amenable to the success of such a case, and the legal precedent stemming from a negative decision would hamper them for years. Additionally, when Sakshi first submitted its gender neutrality recommendations to the Law Commission in 1999, that group too faced angry protest. Other women's NGOs criticized it for failing to consult with them on matters that would change the very face of, and philosophy underlying, Indian sexual assault laws. The Lawyers Collective claimed that its attempts at transparency, demanded by past experience but found wanting by activists like Jaya and Lesley, failed not for a lack of effort but for a lack of knowledge and interest on the part of gay activists about the workings and language of the law. Such an interest was certainly piqued when the petition became public. At issue for many queer activists was the irony—or worse—of ostensibly trying to protect men who habitually or recreationally have sex in public parks by basing a legal argument on the claim of a right to privacy.

Like ABVA before it, Naz argued that s.377 is in violation of the fundamental rights to equal protection under the law as well as to life and liberty, which the group claimed includes a right to privacy.[26] Naz supported its right to privacy argument in part by citing *Rajagopal v. State of Tamil Nadu*, a 1994 case in which the court asserted a citizen's "right to be let alone." Naz went on to suggest that "no aspect of one's life may be said to be more private or intimate than that of sexual relations," and it follows that "the right to private, consensual sexual relations is entitled to protection as a fundamental right" within that established right to privacy.[27]

One issue that arises here for a feminist critique concerns the continual reentrenchment through legal discourse of a public–private distinction—a construct that, historically, has been used to justify the second-class status of women and to put the violations they face within the space of the home outside the sphere of legal intervention. Much Indian feminist scholarship on the relationship between social movements and the law has focused on this particular liability of legal reform efforts.[28] The point is not just that law works to reinforce the division between the public and private, as if such realms were pre-existent. Rather, it is that the law, as Nivedita Menon (2004) argues, by delimiting the realms into which it cannot intervene, actively constructs the private sphere and defines it as a space exempted from the values of justice and equality (see also Rao 1996). Privacy is not the reason for state noninterference; it is its effect. Menon, for example, cites a 1984 Delhi High Court judgment that was later upheld by the Supreme Court. The court, as the feminist scholar Nandita Haksar notes, claimed that "introduction of Constitutional law into the ordinary domestic relationship of husband and wife will strike at the very root of that relationship" and that "in the privacy of the home and married life, neither . . . [right to life] nor [right to equality] has any place" (quoted in N. Menon 2004, 13–14; see also Haksar 1986, 58). It is within such a history of the legal demarcation of a terrain of inequality known as the private that Naz argued, "a citizen has a right to safeguard the privacy of his own, his *family, marriage, procreation* . . . and education among other matters." Many Indian feminist and queer activists read this as an antiwoman—and even antipoor—political compromise, made to safeguard a new class of newly respectable sexual citizens.

These debates, seemingly abstract, are keenly felt even beyond the sphere of public queer advocacy or feminist legal scholarship. At a Sangini support group meeting in August 2002, for example, twelve of us had a discussion on Naz's legal intervention and its relevance to Sangini's members. Nearly everyone felt that neither the antisodomy statute nor the petition to amend it had much bearing on their lives or the daily fears that they live with. The facilitator that day, Cath, asked what those real fears are, and the answers came down, quite simply, to compulsory marriage and the alienation that would result from its eschewal. The fight that Naz was waging—to ensure a domain of privacy in which a man is beyond the law's reach when determining the configuration of adult relationships within his home—was precisely antithetical to the fight these women were waging against fathers, brothers, and mothers alike. They didn't need the further downing of shutters on the domain of the home; they needed the doors to escape it.

Still others found the petition irrelevant because having a domain of their own, defined by liberty and autonomy, was nothing more than fantasy. Four days later, I was at the Sangini office taking phone calls on the help line with Betu. Toward the end of the evening, Cath walked in, smiling and teasingly waggling her eyebrows. "I've figured it out," she said. Naturally, we asked what that was. She told us she had been struggling to understand the previous meeting, still searching for an answer to what Sangini's attendees need. Finger in the air, she announced her answer: "A place to bonk!" We laughed and looked skeptical, I'm sure, but it turned out that she was quite serious. What she was arguing is that the concerns that women come to Sangini with—of marriage pressure, coming out, and loneliness—would at least be assuaged if they had the space and freedom to simply be alone with someone they love, and to realize whatever pleasure there is in what they too often experience as sorrow. Cath was certainly right that women lacked spaces of their own. I thought of the married women I sometimes spoke to on the help line, who would rush desperately through five minutes of talk before a husband, grown son, or mother-in-law could become suspicious about their absence. These are women without dominion, women incarcerated by the private and never lords of it.

Betu, too, came to see Cath's point, recalling an exercise we had done in Sangini months earlier, in which everyone created an image of her personal utopia. The exercise exemplified what José Muñoz calls "queer world-making," which "hinges on the possibility to map a world where one is allowed to cast pictures of utopia and to include such pictures in any map of the social" (2009, 40). The unifying theme of these images, or maps, was space: dreams of homes, rooms, and quiet solitude. Betu talked about one of these pieces in particular, in which there was a large, grassy expanse and a woman lying on her back, undisturbed, under a tree. Its author was Veronica, a lesbian woman in her early forties. Because she is unmarried, she continues to live at home with, and is helping to support, her mother and adult brother. Loneliness is a subjective thing, and its phantoms are difficult to communicate. And so on the day of the exercise, she described the feeling of returning at the end of the day to a space she shares with people who will never know her, where she must walk to the corner paan shop even to call a friend. It is not simply that she has no place to "bonk," but that she has no place to be. The point, argued by Cath and illustrated by Veronica, is simply that the privacy the petition sought to protect is an unequally distributed privilege, one that is unattainable by, and yet haunts, the lesbian women who haven't a room of their own. As for the men who have their sex in public parks, the privacy argument does more than haunt; it actively stigmatizes them—and even worse, that stigma is furthered by gay activists themselves. In the context of progressive activism, legal reform efforts necessarily invoke a theory of how law should be used (differently than it is), and thus offer up an alternative vision of social ethics.[29] The underside of the right to privacy argument is that sex acts that do occur in the excess spaces of the so-called private are not worthy of protection by the law, which reaffirms the criminality of so much of queer male sexual existence in India.

Legal Activism, Symbolic Violence, and Ethics of Talk

It was the perception of a gendered and classed elitism in the Naz effort that inspired several queer groups to call a national strategy meeting in Pune in January 2002. The groups all proudly see themselves as existing on the peripheries of the big-name, well-funded NGOs like Naz and Humsafar, and they hoped to form a national alliance of pro-feminist, anti-classist, anti-communal queer collectives. Among the specific issues they were allying around were opposition to Sakshi's gender-neutrality proposal and, most of all, opposition to Naz's s.377 filing. It was only my second month in the field, and PRISM members suggested that I attend the meeting in order to get better acquainted with the national queer political scene. Before heading for the train station, I asked Lesley if she had an extra copy of the Naz petition she was reading at her desk. She did not, but insisted that I take her copy. I did.

On the second morning of the three-day meeting, Chayanika, an activist from Bombay's Stree Sangam and the Forum against the Oppression of Women, was laying out, point by point, a sophisticated critique of Naz's right to privacy claim. We all sat in a large circle on the floor and listened attentively. I was following along on Lesley's copy of the petition when, sensing eyes on me, I looked up. I saw five women across the room, frowning and alternately gesturing at my document and making a flicking motion with the wrists of their open right hands as if to say, "What is that? Explain it!" Confused, I pointed to myself to claim its ownership, not sure what else they could be asking. Others began to notice our gesticulations, and someone finally interrupted Chayanika's presentation to ask what was going on. "She has a copy of the petition!" someone shouted. At least according to my still-reeling mind when I wrote my field notes that night, people throughout the room began pointing and yelling. I explained in my overly careful Hindi that someone from PRISM had lent me her copy of the petition. Two men I had never met before began denouncing "arrogant foreign spies" and urging that I be removed. Most, however, were more concerned about what my possession of the document indicated about the relationship between PRISM, an ostensibly autonomous collective that supposedly was critical of the petition, and Naz and Lawyers Collective, a well-funded NGO and the legal engine behind this divisive petition, respectively.

The right to privacy argument was not the only reason these groups opposed the action of Naz and Lawyers Collective. They also opposed it because they felt they had not been consulted on matters of importance to their politics and lives and matters on which they would certainly have contributions to make. If PRISM had a copy of the petition that others reported having difficulty obtaining, the implication was that PRISM was deemed worthy of consultation and the other groups were considered politically inconsequential. These groups were not alone in protesting their marginalization from the means of political production and the opacity of legal engagement. A reader might wonder what ever happened to ABVA, the precursor to the groups assembled in Pune that day. It, too, had been caught unawares by Naz's efforts and reappeared at the Delhi High Court to insist on being remembered and involved.

The first hearing in *Naz v. Govt. of Delhi* was on April 23, 2002. Although it was to be no more than a procedural affair, I was surprised that there was no conversation about it on the LGBT-India e-list and that there were only two queer activists at the court that day (granted, they had traveled far to be there, one from Calcutta and the other from Bombay). PRISM was not even aware that the hearing was happening until the day before, when I mentioned my plans to attend.

The hearing was mostly predictable, with the state asking for an extension to respond to the petition, and the request being granted. Somewhat less expectedly, a group called Joint Action Council Kannur (JACK) attempted to intervene in the case. JACK was represented by a tall, pony-tailed citizen activist named Purushothaman Mulloli, who argued that there is no proven link between HIV and AIDS, and that Naz was trying to achieve sexual minority rights on a false premise. The judges, laughingly, dismissed him. They were not dismissive of Shobha Aggarwal, ABVA's representative, who reminded the court that another PIL on s.377 had been filed in 1994. One of the judges, surprised and a bit confused, asked both Aggarwal and Grover if the two petitions were in opposition. Grover sighed and said: "No. But they might seem to be."

I met with Shobha just after the hearing to discuss her thoughts on the Naz petition. We stood outside the court in the shade, behind a tea stall doubling as a photocopy shop, she smoking and both of us casually dodging people and motorbikes. She told me that ABVA had begun talking with activists, NGOs, and lawyers as early as 1992, well before the Tihar Jail story came to light, about an effort to repeal s.377. Grover had declined to represent ABVA in 1992, as had his partner, Indira Jaisingh, in 1994. Shobha asked me, hypothetically, what might have changed for them between 1994 and 2001. She rubbed her thumb and two fingers together pointedly. She was referring to the European funding. It is a common enough belief among queer groups that the Naz petition was an intervention driven by donor funds and the desire for prestige, poorly concealed as martyrdom. But the bigger question for ABVA, in every such conversation I had, was, "Why were we not consulted?"

Political divisions based on a lack of consultation are not unique to queer politics, emerging in every contesting community from disability rights and land rights to the women's movement. Of course, such protests are sometimes based on simple egoism and envy, or even personal vindictiveness. But there is something else at stake in battles over consultation: the very process through which people imagine themselves as belonging to a community of political practice that is, in turn, engaged in the production of new forms of valuation. Debates about the circulation of knowledge, in other words, are about activists understanding themselves as subjects of consequence and understanding their activism as ethical engagements.

Language is constitutive of social life, and that which is shared is an emergent property of dialogue. Furthermore, it is the hierarchies and boundaries within communicative engagement—hierarchies of relative competence and boundaries to the equal distribution of social knowledge—that determine the limits of what can be shared, among whom, and to the exclusion of which classes of people. The idealized notion of a speech community—a group of people who are bound together through a shared language (and, thus, a shared interpretative and productive relationship to the world)—is belied precisely by those economic and social conditions that shape the uneven acquisition of what Pierre Bourdieu refers to as "legitimate competence" (1991, 44). In the case of the activist engagement I am examining here—with the state, and executed through efforts at legal reform—this legitimacy reveals itself as conferred through the competence to speak in the rarefied and opaque language of state authority. (In chapter 1, however, legitimacy was conferred through the ability to dialogue, and not just desire, within the sphere of lesbian collectivity.) Those who can (and do) speak this language become the bearers of representational authority and stake their claims to a privileged means of sociopolitical production; those who cannot (or do not) find themselves voiceless in the newly valued sites of political action. It is this symbolic violence of exclusion—an effect of benign or purposeful neglect, that in turn has the effect of rationalizing divisions of political labor between those who are connected and those who are not, between the speakers and the spoken of—that is brought into focus through the question: "Why were we not consulted?"

Hierarchies of Competence and Consequence in Legal Activism

I gained further insight into the queer contests over the petition at the next *Naz v. Govt. of Delhi* hearing, in late August 2002. My farcical experience at the court's entrance that morning reminded me of the gender and sexual normativity that Naz was up against. I joined the security line and had begun to walk through the metal detector when I was stopped and asked if I were perhaps a lady. I assented and was sent to the empty ladies' queue, where I was brusquely turned back to the men's line. I protested until someone believed me. The female officers laughed amiably and called over a third. As I was patted down, all three interrogated me: Why do you look this way? What do your parents say? What will your husband think? As if all of this were not enough, another guard at the door, assuming that he was frisking a young man, reached out and placed his hands squarely on my breasts. He looked up in shock and deep embarrassment. I tried to reassure him that it was okay, only thankful that I had gotten used to this kind of thing, and anxious to get to the courtroom in time.

Naz's case had yet to be called, and I found a seat in the back of the courtroom with Shobha from ABVA, Shaleen from Naz, and a visiting activist from Bombay (one of only three queer supporters at the court that day). An Indian courtroom is a loud, chaotic place, with the door forever opening as people come and go—observers, plaintiffs, defendants, and attorneys, the latter of whom walk about freely and authoritatively in black robes, starched white shirts, and ties in the shape of inverted Vs. Lay people are not allowed to write during the proceedings, so reporters stand in clusters in the back, observe their case, and then dash out to conduct interviews as the people involved in the case leave the courtroom. The two judges sit on high at the front of the room, surrounded by daunting stacks of loose or loosely bound paper. There are no court reporters because transcripts are not made of interim hearings. Each case that morning was heard in ten minutes or less, with about forty-five seconds of loud commotion between the cases as one batch of participants replaced another.

When Naz's case was called, my party scrambled for the closer seats being vacated so that we could hear amid the din. Additional Solicitor General K. K. Sud was representing the government and remarked, predictably but only unofficially (the government had not yet presented its formal response), that homosexuality is "abhorrent" and unnatural, and that India is too traditional a society to stand for such radical change. Eliciting much laughter, a judge shot back that India is traditional when it comes to preaching, but all too modern when it comes to behaving. Sud closed by asking for another extension, which was granted.

The representatives from Lawyers Collective, two activists, and I left the courtroom and went to the court canteen for coffee and samosas. We were all bonding in our shared optimism until one of the activists expressed surprise that a group of lesbians had not attempted "disruptive tactics" at the hearing. She was referring to Stree Sangam, one of the organizers of the Pune meeting and a group that had been openly critical of the petition on the grounds of the right to privacy claim, the lack of consultation, and the privileging of elite gay male concerns over those of other LGBT people. I was clearly incredulous that they would attempt to disrupt the hearing, so someone told me what was supposed to be a convincing story. At a protest about the Lucknow incident, in Bombay in June 2001, "those women" had objected to the centrality of s.377 in the protests and argued that the platform should be broadened to be more inclusive of lesbians. The person told me, sweeping his hand in a light, dismissive gesture, "I said, 'Feel free to do your little lesbian things! Just please at least show support for the *pressing* issues!'"

He was, he went on to say, surprised that lesbians who argued that law reform was not a queer priority were also so intent on critiquing the petition: "377 doesn't affect lesbian women at all. Why do they care so much?" We all disagreed, pointing out most simply that s.377 is used as a threat against women, just as it is against men. The person shrugged: "Then perhaps they just all hate men." Either way, he went on, the drafters of the petition have learned expertise while the dissenters demand to be consulted on matters that they cannot understand: "It's not enough that we're decriminalizing private sexual behavior. They want to make it public, too!" This was followed with some obsequious laughter.

Such rationalized productions of hierarchies between the competent and the incompetent in communities of social activists are an inevitable consequence of legal-centric engagement (and, as I've shown in previous chapters, of community formation, alliance building, and public visibility). But to claim that this is an inevitable consequence is to miss an important point: a division of political labor is necessary for legal reform efforts, but that division is also what those efforts must overcome and undo in order to become what activism promises to be (and, pragmatically, in order simply to succeed).

This paradox of activism became clearer to me several months later. In January 2003, the *Times of India* ran a front-page story by Shobha John, suggesting that the repeal of s.377 would come at the expense of male street children who are routinely sexually abused by older boys and men.[30] Her source for the article was Amod Kanth, joint commissioner of police and general secretary of a child rights NGO called the Prayas Institute for Juvenile Justice. Outrage over the article lit up the LGBT-India e-list. Once the outrage subsided, what was left was anxiety; the pitting of gay rights against the innocence of street children was certain to lead to a swell of public opinion against the s.377 petition.

Kanth did his part to sink the petition. Prayas organized a seminar for politicians and journalists, explaining that homosexuals are "a small discrete group of freaks and perverts," and that "sanctified homosexuality" would destroy Indian civilization.[31] The *Indian Express* published an article on the seminar on February 3, 2003, under the fear-inspiring headline, "Kids at Risk if Homosexuality Is Legalized." The piece reported that Kanth was drafting a formal letter to the law minister urging that Naz's petition be denied, "on behalf of street children." This was clearly a new moment in the s.377 legal reform effort, one of great (if undesired) visibility and a fierce campaign directed at recruiting opposition from even the secular middle class. So why did queer activists do almost nothing in response?

One reason was that many queer people did not feel equipped to combat an effort being promoted by a joint commissioner of police in dialogue with cabinet ministers about a legal petition they still knew very little about. Another reason was apathy. They didn't care what became of the petition because they had not yet been convinced that the decriminalization of adult, consensual sex acts in private would make their families take them in again, bring them happiness, or relieve the fear they feel at the sight of a police officer in a park. And yet the ever sincere activists at PRISM, however opposed they were to the processes by which the petition was produced, were deeply concerned. They posted on LGBT-India; they (and I) wrote a letter to the editor of the *Times of India*, making it plain that the Naz petition did not seek to decriminalize nonconsensual sex acts, which includes the sexual abuse of children;[32] they drafted a letter and circulated it, with pleas to queer people across India to copy, sign, and forward the text (this did result in a few additional letters to Shobha John); and they tried, unsuccessfully, to organize a joint press conference with feminist and child rights allies to refute Kanth's claims. Despite the fact that they were now having to defend a petition they were once deemed unfit to contribute to, they turned to Naz and Lawyers Collective for advice on how best to support them. A representative from Naz said that members of that group could not speak to the press or generate activity while the petition was being heard; their hands were tied. "It really hurts us," the representative added, but PRISM was free to act if, and however, they saw fit.

Even the government of India was aware of the lack of queer mobilization around Naz's effort and exploited that absence in the counteraffidavit it filed on September 8, 2003.[33] The government's main argument for dismissing Naz's petition was that Naz has no *locus standi* in the case—the petitioners had failed to show, the government argued, that the antisodomy statute directly affected them.[34] The government also claimed that consent is impossible in cases of sodomy[35] and agreed with Prayas that the state has a responsibility to ensure that "childhood and youth are protected against exploitation" (*GoI*, 5–6). These were predictable arguments. Less predictable was the fact that the government claimed to be open to the possibility that public opinion on homosexuality had shifted, but then concluded that queer activists had not yet accomplished that shift. The government wrote: "Acts, which have been glorified in the past, like dowry, child marriage, domestic violence, [prohibition on] widow re-marriage etc. have now been brought under the purview of criminal justice. Therefore, changes in public tolerance of activities lead to campaigns to either criminalize some behavior or decriminalize others. *There is no such tolerance to the practice of homo/lesbianism in the Indian society*" (*GoI*, 11; emphasis added).

The absence of protestors on the sidewalks outside the court, or of street protests throughout the city, could have supported the government's position. (Of course, it was convenient to ignore the fact that, unlike women and the defenders of children, queer people do not have the same luxury of public visibility as queer people; moreover, this imposed invisibility is partly an effect of, rather than a justification for, s.377.) But the government even went so far as to offer Naz advice on how to start a social movement: "The petitioner may well lobby with the Parliament and involve doctors, psychiatrists, criminologists, sociologists, and legal experts so as to mobilize public opinion" (*GoI*, 2).

PRISM certainly tried. As a true sign of the nation's attention, the popular television news station, Star News, called PRISM the morning after the government filed its affidavit, requesting one or more "gays" for its evening broadcast. But PRISM didn't have a single gay to give. Most of the very out gay activists in Delhi were too closely associated with the petition to speak publicly about it. And other queer people who were quite out to their families and co-workers were not able or ready to appear on television—they had extended families, bosses, and neighbors to worry about. By the end of the evening, one hour before taping time, Jaya was literally in tears, landline phone in one hand, cellphone in the other, pleading with people to appear. One newer PRISM member finally acquiesced, perhaps more concerned about Jaya's state of mind than the petition itself. He appeared on the show for twenty wonderful seconds. When he returned from the studio, we served cake and treated him like a hero.

The rest of queer India—its activists anyway—having been chastised by, of all institutions, the national government for not having a proper movement, now attempted to forge a temporary solidarity where the petition had (necessarily) divided them. It happened that Lawyers Collective was to hold an unrelated national consultation in Delhi in October 2003 that several queer activists would be attending. PRISM and a few of its allies decided to use the opportunity to discuss a mass national campaign around s.377. Our first gathering was held on the lawns of a meeting hall in Delhi's embassy district, Chanakyapuri, where Lawyers Collective was holding its consultation. Around twenty-five of us sat on the grass in a circle as the sun set, eager and yet also skeptical. Alok, from Gay Bombay, opened the meeting: "I have been hearing about opposition to get together because of this business about being angry with Lawyers Collective [dramatic pause]. Come on! We're a community with no strategy! We don't know how to use the media to our benefit! We must use this meeting to strategize . . . to show India that there is a large community of queer people who want legal reform. There is too much at stake now. We must be unified!"[36]

Shaleen from Naz agreed, asking the assembled activists to put old hurts aside, to rally, and, most important, to provide volunteer affidavits testifying to harassment, extortion, or other trouble related to s.377 that could bolster Naz's case. Grover, a rare presence at such gatherings, added that "while there is no need for panic," the argument that a petition "should grow from a movement . . . has now become reality." That admission was, for Jaya, a shameful understatement: "What did the government say about a lack of a gay movement? Yes: clearly a petition is not just a technical thing that can be handled by only the 'experts.' It's not that we're so angry that we're staying out of this. We've already started without you and on our own terms. But we have to talk about past mistakes while at the same time responding to the government." Another activist from Bangalore tried to strike a conciliatory note, saying that at least they all had more in common with one another than with nonqueers. This was dismissed with loud snorts, and that was our cue to disband.

We reconvened the next day, on a bright Sunday morning, this time meeting indoors due to the heat of the midmorning sun. We arranged folding chairs into a circle of twenty-five or so in an empty dining hall and looked at one another expectantly, excited about our upcoming drama. Alok stood. Forget one unified voice, he suggested in a tone of compromise. Instead, he endorsed PRISM's suggestion of a campaign with two distinct agendas and camps: one that would work closely with Naz on the petition itself (for example, soliciting and collecting affidavits), and one that would conduct a wider and public campaign on queer politics more generally. We then solicited ideas about what such a campaign could include. A kothi from a South Indian group demanded inclusion of those who are not "full-time activists" or well-versed in law; another activist suggested getting at least one progay story or editorial published in English-language and vernacular papers every two weeks; someone else thought the campaign should stress the fact that heterosexual sodomy is also criminal under s.377.

The common theme that arose through everyone's brief monologue was that of forging a "common minimum understanding." But that was not easy to achieve, largely because of the usual, heated politics around allegiance to and disdain for Ashok Row Kavi. Members of PRISM made it clear that they would not "work with communalists," by which they meant Row Kavi and his Humsafar Trust. People stood up from their chairs, and even on top of their chairs, shouting and pointing at one another as they argued about Row Kavi and whether he is indeed anti-Muslim, until Alok dramatically threw his notebook to the floor with a loud, echoing bang. He mourned his days in South Africa, when he was among queer activists who managed a sustained, national campaign for three years to overturn that country's antisodomy statute.[37] But such solidarity would not be found on this day. Below is a fragment of dialogue from the meeting's final minutes:

Bombay activist:	I'll help coordinate in Bombay with everyone but Humsafar.
Alok:	Fine. No activism in Bombay, okay? I see nobody's ready to compromise.
Aditya:	Let's have two camps in Bombay. It's no big deal.
Alok:	Why are you encouraging this?
Bangalorean:	We [also] do no work with people who hate Muslims.
Humsafar employee:	You know that Humsafar has always taken the lead in everything!
Bombay activist:	Who are you? What shit!

[Alok leaves, saying nothing.]

With that, this attempt at a national-level queer activist consensus around the s.377 campaign ended. I went home with PRISM members after the meeting, most of them more amused than shaken by the morning's conflict, and over lunch around Jaya and Lesley's dining table, they resolved to go forward with at least a Delhi-level campaign. Only two days later, PRISM hosted a meeting with a number of autonomous women's groups, women's NGOs, and representatives from Lawyers Collective. We crowded into Saheli's tiny, boxlike office under an overpass, drinking chai, sharing water out of large, old plastic soda bottles, serving up both impassioned critique as well as a commitment to go forward together. Some perched on window ledges, some sat with legs folded on the floor, and many of us lined the walls; it was hard to breathe in there, and yet I remember a feeling so deeply affirming. I know the feeling was shared because the people present decided, despite their many differences about the petition, to form a new collective. The group named itself "Voices," short for "Voices against 377." The concept of "voices," the members suggested, would express their multivocality as well as their solidarity.[38]

After weeks of manic labor, shared largely by all, Voices had its own coming-out party in mid-November. The event was a press conference, held in the legitimizing Central Delhi hall of the Women's Press Corps. Delhi's most sought after activist celebrity, Arundhati Roy, sat in the audience along with reporters from all of the major English-language, and many of the vernacular, daily newspapers. Each reported the next day on the birth of a new, vocal coalition—ranging from PRISM and Saheli to the National Campaign against Child Abuse and Amnesty International—calling on the government and judiciary to end discrimination against India's lesbians, gays, bisexuals, and transgendered people.

Their voices were, altogether, in the hundreds (Narrain and Bhan 2005; Bhan 2006). They would continue to speak—in online petitions, on television and in newspapers, on the streets with placards and fliers, with legal interventions, and through the familiar faces of the intellectuals of India's glitterati, such as Vikram Seth, Nandita Das, and Arundhati Roy—until the High Court issued its historic decision on July 2, 2009. And the plurality of voices that constituted this collective was the result, much like CALERI, of interpellation, an emergent world coming to speak in and through the language in which they were spoken to, becoming who they were in the moment they recognized themselves as addressees of a once unfathomable enactment of public speech. What then becomes important for an analysis of such emergent worlds is to understand the contest between possibility and containment that is newly introduced in social emergences. In the emergence of queer people as legally recognizable subjects, as interlocutors with the state, the struggle between possibility and containment might be summarized as one between justice and law. The story of how queer activists were called to speak in the context of the gender neutrality debate —and in its coincidence with the early debates about s.377—throws light on the forms and consequences of the contest between law and justice, as well as the many other impossible choices that fall within.

Gender Neutrality

The process of amending Indian sexual assault law began in 1996 with the case of a politician prosecuted for fingering and receiving oral sex from his six-year-old daughter (Agnes 2002a).[39] Because there was no penile penetration, the police did not charge the man under s.377. Further, the Delhi High Court refused to charge him under existing rape law, Sections 375 and 376, because there was no "sexual intercourse." The court found him guilty only of a "violation of modesty," for which the maximum sentence is two years. A Delhi-based women's NGO, Sakshi, responded promptly and petitioned the Supreme Court to direct the Law Commission of India to draft recommendations for a new sexual assault law. After consulting with Sakshi, another NGO called IFSHA, an affiliated women's group, and the National Commission for Women, the Law Commission of India submitted its 172nd Report on Review of Rape Laws in March 2000, largely accepting the suggestions of these women's groups.[40] The main recommendation was to replace the offense of rape with that of sexual assault, which would incorporate "all kinds of penetration in the vagina, anus, or urethra of another, whether by a part of the human body or by an object."[41] A significant collateral argument was to delete s.377 because the newly broadened scope of (gender-neutral) "sexual assault" would be sufficient to prosecute the sexual abuse of male children by adult men. The unnatural offense would be an unnecessary relic.[42]

Autonomous women's groups, including NGOs, reacted angrily, protesting both the lack of consultation and transparency in the process, as well as the consequences for women if the changes were implemented.[43] Thirty-two of these organizations came together in a national coalition, and in their first collective act, a letter to the Law Minister, they put forward their opposition to Sakshi's—and now the Law Commission's—recommendations for gender neutrality. "In cases of sexual assault," they wrote simply, "men are the perpetrators and women are the victims."[44]

Queer groups were, from the beginning, integral to the consolidation of dissent against the 172nd Report on Review of Rape Laws. Nearly a third of the thirty-two organizations were queer—and most of these were lesbian-focused—including CALERI, OLAVA, Sangini, and PRISM. As I discussed at the beginning of the chapter, there were certainly many reasons why gender neutrality in sexual assault law was, and could be, seen as furthering queer causes, such as deletion of s.377, legal redress for male victims of sexual assault, and the aspiration for a gender neutral society. Still, a majority of queer activists in India stood united in opposition to a gender neutral law. Why and how did this voice emerge?

PRISM was one of the most vocal queer groups opposed to Sakshi's plan, but the heated and often tortured conversations I observed within PRISM from the beginning of my fieldwork showed how much reflection went into that opposition.[45] In my first week in Delhi—just a few days after the s.377 fight between Akshay and Lesley—Jaya, Lesley, a third PRISM member, and I stuffed ourselves into Jaya's Maruti car to go to what would turn out to be a critical meeting. As we drove to our nearby South Delhi destination in the thinning, late evening traffic, I asked them to fill me in on what we were doing and where we were going. This meeting had been organized by Kirti Singh, a prominent Delhi lawyer and member of AIDWA, one of the affiliated women's groups involved with Sakshi in the campaign in favor of gender neutrality. When we arrived at her house, we were greeted respectfully by a servant and led downstairs to Singh's book-lined, low-ceilinged office, where we sat around a large table and were served with tea. Singh folded her hands and looked at each of us kindly (though she was a bit confused about my presence), and asked my companions how she could convince them that gender neutrality is good for gays and lesbians. The three PRISM members were skeptical, but, because they were also pleased to have been invited to Singh's house, open to debate. Singh presented them with the expected arguments, from the deletion of s.377 to the simple matter of justice for everyone, regardless of gender. The argument she seemed most convinced of was that the legal recognition of sex (even if in the context of assault) between women would constitute a "foot in the door" and a step toward wider societal recognition of lesbians.[46] The three PRISM members nodded thoughtfully, offered mild counterarguments, and thanked Singh for her invitation.

We walked outside and started debating before even getting into the car, comparing Singh's arguments with what PRISM had heard from the Forum against the Oppression of Women, Saheli, and the many other, more lesbian-friendly, women's groups that had been busy recruiting PRISM to their side. The four of us continued to talk animatedly in the car, back at home, and over the next several days. By the PRISM meeting on the following Thursday the other three were committed to their position.

The coalition of thirty-two groups was meeting that weekend in Bombay, but PRISM was unable to send a representative. The group decided to send a letter instead. Despite the fact that there was a Madonna concert on television that we had planned all week to watch, we stayed at the Lawyers Collective office well into the night, bent over a computer and debating each line of the letter. It began with strong words about the Law Commission's lack of consultation with a "young, but vibrant" sexual minorities movement and went on to critique the substance of the recommendations along four lines.[47]

First, the letter argued that the law should be based on social reality rather than on aspiration or ideology: society is not gender neutral, and therefore the law should not be either. (Activists who came to support the s.377 petition, including members of PRISM, made the counterargument in that case: that the law must not simply mirror social relations and prejudices but should lead society along a more just path.) Second, and also in line with PRISM's feminist allies, the letter argued that one of the few "rights" that Indian women currently had was to be acknowledged as only victims, and never perpetrators, of sexual assault, adding that "women who are raped will find that they are being prosecuted for sexual assault by their rapists . . . disempowering women even further." The law here is a powerful tool of justice, and must continue to protect the weak from the strong. (In their opposition to the s.377 petition, PRISM members made a different sort of argument: the law means little to nothing to real people on the ground.) In another nod to the power of the law, and in an argument now specific to queer concerns, the letter's third argument revealed a worry about third-party false accusation, arguing that a gender-neutral sexual assault law would enable scornful neighbors and colleagues, angry fathers, or jilted male lovers to express their homophobia by accusing lesbian women of sexually assaulting each other.[48] (Ironically, the specter of false accusation, as the letter writers and the feminists who comprised the coalition knew only too well, had long served as an impediment to more powerful, gender-specific, rape law.) The letter's fourth strand of argument concerned timing and priorities, a fault line in all social movements. Now is not the time, the letter writers suggested, to openly discuss or raise awareness about same-sex sexual assault. There was as yet no positive legal recognition of queer lives and relationships; furthermore, "none of us [is] in a position to really understand the contexts and issues of same-sex violence—we are still grappling with sex, sexuality, and gender." (This sounded, even to PRISM members themselves, like a disturbing echo of early women's movement arguments against addressing lesbian concerns.)[49]

Impossible Choices

PRISM and its queer (mostly lesbian) allies had many convincing reasons for taking the stands that they did, among which were showing solidarity with autonomous women's groups from whom they had so long sought recognition, and representing lesbians and other queer people in the face of their newfound vulnerability to the law. But at the same time, members of PRISM engaged in countless debates about their position throughout the two years of my fieldwork, annoying the group's feminist allies in Delhi, who considered the matter closed, and angering lesbian allies such as Stree Sangam and OLAVA, which interpreted PRISM's waffling as a sign of PRISM's unfortunate willingness to compromise. But organizational positions do change, especially quickly in groups that are so small and have so dynamic a constituency. Lesley, PRISM's most adamant proponent of gender specificity, had essentially left the group by mid-2002. Some people who had become newly active in PRISM, like Gautam, were equally influential (and equally vocal). Gautam, for example, felt none of the passion that PRISM had once demonstrated against gender neutrality and, in fact, questioned the idea's ethics and rationale. But the biggest factor in PRISM's transformations was its rigorous interrogation of the politics of identity.

As I discussed in chapter 2, after several of its members had attended the Sexuality and Rights Institute, PRISM had become increasingly committed to a politics that transcended the usual domain of LGBT concerns. They sought not to defend the boundaries between lesbian and not lesbian, or between male and female, but to work to dissolve those boundaries, creating a world of possibility rather than imperative. The questions about gender neutrality that came to nag—even to torment—PRISM were: How can we insist on the stability of male and female and, furthermore, the stability of power's circulation between them? How can we demand that the law be a representation of unjust social realities, rather than of the ideals that we ourselves hold?

In seeking answers to these questions, PRISM formally reopened the

Delhi debate on gender neutrality in mid-2003, while the Law Commission's recommendations were still stalled.[50] They held a meeting at Saheli (several months before Voices would be founded there), the office filled to capacity with university students, representatives of women's NGOs, and human rights activists. Uma Chakravarti, the eminent historian, accepted PRISM's invitation to facilitate the meeting, which PRISM opened with a position paper offering two problematics for rethinking gender neutrality. I'll paraphrase them as law as a gendering practice (see Smart 1995) and law as a means to ideal justice. These problematics are, as I see them, what Joan Scott calls the "impossible choices" (1988, 136) of feminist legal engagement.

Much feminist scholarship has examined law as a gendering practice (see Smart 1995): that is, how legal discourse actively constructs gender and, thus, how feminist activism through the law can wind up legitimizing the very gendered norms that feminism seeks to disrupt. The central binary through which law acts as a gendering practice is that of similarity and difference. The liberal legal approach of sameness, or of creating social equality through the legal sameness of men and women, is not historically common in Indian feminist activism (or, for that matter, in Indian law generally, outside of the formal equality enshrined in the Constitution). Both feminists and the judiciary insist on gendered and sexed difference—with different ends in mind but, as the legal scholars Ratna Kapur and Brenda Cossman (1996a, 1996b) have shown, with similar consequences for women and feminism.

Where Indian feminist activists have historically argued for the acknowledgment of difference between men and women, their position falls within what Kapur and Cossman call "correctivism." The difference these activists insist on is not one of physiology, but of historical, systemic disparities that must be corrected in order to eventually achieve social equality. Correctivists argue that "it is unjust to treat unequals equally" (N. Menon 2004, 4). Indian jurisprudence has long demonstrated a willingness to treat unequals unequally, but in a manner that, Kapur and Cossman believe, "reinscribe[s] the very familial and legal discourses that have constituted women as different, and as subordinate" (1996b, 79). Indian jurisprudence has interpreted the constitutional guarantee of sex equality as justification for differential treatment: to treat men and women differently is, ultimately, to act in women's interests (Kapur and Cossman 1996b, 79). Adultery, for example, is a crime only when committed by a man. In a challenge to the law, a court upheld its constitutionality, claiming that "it is commonly accepted that it is the man who is the seducer and not the woman" (quoted in Kapur and Cossman 1996a, 171). As PRISM argued in its letter to the groups in Bombay, women have long benefited from not being thought capable of sexual criminality (the principle applies to lesbians as well in the context of s.377), and this one measly advantage should be left unaltered. But at what larger costs?

The positions against gender neutrality advanced by the coalition of thirty-two groups and, at least at one point, by PRISM are correctivist in philosophy but, given their legal and historical context, reinforce state protectionism as well. The coalition's argument that India is not a gender-neutral society is undeniable and, in fact, is a point of departure for feminist and queer projects: gender matters in India, and often in violent, tragic ways. The proposition, however, that "in cases of sexual assault, men are the perpetrators and women are the victims of abuse,"[51] might well be a point of departure, but it also threatens to undermine the very project of feminist activism. Nivedita Menon (2004), following Judith Butler, argues that the jurisprudential linking of women with sexual victimization, and of men with sexual aggression, posits the sexed body and its capabilities as prior to discourse. And if sex and gender are prior to discourse, it renders feminist social transformation unimaginable.

The upshot, as PRISM came to see in the course of its many debates, is that activism as ethical practice is not easily aligned with the binary of sameness–difference. Joan Scott argues, as an alternative to that binary thinking, for an "unmasking of the power relationship constructed by posing equality as the antithesis of difference" and, through that project, exploring what is foreclosed and what possibilities for politics lie beyond (1988, 172). Such was PRISM's project of problematization, shared by dozens of others—however reluctantly—at Saheli that summer evening in 2003.

If interrogating the impossible choice between sameness and difference was PRISM's first problematic that evening, the second was interrogating the impossible choice between ideal justice and real vulnerability. PRISM wondered to the group what sorts of ethical questions are foreclosed by their worries about both false accusation against lesbians and about bringing actual incidents of same-sex sexual assault to light. In calling to "postpone" discussion of sexual assault between women and between men, as PRISM did in its letter, Gautam argued that what was at stake for queer groups was not justice at all, but presenting a uniform respectability in the interest of attaining legal rights. Much as Sakhi in chapter 1 sought to present lesbians as stripped of desire and embodying only the rationality of political discourse, queer people now, perhaps at the cusp of their decriminalization, sought to present themselves as stripped of violence and embodying only the respectability of civil engagement. These impossible burdens of presentation are, of course, among the burdens of marginality everywhere. For PRISM—one of the few collectives in the country advocating for lesbians and gay men, a group whose identity is based on being involved and invested in these people's lives, struggles, and relationships—this burden raised an extremely important question. For the sake of protecting some lesbian women from false accusation and state interference, was the group willing to argue that those who are assaulted at the hands of their partners have illegitimate claims? This was not, of course, merely hypothetical. Stories and rumors circulated of lesbian abuse—psychological and physical, if not sexual; they were not many, but we were aware of them. I told a story in chapter 1 of the Sangini support group's indifference to a presentation by a North American group, Incite!, on lesbian domestic violence. After that meeting, Maya had told me that the support group is not "interested in all this heavy politics and analysis. First they have to deal with the basic stuff." PRISM, which understood itself as a departure from Sangini, wound up arguing for a similar separation between the urgency of the now and that which must wait for recognition. In both cases, the problem arises of who decides when that better time has come, and based on what conditions.

The meeting between PRISM and local activists did not lead to any immediate action on gender neutrality, but that was never really the point. The exercise that PRISM offered was one simply of problematization, of facing the ethical limits posed by the false choices between neutrality and specificity, sameness and difference, law as faithful reflection and law as lodestar, seeking justice and seeking rights, and then undoing those very limits through reflective critique. That critique was itself the action, recalibrating PRISM's relationship with itself, its movement, its allies, and legal engagement more generally. The last was an especially important task for the group, as law reform would continue to be an ever more privileged site for queer activism in India, from the indifference of the days of ABVA and Naz's tortured efforts to build a movement to an all-hands-on-deck approach to decriminalization. In the following section, I want to turn to what feminist and queer activists in India are making of this imperative to transform their worlds through law.

Conclusion

Late in 2003, just a month before I left India, Jaya and I were reflecting. She had accompanied me to a Sangini meeting, and we were remarking afterward about all the foreigners who seemed to be doing projects on Indian queer politics (two such people had been at Sangini that day, soliciting interviews). This reminded me of an awkward conversation Jaya and I had when I first arrived, in which I had apologized for my Western privilege and assured her I would not impose "Western" terms like "lesbian" or "queer" on her. Jaya had rolled her eyes then and told me to grow up. She had, I was pleased to learn, forgotten about this exchange and assured me that I had grown up nicely. But I had wondered about that conversation many times, and I asked her why she had been so welcoming of me then. Hadn't she been at all annoyed by the presumptuousness of my fieldwork, or by the number of foreign students and activists who show up, become deeply involved, and then leave to write theses about what she had helped to create? I reminded her of stories about the exclusion of foreigners from the early Women to Women/Stree Sangam retreats as well as the Tirupati meeting. Why hadn't she shared that suspicion, or at least annoyance, about the involvement of an "outsider?"

Jaya responded by saying that *Fire* had changed many things, one of which was to demonstrate to Indian lesbians and to NRIS that lesbians in India had a politics of their own. And as lesbian—and queer—activism built from that critical moment in 1998, something else became clear: That India is where it's at. She clarified, though, that this was true when I arrived in 2001 but perhaps was no longer so. Queer activism immediately after *Fire* seemed then to have infinite possibility, particularly in comparison to queer activism in the United States, which was so consumed with gay marriage and other liberal conversations about equal rights. For Jaya, Indian activism was not so constrained, and nothing demanded that it be so. To start a queer café, to throw parties, to organize film festivals, to argue, to give shelter: this was the stuff of activism, extraordinary for how it felt and not because of its strategic use. I asked what had changed since then. It was the movement to repeal 377. India no longer felt like "where it was at." Indian queer activism was on the rights trail, for better and worse.

I relate this conversation not to create or romanticize a simpler time in queer activism before the—perhaps inevitable—prioritization of legal reform. Nor did Jaya wish to salvage a more diverse, tenuous moment in which smaller actions produced bigger feeling, or activists were expected to contest agendas and not simply consent to them. The point is to show how engaged queer activists in India are in thinking about the transformations in their landscape, and how the extraordinary achievements of increased public visibility and (limited) state legal recognition challenge the creativity of their lives and of their politics.

In January 2003, at the Asia Social Forum in Hyderabad, several LBGT groups from across Asia gathered to discuss the place of law and human rights efforts in their activism. This was a group with varied critiques, which together illuminate four strands of feminist, queer, and poststructuralist critique of the role of law in social change: distrust of state power; supplementing law reform with mass movements; distrust for the "ease" of legal reform; and the symbolic violence of law.

The first person to speak at the meeting was Tejal, a visual artist and activist with Stree Sangam (later with LABIA): "Our movement is now ten years old. But where are we? Not far. And if 377 goes, is that going to be some magic mover? After Gujarat [the site of mass killings of Muslims by Hindus in 2002], what do rights even *mean* in this country? Is *this* really where we want to devote our energies?" In arguing that activism directed at the state affirms the legitimacy of a state she sees as unlawful and also fails to guarantee the practical exercise of rights, Tejal echoes arguments by feminists like Madhu Kishwar and Ruth Vanita (cited in N. Menon 2004) and Flavia Agnes (1992). They all critique the privileging of legal campaigns on the grounds that these legitimize state regulation of women's lives without the balancing power of implementation (N. Menon 2004, 4).

One way to ensure the practical exercise of rights, as two later speakers suggested, is to first build a mass movement. Arvind Narrain and Tarunabh Khatain, both graduates of India's National Law School, cited the influence of Nandita Haksar, an Indian feminist, and offered her mantra as their own: "A petition is not the basis of a movement." The Haksarian position departs from Tejal's in the recognition that law reform is necessary (even though it must necessarily be secondary). Haksar argues: "We should resort to the law only when the movement is strong enough to carry the law reform forward" (1999, 87). What is operating here is an ethic of scale: begin in the spaces of intimacy and move forward only then.

Anish, the young gay director of an HIV/AIDS program in Hyderabad, made a similar plea for directing queer activism to everyday spaces of intimacy. "What will this petition really mean to me?" he asked us. "What is it in everyday terms? Will I be able to go to my parents that same day [of a repeal] and shout to them, 'I'm gay! Isn't it wonderful?'" The law will not, he reminded us, magically transform discrimination into honor or a mother's disdain into repentant, open-armed welcome.[52] As Arvind has written, those are the sorts of transformations that are fought for between people, and not simply enacted through law: "The . . . only way forward is to mobilize and convert the [s.377] petition from a narrow legal struggle to a wider political struggle. . . . The petition should be the peg on which hangs a campaign, whose objective is to question the homophobic resilience of s.377 in the structures of . . . public opinion" (Narrain 2004).

His argument for a simultaneity of legal and "social" reform is a pragmatic one. But it ignores the myriad ways in which legal reform efforts necessarily foreclose certain kinds of solidarities and politics. This is the problem Tejal alluded to when she confessed that she's simply "against the movement to repeal s.377. What we need instead is *vision*." She echoes Haksar here, who argues that in the Indian women's movement, law reform has been a "substitute for the other harder option of building a movement for an alternative vision" (1999, 76). We could characterize this as a conflict between the political model of visibility and an ethic of envisioning. Tejal and Haksar are critiquing how the premium on visibility, the making visible of identities and lives as they already are, substitutes for a less certain and more laborious process of envisioning, or creating the conditions under which new imaginations can be creatively practiced. The "already is" of visibility (or legal legibility) usurps the "what may be" of envisioning.

Critics might see law reform as an easier proposition than the imaginative labor of envisioning because the former's methods are already given, its promises secure for rendering fixed what is uncertain. Sure enough, the legal transformation of the uncertain to the fixed appears to hold where it is most troubling for queer politics, and to be most elusive where it is most desired. As many scholars have argued in a Foucauldian vein, the force of the law lies not in its ability to emancipate, but in its imperative to still. Veena Das and Deborah Poole, for example, are interested in the relationship between the potential of political creativity (2004), on the one hand, and the imperative to rationality, legibility, and indifference in making formal claims to the state, on the other. Talal Asad says of this juncture that the "authority of law seeks to make things definite within the continuous flow of uncertainty by imposing itself from the outside" (2004, 287). The stories in this chapter reveal many ideas that queer activists would like to treat as uncertain and yet are urged to define through legal reform: the supposed truths of gender and sexual identity, the sanctity of the private, and the legitimacy of forms of pleasure.

Asad treats uncertainty as a good in itself, as something to be preserved, but it is worth asking what it is about uncertainty—or, perhaps, the unfixed —that is so fine a thing for queer politics particularly. It might be useful to turn to Derrida (as many of the activists did) and his troubling of the as-sumed oneness of law and justice. Law, he argues, is not justice. Justice is that which is "incalculable" (Derrida 1992, 16), that which "must not wait" (Derrida 1992, 26), that which requires identification of the self with the other. Law, which claims to speak for that which is just, is not only a calcula-tion among rules, but a calculation over time during which justice must wait. Justice, then, is always an experience of aporia—impossible because its universality erases singularity (and thus is not just), and impossible because it is always beyond what actually is and never, as Drucilla Cornell puts it, the "endorsement" of what is (1992, 87). It is thus that the "compro-mise is fatal" between the idea of justice that is always yet to be and always radically singular, and the law that codes justice as abstract, general, and fixed (Derrida 1992, 61–62). In understanding justice as necessarily un-certain and unfixed, uncertainty is more than mere resistance to conven-tion: it is the very stuff of belief, and the motor for ethical and political action.

That said, one of the points I have emphasized throughout this book is that containment—the fixing of potential into certain normative forms—is an inevitable part of activism, and one that is productive of ethical engagement rather than its closure. It is only in the face of limitation that problematization is demanded, leading to the invention of new kinds of relational practice. Furthermore, and less abstractly perhaps, it is in containment that there is security, which is not always identical with normativity. It would be wrong to burden emergent radical worlds with a prohibition against moments of fleet-ing belonging. The Delhi High Court's decision to read down s.377 shows some of what such belonging—however fraught the process of achieving it— can mean. The justices wrote that at the heart of the Indian Constitution is "inclusiveness" for all, including those whom the majority perceives as "de-viants." They invoked the language of India's first prime minister, Jawaharlal Nehru, the father of Indira Gandhi, to claim that a democracy is greater still than the formal words—such as "inclusiveness"—that define it: "Words are magic things often enough," Nehru said in 1946, and the High Court quoted sixty-three years later, "but even the magic of words sometimes cannot convey the magic of the human spirit and of a Nation's passion."[53] With that reference paving a historic path, the justices formally declared lesbians and gay men in India "included" in and embraced by the nation of India. For a once-unimaginable moment, law and justice seemed reconcilable. But only for a moment. Only hours later, Jaya was drafting an article to send to local papers: critically interrogating how she, of all people, came to be crying with joy in a New Delhi courtroom. The horizon of justice continued to compel critique. This was still not a time to rest.

appendix: cast of organizations

Organization	Focus	Signature activities	Years	City
ABVA (AIDS Bhedbhav Virodhi Andolan)	People with HIV/AIDS; sexual minorities; professional blood donors; sex workers; social justice broadly	Nonfunded; filed the first PIL against s.377 in 1994	Founded 1988	Delhi
CALERI (Campaign for Lesbian Rights)	Lesbians	Visibility; activism around *Fire*; public leafleting	Founded 1998, no longer meeting	Delhi
Lawyers Collective	People with HIV/AIDS; LGBT; women; other socially marginal groups	Filed PIL in Delhi High Court in 2001 against s.377, representing Naz	Founded mid-1980s	Bombay, Delhi
Naz Foundation (India) Trust ("Naz" or "Naz India" or "Naz Foundation")	MSM (men who have sex with men); gay men; kothis	HIV outreach; parent organization for smaller groups, including Sangini at one point; petitioners in successful 2001 PIL against s.377	Founded 1994	Delhi

Organization	Focus	Signature activities	Years	City
OLAVA (Organized Lesbian Alliance for Visibility and Action)	Lesbians and bisexual women	Protest of MASUM; telephone help line; visibility	Founded 2000, no longer meeting	Pune
PRISM (Originally People for the Rights of Indian Sexuality Minorities, now simply PRISM)	LGBTKQH; sexual minorities; humanity	Alliance building; critique of identity politics; study groups and public meetings; public activism	Founded 2001	Delhi
Sakhi	Lesbians	Letter writing network; resource center; drop-in center; lesbian guesthouse	1991–97	Delhi
Sangini	Lesbians and bisexual women	Telephone help line; support group	Founded 1997	Delhi
Voices against 377 (Voices)	LGBTKQH; humanity; decriminalization of all adult, consensual, same-sex sex	Progressive coalition for the striking of s.377.	Founded 2003	Delhi (national coalition)

Notes: LGBT is lesbian, gay, bisexual, and transgender. LGBTKQH is lesbian, gay, bisexual, transgender, kothi, queer, hijra. PIL is public interest lawsuit.

notes

Introduction

1 I discuss court cases in this book that are being heard, or have been heard, at both the High Court and Supreme Court levels. High Courts are the courts of states and territories in India. The Supreme Court, a federal court, is the highest court of appeal in the country. In addition to hearing appeals against High Court judgments, the Supreme Court also accepts writ petitions concerning human rights and other urgent violations. The Delhi High Court ruling to decriminalize same-sex sex is now, in March 2012, being appealed in the Supreme Court. I say much more about this case, and about Indian jurisprudence more generally, in chapter 5.

2 Michael Lambek (2010), in his introduction to a collection of essays exploring the role of ethics in ordinary life, writes persuasively against distinguishing between ethics and morality. However, from my ethnographic perspective—that of analyzing a social movement whose counterforce is deployed through norms about proper moral sexual behavior—the distinction between ethics and morality is an important one.

3 For other work in the field of the anthropology of ethics, see Das (2006), Faubion (2011), Hirschkind (2006), Keane (2007), Laidlaw (2002), Lambek (2010), Mittermaier (2010), Pandian (2009), Pandian and Ali (2010), Povinelli (2002 and 2006), and Prasad (2006).

4 I prefer describing this ethic as "radical" rather than "homosexual." I am not arguing that homosexuality is inherently ethical or has an especially privileged

relationship to what I'm referring to as the ethical (cf. Blasius 2001; Hoagland 1988). Instead, I am interested in ethical aspirations as they are common to all emergent radical worlds.

5 But let me add a caveat: the ethics I describe here are at the center of any activism that seeks to transform and multiply existing social relations, or the sort of activism that might be thought of in shorthand as "liberal" or "progressive." Mahmood, as I discuss earlier in the chapter, also sees the relevance of a Foucauldian ethics to nonliberal activism.

6 Kamala Visweswaran (2010) writes about contemporary transnational activism in terms of the creation of a commons or "common cultures." The commons, like the PRISM home, is marked by a play between singularity and the reproduction of common values.

7 See also Cooper and Stoler (1997) on methods for reading emotional hesitancies and productive frictions, in this case of colonial agents.

8 Hijras are, generally, genotypic males who dress in female clothing and, sometimes have undergone ritual castration in order to achieve a spiritual ideal. Some hijras are also hermaphrodites by birth. See Reddy (2005) on hijra identity in contemporary India as well as their intersections with the Indian queer movement.

9 Scott (1985) argues that everyday forms of resistance are necessarily class struggles. See also Sivaramakrishnan (2006, 347).

10 John Fiske's notion of "semiotic resistance" (1989) involves the appropriation of dominant texts and images in order to forge subjective meaning. This draws upon Michel de Certeau's notion of everyday resistance through "tactics" (2002) —which, like Foucault's turn to the aesthetics of resistance, offers a corrective to theories of modern power that imply a surrender to a dispersed disciplinary apparatus. It is important to think about such forms of resistance, but I argue that they are both excessive and insufficient for the forms of politics that queer people in India engage in.

11 Among the work on so-called third genders that helped to legitimize studies of same-sex sexuality in anthropology are Herdt (1984), Blackwood (1984), Nanda (1986 and 1990), and W. Williams (1986). See Elliston (2002 and 2005) for critiques of this literature, specifically its slippage between sex and sexuality.

12 Alpa Shah, in a similar use of Appadurai's "incarceration," describes indigenous people as being "eco-incarcerated"—that is, romantically linked to "their" land—by otherwise well-meaning advocates (2010, 127).

13 Some English-Hindi dictionaries now give *samlaingikta* as the Hindi term for "homosexuality." The Lonely Planet guidebook to India also advises travelers to use the term *samlaingik*.

14 See Sinnott's (2004) examination of the politics of (female) queer naming in the context of "toms" and "dees" in Thailand.

15 This is just the vocabulary for love between women. Many premodern texts

discussed sex between women, often in order to condemn it. Take, for example, the following passage from the *Laws of Manu*, composed around the third century CE: "If a virgin does it to another virgin, she should be fined 200 [*panas*], be made to pay double [the girl's] bride-price, and receive ten whip [lashes]. But if a [mature] woman does it to a virgin, her head should be shaved immediately or two of her fingers should be cut off, and she should be made to ride on a donkey" (quoted in Doniger 1991, 191).

16 "Bombay" was officially changed to "Mumbai" in 1995 in an act of linguistic nationalism. I use both names for the city in this book, but not interchangeably. I tend here to use "Bombay" when I am speaking about my fieldwork or the lives of my interlocutors (for that is what they call the city) and "Mumbai" to speak of the city in official terms.

17 Communalism, in South Asia, refers to violence between religious communities, most often between Hindus and Muslims.

18 Vanita (2005) later critiqued her own usage of this term.

19 See Reddy (2005) and A. Gupta (2005) for analyses of kothi identity. Gupta is particularly interested in the class dynamics between gay activists and kothis.

20 Dozens of such ostensibly local, behavior-oriented terms for male-male sex have been "found" or implemented. For example, terms for those who will both penetrate and be penetrated include *do-paratha, chhakkas*, double-deckers, and AC/DC. Even within one category—such as kothi—there are multiple types (see Reddy 2005).

21 Paola Bacchetta (2002) has dealt with this representational dilemma in the following way. When speaking of same-sex desiring women in India who do not call themselves "lesbian," she refers to them as "lesbians," with quotation marks intact; when referring to same-sex desiring women in India who do voluntarily call themselves "lesbian," she calls them lesbian, without quotation marks.

22 But see, for example, Duggan (2002) for an analysis of the many ways by which the queer becomes the normative, particularly under neoliberalism.

23 Elizabeth Povinelli and George Chauncey, likewise, criticize the queer globalization literature on the ground that "with all the focus on external social forms—flows, circulations of capital and people—there is little model of subjective mediation" (1999, 445).

24 It was not out of an inflated sense of my own influence that I would sometimes limit my participation. There were times in the demographic ebb and flow of this little independent organization when there would be only three or four of us attending meetings. Furthermore, in spite of the group's size, PRISM's decisions were of considerable importance at the national level.

25 Other anthropologists have written about the conflicts of writing critically about activists with whom we share certain solidarities. See Chari and Donner (2010), A. Shah (2010), Baviskar (2004), and Jean-Klein and Riles (2005).

26 Indeed, several activists in India, many of whom I write about here, have written their own analytic accounts of queer activism in the country. See, for example, J. Sharma and Nath (2005), Narrain and Bhan (2005), and Narrain and Gupta (2011).

27 See Nagar's contribution in Swarr and Nagar (2003), discussing rural lesbians in North India, their exclusions from urban lesbian politics, and their distance from urban lesbian priorities.

Chapter 1: Rendering Real the Imagined

1 In analyzing the normalizing and exclusionary practices central to the production of political community, this chapter is part of a long lineage of feminist and postcolonial scholarship. Cherrie Moraga and Gloria Anzaldua (1983); Gloria Hull, Patricia Scott, and Barbara Smith (1982); and Shane Phelan (1989) all pointed out the racial, sexual, and class-based exclusions inherent in the notion of a "community of women" within North American activism. For a transnational activist context, see Chandra Mohanty, Ann Russo, and Lourdes Torres (1991). In anthropology, David Valentine (2007) has recently extended this feminist critique of political identification to analyze the production of transgender community in New York. Here, I critique "community" by way of understanding the consequences of its exclusions through ideas of affect and attachment, ethics and loss, and combine feminist ethnographic work with analytics offered by such scholars as Judith Butler (1997) and Elizabeth Povinelli (2006).

2 In describing this nascent social world as an "imagined community," I draw on Benedict Anderson's understanding of imagined collectivity in which "members . . . will never know most of their fellow-members, meet them, or even hear of them, yet in the minds of each lives the image of their communion" (1991, 6). Anderson's view that "community" is "always conceived as a deep, horizontal comradeship" is what I am interrogating here. Furthermore, the letter writers described in this chapter were connecting, though not in real time, in ways that Anderson's newspaper readers never did.

3 Although these women varied widely in their access to cultural and economic capital, all were able to read and write in English, thus indicating some access to education across this group. (Exceptions to the English norm were eight letter writers who wrote exclusively in Hindi, and two who solicited others to write their letters.) I am thus not arguing that these writers represent the full class spectrum of same-sex desiring women in India, but that Sakhi's potentially anonymous and placeless network democratized access to lesbian community from the days of local activist groupings and compared to later forms of face-to-face community. For a critical engagement with questions of representation and lesbian politics among "unprivileged India"—a category the author partly defines through a lack of sustained education—see M. Sharma (2006).

4 Arati Rege calls this time in the women's movement the "taciturn phase"—one of quiet acceptance of lesbians on the condition that they do not declare their lesbianism (Rege 2002, 144).

5 Interview with Abha Bhaiya, November 20, 2003, New Delhi.

6 This information comes from a letter Sakhi wrote in 1995 to an unnamed funding agency, a copy of which Thadani gave me.

7 See L. Cohen (2005) for more on Row Kavi's public eccentricities.

8 However, three lesbians joined the editorial board of *Dost* in 1991 (Fernandez 2002, 183).

9 Miss Kumar to Sakhi, May 10, 1994. All letters and other materials from Sakhi that I cite in this chapter were given to me by Thadani and are in my possession. All names of letter writers (other than those who were activists) are pseudonyms. I have chosen not to edit these excerpts for grammar or spelling. One of the most interesting aspects of these letters is that they were written by women from a range of social positions, showing the short-sightedness of those who think of lesbianism as an activity of only the elite. I reproduce the excerpts as they are to highlight the fact that there is no simple equation of lesbian affinity in India with social status or with mastery of the English language.

10 Ms. Kapur to Sakhi, 1993.

11 IJ to Sakhi, 1993.

12 However, lesbian organizing in India has grown through what Cindy Patton calls the "AIDS service industry" (1990). Sangini was only made possible through the assistance of Naz, an NGO focused on the prevention of HIV. As I will discuss in the next chapter, Sangini's reliance on Naz's terminology and resources had limiting consequences for the group and its attendees. A theme throughout this book is the relationship of dependence lesbian women have with gay men and feminist women.

13 Cath, personal conversation with author, 2002.

14 Anuja to Sakhi, 1991.

15 Ms. Nandita to Sakhi, November 11, 1991.

16 Ms. Bhan to Sakhi, 1992.

17 Yogini to Sakhi, 1996.

18 For more on their case, see Bhaskaran (2004), John and Nair (1998), Patel (2004), Puri (1999), and Thadani (1996).

19 Partha Singh, "Unbecoming Conduct," *Bombay Indian Post*, February 29, 1988. Eating off the same plate and sharing a bed are common practices between women in India, which is not to say that the practices are devoid of eroticism. See Trawick (1992, 202–3).

20 Ibid. Public fascination with the perceived pathos and gender non-normativity of female same-sex relationships extends far beyond India. The depictions of Urmila and Leela in the Indian press in 1987–88 are very similar to Japanese

depictions in 1935 of Masuda and Saijo, lesbian partners who attempted a double suicide and garnered much undesired publicity (Robertson 1999).

21 Nachiketa Desai. Marriage with sex convert challenged. *The Independent.* January 9, 1990.

22 A condition for marriage under the Hindu Marriage Act of 1955 is that neither spouse suffers from a "mental condition" that renders him or her unfit for procreation.

23 "With Gay Abandon," *Indian Express*, August 5, 1990.

24 Parvez Sharma, "Emerging from the Shadows," *Statesman*, July 3, 1994. The *Statesman* is an Indian English-language newspaper and its Sunday Miscellany section, in which this article appeared, has a circulation of around two hundred thousand.

25 See L. Cohen (2005, 286) for more on Thadani's opinions about sex.

26 P. Sharma, "Emerging from the Shadows."

27 RS to Sakhi, July 22, 1994.

28 Ms. Sen to Sakhi, July 5, 1994.

29 Funding proposal to Mama Cash, Sakhi, 1995. In my possession.

30 I am alluding to Pierre Bourdieu's (1979, 126) notion of political competency, though not in his context of polling practices. The larger concern I share with Bourdieu is the unequal distribution of various forms of capital (cultural, social, and symbolic), and how that distribution produces different kinds of political subjects.

31 Sumana to Sakhi, 1995.

32 Sakhi to Sumana, 1995. The letters contain many other examples of a growing divide between politics and desire. For instance, Sakhi wrote in response to a writer who received letters with sexual fantasies that "we also get some letters from women who write about their desire for other women—I guess there is no exposure to our kind of 'lesbian politics' for many women" (Sakhi to Lesley, November 16, 1994). And Mrs. Nandini from Orissa contacted Sakhi with the offer to "write all my hot true stories to you and you must give financial help for my nice hot sexy stories. . . . And also I can able to send you nud[e] photos if you will send some of your friends nud[e]" (Mrs. Nandini to Sakhi, July 18, 1994). Sakhi's response, decidedly professional, was as follows: "Your request for photographs . . . we cannot fulfill although we have been producing postcards and silk-screened letter-writing paper with images taken from temple iconography, which are either woman-centered or lesbian. Perhaps you might be interested in buying some?" (Sakhi to Mrs. Nandini, August 10, 1994). Finally, the cleavage between politics and desire is explicit in this letter: "Do you also receive letters from women inviting you to their homes, or just for sex? Is there anyone who seems less into physical relationships and is more into joining a movement, so to speak?" (anonymous to Sakhi, November 30, 1994).

33 Sakhi to Mama Cash, 1995.

34 Miss V. Kumar to Sakhi, May 10, 1994.

35 For another story on the homoerotics of urban Indian beauty parlors, see Kumani (1995).

36 It is common in South Asia to refer to pornographic films as "blue films." See Liechty (2001).

37 Miss V. Kumar to Sakhi, June 24, 1994.

38 Miss Kumar refers elsewhere to an article she had read on lesbian sex in hostels. She was probably referring to Deepal Trivedi's "Lesbian night-outs a lucrative proposition" (*Indian Express*, September 14, 1993). A choice paragraph in the article reads: "The number of lesbians in city hostels is astronomical. Ask any hostelite staying at ladies' hostels in Navrangpura and Paldi [middle-class, primarily Hindu neighborhoods in Ahmedabad] and they will 'entertain' you with a number of incidents. The most popular one is that of Mani and Ratan . . . They have been caught together in bathing rooms and in the TV viewing room in awkward positions. They have no qualms about it."

39 Miss V. Kumar to Sakhi, July 18, 1994.

40 Ibid.

41 Miss V. Kumar to Sakhi, 1995.

42 Lesley would become a founding member of PRISM. See chapter 2.

43 Lesley to Sakhi, September 1994.

44 Sakhi to Lesley, September 28, 1994.

45 Lesley to Sakhi, October 3, 1994.

46 Lesley to Sakhi, October 3, 1994.

47 As was the case in Delhi before Sakhi's advent, same-sex desiring feminists had already been meeting in Bombay informally (Rege 2002).

48 Lesley to Sakhi, May 19, 1995.

49 The group opened a post office box, like Sakhi, and also gave interviews to the popular press. Sarah Singh—a Punjabi American member of Women to Women—would be featured in the next issue of *Savvy* magazine. Lesley also described the structure of the group: it was run by a working committee of six members, all of who were unpaid volunteers. The composition of the committee would change on a rotating basis to avoid concentrations of power.

50 Lesley to Cath, 1995.

51 Interview with Lesley, December 7, 2003, New Delhi.

52 Monisha Das Gupta describes how members of diasporic groups like the Massachusetts Area South Asian Lambda Association also had internal conflicts about not being "political" enough, especially in relation to other organizations (2006, 172). Tensions about whether a group is "political" or offers "support" are common across South Asian queer organizations in India and elsewhere.

53 The contours and constitution of the categories of "competent" and "incompe-

tent" are in a continuous state of construction as political groups move toward success, as normatively understood. At this early stage, "competence" was being defined as the ability to engage in political talk, but "competence" would later be defined by different abilities: to delink identity from affect (see chapter 2), to compromise for the sake of alliance building (see chapter 3), to become visible and public (see chapter 4), and to demonstrate expertise in the language of law and rights (see chapter 5).

54 As an anonymous reviewer of an earlier draft of this book rightly pointed out, the desire to exclude foreigners is also sometimes based on the reality of racism in interracial relationships and settings. See also Das Gupta (2006, 178).

55 Lesley to Sakhi, January 3, 1996.

56 On the analytic utility of spacetime, see Massey (1994, 249–72).

57 Ms. Sunita to Sakhi, September 24, 1994.

58 Ms. K to Sakhi, 1994.

59 Embracing gay narcissism has been an important strategy in queer politics and theory. See, for example, David Halperin's proclamation in his introduction to *Saint Foucault*: "In short, *Michel Foucault, c'est moi*" (1995, 8). Lee Edelman, in his polemical *No Future* (2004), urges queers to embrace their status as narcissistic, nonreproductive, and unconcerned with the child as future. This acceptance would enable queers to realize their radical potential, a relentless pursuit of *jouissance* and death.

60 JD to Sakhi, 1995.

61 Interview with Prerna, June 14, 2003, New Delhi.

62 My project resonates with Miranda Joseph's (2002) critique of the "romance of community." I address these connections further in the next chapter.

Chapter 2: Within Limits, Freedom

1 Interview with Betu, August 17, 2002, New Delhi. All of the following quotes and comments from Betu are from this interview.

2 Queer literature, scholarly and otherwise, often assumes the universality of coming out as the organizing rubric for queer life, and this is due in part to the focus on queer politics in Western locales. Mark Blasius (2001), for example, is interested in questions similar to mine about ethics and queer politics, but he assumes that coming out is the fundamental gay act through which queer people enter into shared ethical practice. What my story shows is that leaving home is both a more salient rubric to most Indian women than coming out, and that it is a means to ethical practice. At the same time, while I am critical of the assumed centrality of coming out for queer politics, I think some have gone too far in claiming that nonwhite queers cannot or do not want to come out or leave home. Ann Pellegrini, for example, faults John D'Emilio (1993) for claiming

that leaving family behind is a "nonnegotiable condition" (Pellegrini 2002, 139) of gay identity. Pellegrini argues that this might "articulate gayness with or even as whiteness." Her cautionary point that we mustn't assume the same nonnegotiable conditions for all queers everywhere is well taken, but for some of the most disempowered queer people in the world, leaving home is not only a hope but an act of ethical and literal survival. See Martin Manalansan (2006) on the importance of migration to queer people in contexts outside Europe and North America.

3 But see Sedgwick (1992) on the "epistemology of the closet."

4 This echoes Lesley's comments and my discussion in chapter 1 of the ascendance of political dialogue as a marker of lesbian identity.

5 Interview with Veronica, August 30, 2002. All of the following quotes and comments from Veronica are from this interview.

6 Foucault's story of the nineteenth-century French hermaphrodite, Herculine Barbin, makes an alternative, but similar, point about the sex-gender-sexuality alignment. In Herculine's case, before anyone could determine that Herculine's genital (male) sex was out of alignment with Herculine's social (feminine) gender, people recognized that Herculine's sexual desire for women was out of alignment with Herculine's feminine gender. It was the recognition of a desire for women that led to the transformation of Herculine's homosexuality into heterosexuality through the medical and legal determination of Herculine's sex as male. Thus declared, Herculine was now in alignment: "his" new male sex predicted "his" masculine gender, which comfortably predicted "his" love for girls. Everyone was finally happy, except for Herculine, who committed suicide in an attic (Foucault 1980).

7 Susan Talburt (2004) discusses how young queer people learn to create seamless narratives of personal sexual liberation through coming out. She problematizes this practice as an exercise of queer normalization and reductionism.

8 Interview with Cath, June 1, 2002, New Delhi. All of Cath's comments and quotes in this chapter are from this interview.

9 Akhil Katyal (2009) cites this interview (from Dave 2006) to argue that this rendering of a "raw" "dyke" (Dave 2006: 115) body, stripped of ideology, recalls a raced sexological discourse that sought to render same-sex desire visually configurable.

10 Sangini Report for 1997–99. In my possession and also archived at Sangini. *The Sangini Project: A Support Project for Lesbian and Bisexual Women in India.* Report 1997–99.

11 In their effort to avoid the imposition of "lesbian," however, they do not elide sexual subjectivity or identity altogether. The woman of their ad is a *type of* (implied in Hindi by *aisi*) woman rather than a woman who simply behaves a certain way.

12 Most lesbian support groups in India schedule their meetings based on this rationale. One group in Bombay even located its office in an "A/C market," or air-conditioned mall, so that if a woman ran into a relative or co-worker on her way to or from a meeting, she could claim that she was shopping. Unfortunately the mall was well past its prime, occupied primarily by used auto supply dealers and mechanics.

13 See also Curtis (2004) on the market politics of sexual subjectivities.

14 Lamia Karim (2008) argues that micro-credit NGOs in Bangladesh construct and appropriate female honor and shame in pursuit of their own—capitalist—agendas.

15 Sangini Annual Report 2000–1. "Sangini Report for 1997–99." In my possession and also archived at Sangini.

16 Monisha Das Gupta (2006), drawing on Ann Pellegrini, is critical of Joseph's linking of queer community with capital. Pellegrini argues that such cautions against community are based on an "unmarked whiteness" (Pellegrini 2002, 139), and Das Gupta adds that they obscure the alternative, disruptive structures that queer communities produce from within capitalism. The point is well taken, and Sangini is certainly a space of queer inventiveness. But the queer of color critique that Das Gupta argues for, one that takes into account "migration, colonization, and racialization" (Das Gupta 2006, 165) also, in my analysis, can point to the uncomfortable self-commodification of racial difference.

17 Though the group's aggression toward Rani may have been unfair, Sangini had reason to keep its address confidential and occasions to fear infiltration. In August 2002, for example, a Hindi magazine called *Madhur Kathaien* printed the address and times of all the support groups at Naz. Worried, we packed up Sangini's books and films and stored them at the directors' homes until the panic died down. The directors decided not to tell the support group members about the breach of security, fearing their fear.

18 Sangini does not have a formal policy on the complex matter. Sam is transgender but not transsexual; he is biologically female and free to attend support group meetings. Raj, however, complicates things. He is young and boyish and dropped out of school because of a requirement to wear skirts. Raj is a beloved group member because of his youth, but he is macho and derisive of women, loudly decrying female drivers and making all manner of other sexist remarks. Raj was transitioning from female to male during my fieldwork but had not yet had bottom surgery (that is, he did not yet have a penis) and was thus allowed to attend meetings. But when he surgically transitioned, he would have to leave the group. Aishwarya, on the other hand, is biologically male but transitioned to female and identifies as a lesbian woman. She was not allowed to attend meetings because she still had a penis. Sangini prioritizes biological females—a concept that itself is a convenient fiction, as Anne Fausto-Sterling (2005) and others

have explained—even if those females identify as men, are becoming men, and are men. Cath's reason for this is that few women in India know that they can be lesbians; they conflate desire for women with "gender trouble" and assume that they are "really" men. Part of Sangini's mission with Raj was to coax him away from surgery and into butch lesbian identification. At the same time, the Sangini directors were fully supportive of Raj's decisions. See Sukthankar (2005) on the rights and struggles of transsexuals in India.

19 Interview with Maya, June 17, 2002, New Delhi.

20 I address activist debates around same-sex violence in India in chapter 5.

21 Dhabas are small roadside restaurants that serve simple, usually North Indian food. Seating is often on cots which double as beds for resting truckers. Paan is betel leaf usually filled with tobacco and spices.

22 See Corie (2009) on the Western cultural politics of impersonal lesbian sex.

23 Maya's understanding of Sangini as "the subversives," deploying everyday acts of subversion while appearing to comply with top-down laws of normativity, might seem comparable to Michel de Certeau's "tactics" (1984) or James Scott's "weapons of the weak" (1985). The similarities are limited, however, because the efficacy of tactics or weapons of the weak is derived from the sense of empowerment they produce in the actor. In contrast, the support group's strategic calculus, as I have been trying to show, tends to work against the cultivation of creative invention and requires instead adherence to a discourse of danger and fear. Maya's "subversiveness," then, could better be compared to Pierre Bourdieu's "succession strategies" (1975, 30), acts of adaptation that are born of a perception of positional weakness.

24 Interview with Roshni, December 2, 2003, New Delhi.

25 This is clear in PRISM's mission statement: "The events surrounding [the Lucknow outreach workers'] arrest underlined the reality that groups working on issues such as sexuality . . . cannot 'afford' *not* to engage with other groups. Equally important was the recognition that all struggles for social justice needed a politics of inclusion and collaboration."

26 One of these two comments was made to me in a casual conversation, and the other in a formal interview.

27 The understanding of sexual identity by PRISM's members entails a rejection, in other words, of what Stuart Hall calls "the interior mechanisms of assent to the rule" of identity (2000, 26). Hall argues that Foucauldian analyses of identity are aloof to the affective experience of subjection. He sees Judith Butler's (1997) psychoanalytic approach to subjectivity as a corrective to this, one that takes seriously the affective dimensions of our attachment to identity and its norms (see my discussion of passionate attachment in chapter 1).

28 For an overview of intersectionality theory in feminist scholarship, see Leslie McCall (2005). McCall defines intersectionality as "the relationships (and anal-

ysis *of them*) among multiple dimensions and modalities of social relations and subject formations" (2005, 1771).

29 Butler borrows the "necessary error of identity" from Gayatri Spivak.

30 From the PRISM mission statement.

31 Jaya, personal communication to author, 2001.

Chapter 3: Virtuous Women, Radical Ethics, and New Regimes of Value

1 I am using a pseudonym rather than A. Khan's real name because I didn't hear her comments to Jaya firsthand.

2 I should clarify my use of terminology. First, concerning "feminism," there is a vast literature in India (see Chaudhuri 2005 for a strong collection of essays), and in the developing world more generally (see Mohanty, Russo, and Torres 1991) on the use of "feminist" and "feminism" to describe women activists and their politics in the non-West. Madhu Kishwar has rejected the labels of "feminist" and "feminism" because of their links to the West (Kishwar 2005). Kamla Bhasin and Nighat Khan (2005), however, defend the use of "feminism" and "feminist" in India as a means of solidarity and political clarity. The latter position is far more common among women's movement activists in India today, and I accordingly use the terms "feminism" and "feminist." Second, referring to organized women's action in India as constituting a "women's movement" is not uncommon or particularly problematic (see John 2009 on the women's movement and women's studies in India). The relevant question here is whether to refer to a "women's movement" or to "women's movements" in the plural. I explain in some detail that there is no monolithic women's movement in India. Still, I refer to a single movement in this chapter because I am making an argument about hegemonic positions among feminists about virtue, value, and sexuality.

3 Most major book-length studies of India's women's movement published since the early 1990s (see Forbes 1996; Kumar 1993; Ray 1999; and Ray and Basu 1999) make no mention at all of lesbian women or of controversies in the movement around lesbian sexuality. Ray's (1999) omission seems especially striking given that she devotes much of her book to explaining the uniquely feminist, non–victim centric politics of the Forum Against Oppression of Women (FAOW) in Bombay. FAOW has, as I will show, been at the forefront of the women's movement in engaging questions around lesbian sexuality and its relevance to feminist politics.

4 The reform movement in India began in 1818 with Raja Rammohun Roy's launch of an antisati campaign. See Lata Mani (1990) for a thorough analysis of the sati debates and the place of women in them. She famously argues that

women were not the subjects or the objects of the debates, but the ground on which they took place.

5 By the late nineteenth century, reformers' emphasis on women's education had resulted in a growing class of women with university educations, some of whom were instrumental in founding national-level women's organizations such as the Women's India Association and the All India Women's Conference (Kumar 1993). While engaging in elite activities such as fundraising and social work, these organizations also joined British women in pushing powerfully for radical reforms such as women's suffrage, universal education, and the abolition of untouchability (Ray 1999, 179).

6 See Agnes (1992) for a comprehensive analytical review of the antirape campaigns.

7 Rape had been a focus of the feminist nationalist movement before the contemporary phase. Although rape in the Mathura period carried the symbolism of class, state, and gendered violence, rape during the nationalist period of Indian women by British men served as a symbol of imperial violence. During Partition, rape took on ghastly communal dimensions, symbolizing the Hindu penetration of Muslim honor, and vice versa (R. Menon and Bhasin 1998).

8 Understanding silence as a means of resisting global gay hegemony in the non-West is a common theme, from Alonso and Koreck (1989) on Hispanics in the United States and Mexico to Wright (2001) on MSM in Bolivia.

9 Interview with Abha, November 20, 2003, New Delhi. All of the following quotes from Abha are from this interview.

10 It is commonplace to represent rural women as being far less sexually repressed than their middle-class counterparts, and to some extent, the mores are indeed different. Nineteenth-century reform movements targeted the urban middle class, and not the rural poor, for the engineering of respectability. That aside, the language in which Indian rural women's sexual freedoms are romanticized is troubling. The perceived distinction—including the way Abha frames it in this quote—between the sexually free rural woman and the repressed middle-class urban woman is perhaps analogous to Foucault's (1990) problematic distinction between the *ars erotica* of "the Orient" and the *scientia sexualis* of the modern West.

11 Chinu Panchal, "'Lesbian Cops' in M. P. to Challenge Dismissal," *Times of India*, February 24, 1988.

12 Vishwanath Hiremath, "Pairing up to fight exploitation," *Free Press Journal*, March 6, 1988.

13 Pradeep Shinde, "Women Split on Marriage of Lesbian Cops," The *Daily* (Bombay), March 2, 1988.

14 Ibid.

15 Interview with Urvashi Butalia, November 19, 2002, New Delhi. All quotes from Butalia are from this interview. The phrase "articulation of lesbian politics" is Butalia's, not FAOW's.

16 Below is one excerpt from an interview with Urmila, published in the *Illustrated Weekly of India* (Saisuresh 1988):

IWI: Do you hate men?
Urmila: No, I don't.
IWI: Are you attracted towards women?
Urmila: No.
IWI: Do you know what the word "lesbian" means?
Urmila: No.

17 There were, of course, exceptions to this negative critique, such as Jagori's own efforts, described by Abha, of affirming women's pleasure in rural settings.

18 One of the books produced through this project is *Tu Ekal, Main Ekal* (you are single, I am single) (Jagori 1992).

19 Interview with Kalpana Vishwanath, May 19, 2002, New Delhi.

20 The conference was exclusively for autonomous women's groups, with "autonomy" defined as being unaffiliated with political parties or the state. Still, major leftist women's groups such as the All India Democratic Women's Association and the National Federation of Indian Women were allowed to participate, along with the thirty or so autonomous groups. The conference defined "women's groups" as those comprised only of women (Fifth NCWM, 1994).

21 I have not found any audio recordings or minutes of this event, but I believe Butalia's claim that she did not say "there are no lesbians in India." *Trikone* invited Butalia to defend herself against Thadani's allegations, but she declined on the ground that she was too disappointed in *Trikone* for allowing her to be misquoted in the first place.

22 "Lesbian Group in Kerala School," *Indian Express* (date unknown), cited in Jagori letter to the editor of the *Indian Express,* February 1, 1992.

23 Ibid.

24 Jagori letter to the editor of the *Indian Express*, February 1, 1992. Unpublished. Both documents are in my possession. Jagori to the Principal of Government Girls' High School, Thiruvananthapuram, Kerala. February 22, 1992.

25 The NCWM debated about whether to apply for funding but opted to resist that trend. The conference operated solely through donations.

26 Interview with Cath, June 4, 2002, New Delhi.

27 But, as noted in chapter 1, the desire to preserve all–South Asian spaces is also sometimes about avoiding racism.

28 Interview with Ranjana Padhi, June 1–2, 2003, New Delhi.

29 Quoted in "PM Asked to Stop Gay Men's Meet," *Pioneer*, November 1, 1994.

30 Jagori letter to women's groups about Vimla Faroqui, 1994. In my possession. All quotations are from this source.

31 In contrast, a group like PRISM expresses its egalitarianism by *not* insisting on common positions. See J. Sharma and Nath (2005, 97).

32 Interview with Ranjana Padhi, June 1–2, 2003, New Delhi. My discussion of Saheli's approach to Faroqui is based on this interview.

33 See G. Misra and Chandiramani (2005) on feminist struggles over rights discourse in South and Southeast Asia more generally.

34 Mita Radhakrishnan to autonomous women's groups, 1995. In my possession.

35 The Platform for Action for the 1995 Beijing conference can be found at http://www.un.org/womenwatch/daw/beijing/platform/. The twelve "critical areas of concern" are under point 44 (last accessed on March 3, 2012).

36 Radhakrishnan to autonomous women's groups.

37 The tension that Radhakrishnan encapsulates between liberal human rights versus radical approaches to feminist politics has also been central to lesbian movements elsewhere. See Phelan (1989) for a discussion of the lesbian feminist movement in the United States.

38 The debate over including "sexual orientation" in the platform for action sparked sharp disagreement between activists, with many representatives loudly cheering when the phrase was finally dropped from the platform.

39 Interview with Pramada Menon, November 4, 2003, New Delhi.

40 International Women's Day has been a source of tension between feminists and lesbians elsewhere as well. See Diaz-Cotto (2001) and Thayer (1997) on the exclusion of lesbians from March 8 marches in Latin America.

41 Maya Sharma, informal conversation, June 2000 (date unknown). I made it a point to jot this phrase down. The details of this meeting are also recorded in the meeting minutes, which I spent an entire night in 2000 typing up from nearly illegible longhand. It was one of the most memorable nights of my fieldwork; as I typed, Maya narrated for me the history of lesbians in India's women's movement.

42 The fact that gay men (and lesbians) have tried to distance themselves from hijras in the media might be surprising, given that hijras are a much more common sight and concept to Indians than are out gays and lesbians. But what is the case elsewhere is true in India, too. David Valentine (2007) helps us to see how gay respectability is intimately tied with gender normativity and requires a distancing between the concept of gayness (a purely sexual identity, and thus potentially private) and various forms of transgender (a gender identity, and thus more public). At a planning meeting for a South Indian queer press conference, activists decided that hijras would not be invited, on the ground that they are "too flamboyant" and are "camera hogs." Furthermore, Shaleen Rakesh, of Naz, gave talks in Delhi arguing that hijras must become "more ethical" and "less flam-

boyant" if they want gay people to fight for their rights. Debates about the treatment of hijras by gay activists abound on the LGBT-India listserv.

43   Interview with Jaya Srivastava, June 5, 2003, New Delhi.

44   Interview with Rarjana Padhi, June 1–2, 2003, New Delhi.

45   Ibid.

46   Interview with Kamla Bhasin, May 2, 2002, New Delhi.

47   Interview with Indiraben, November 27, 2002, Baroda.

48   Unlike CALERI, whose acronym has no other referent, *olava* is Marathi for moist —which, the group likes to point out, is sexually suggestive.

49   MASUM stands for Mahila Sarvangeen Utkarsh Mandal, or a women's forum for integrated development.

50   MASUM Ex-Employees Association to queer allies and women's groups. Draft report. August 2003. The report is in my possession. Manisha Gupte, e-mail correspondence with the author, February 5, 2011, through March 30, 2011. All of the following quotes attributed to Gupte are from this correspondence.

51   MASUM Ex-Employees Association to queer allies and women's groups. All quotes are from this letter.

52   From MASUM's perspective, of course, OLAVA's case was not a solid case of anything, particularly of discrimination against lesbians. Gupte wrote me: "If truth should be known, we didn't *fire* anyone because they were lesbians; but we certainly did *hire* women because they were." On the charge of dissuading other women's groups from supporting OLAVA, Gupte is similarly adamant: "Nothing could be further from the truth." As even OLAVA acknowledged, Gupte had been nothing short of a champion of lesbian rights in Pune. In our personal communications Gupte was very modest about this, stressing that supporting lesbian rights was easy in Pune because of the city's strong progressive activist culture. Pune groups, from the People's Union for Civil Liberties to leftist organizations and women's NGOs, proudly bore OLAVA's flag during International Women's Day marches (a situation unlike that in Delhi or Bombay) and attended vigils as well as celebrations for lesbian rights issues. The idea that Gupte would dissuade other groups from supporting OLAVA was not just personally hurtful, Gupte suggested, but factually untenable: Pune's progressive support for OLAVA was quite independent of Gupte. Gupte writes: "I say with some sadness that it wasn't Pune that failed OLAVA; it was [OLAVA] that failed a nascent movement for lesbian rights in the city."

53   It is worth noting here, as I noted earlier about Thadani, that Tellis is not an uncomplicated figure. He is brash and outspoken, while also dedicated and incisive. Some people's resistance to supporting him had more to do with his history of conflict than with apathy.

54   Sangama temporarily imploded in 2003, after demanding that its hijra em-

ployees give up sex work and adhere to a more normative dress code. The group had built positive relationships with the local police, and its leaders were loath to allow hijras to jeopardize that relationship. PRISM considered cutting ties with Sangama, as many other progressive queer groups did.

55 Stree Sangam, e-mail message to PRISM, CREA, and CALERI, September 28, 2003.

56 The India Centre for Human Rights and Law was founded by a group of High Court lawyers and human rights activists as a comprehensive resource center for the study of human rights and law. They have sponsored several lesbian and gay initiatives over the years, including providing resources and office space to Aanchal, the Bombay lesbian help line.

57 Interview with Chatura, October 23, 2003, Bombay.

58 Ibid.

59 Ibid.

Chapter 4: Public "Emergence"

1 Interview with Kruti, September 18, 2002, New Delhi.

2 Though she does not refer specifically to the "Indian and Lesbian" sign, activist S. L. describes the ambivalence, excitement, and uncertainty of seeing the word "lesbian" reproduced in newspapers the morning after the Delhi lesbian demonstration: "By the morning of December 8 it had all happened. The word 'lesbian' was on the front pages of every newspaper I picked up in Delhi. LESBIAN. It looked odd and out of place. Why was a word like that being tossed around? A word so loaded with fear, embarrassment, prejudice, a word shrouded in silence, a whisper that spoke of an identity that must be hidden from others, that frightening word that dare not cross any threshold, was on that winter morning landing at the doorstep of millions of households in many parts of the country. At my colleagues' door. At my parents'. At their neighbors'. At my landlord's. . . . The Mother Dairy [milk] man was going to read it. . . . My sister-in-law. . . . They were all going to pick up their morning paper and stare at a word they had possibly not seen earlier in print, and never given much thought to, and wonder what it was doing on Page One. And Three. And editorials . . . Not just that day but for days and weeks after December 8" (S.L. 1999, 17).

3 *Fire* was a $1.6 million venture, conceived and directed by the Delhi-born and Toronto-based writer and director, Deepa Mehta. *Fire* was shot in Delhi with Indian actors but funded primarily through private sources in North America. It made its award-winning debut at the 1996 Toronto film festival and won thirteen more international awards before its arrival on the Indian screen. Much scholarly attention has been paid to *Fire*, from literary criticism (Gopinath 1998 and 2005; Patel 2002 and 2004) to discursive analysis (Bachmann 2002; Kapur

2002). This chapter, however, is not about *Fire*. It uses the critical event of the protests around the film to think about the nexus of affect, commensurability, queer sexuality, and the politics of public culture.

4 One exception was Madhu Kishwar, the well-known women's activist, who lambasted the film and its director for showing Indians in a negative light. In an essay originally published in the journal she cofounded, *Manushi*, Kishwar suggests that Mehta "enjoy[s] pouring shit on the heads of our fellow Indians because it has become a lucrative proposition in the western market" and characterizes her as the ideal (female) mimic man: "Macaulay who claimed that through English education, he hoped to create a class of Indians English in taste and morals, though brown in skin color, would be proud of his achievement if he saw Mehta's *Fire* or heard her pontificate on Indians and India" (http://www.infinityfoundation.com/mandala/s_es/s_es_kishw_naive_frameset.htm).

5 "Thackeray Adamant on *Fire*," *Hindustan Times*, December 15, 1998.

6 I am concentrating on Hindus in this section for three main reasons. First, the violent objections to *Fire* and to lesbians more generally—though couched as protecting India as a whole from Western influence—were inflected with religious, and specifically anti-Muslim, sentiment. I am seeking to underscore the relationship between anti-Muslim and anti-queer politics. Second, even in an anticolonial nationalism that was not premised on Hindutva (the idea of a rightfully Hindu nation) as the Sangh Parivar's nationalism is today, Hindu and Muslim publicists were not equal players. The manner by which Hindu publicists were able to make claims on behalf of all Indians only exemplifies the authority of the imperial-era linkage between "Hindu" and "India." Finally, the mores of sexual respectability that are invoked in the contemporary Hindu nationalist movement are derived from distinctions made between Hindu and Muslim sexuality in the anticolonial period, distinctions that I discuss in this chapter.

7 See, most centrally, Chatterjee (1990). For elaborations upon and critiques of Chatterjee's thesis, see Sarkar (1992, 1996, and 2001), Sinha (1995), and C. Gupta (2001).

8 The vociferous responses to Mayo on the part of Indians demonstrate the depth of their anxiety. For example, Chandravati Lakhanpal, in her *Mother India Ka Jawab* (Reply to *Mother India*), adamantly denied Mayo's allegations of Indian homosexuality, suggesting instead that British males were raging homosexuals, inculcated as such by their education system (Sinha 1995, 45). Similarly, K. L. Gauba's *Uncle Sham*, a treatise on the perversity of American society, and S. G. Warty's *Sister India: A Critical Examination of and Reasoned Reply to Miss Katherine Mayo's "Mother India"* tried to locate queerness within Europe and North America.

9 British India also signed an international agreement for the suppression of obscene publications in 1910 (C. Gupta 2001, 31). This legal attention to obscenity in the colony was linked to a similar trend in the metropole. The 1868 English case of *Regina (The Crown) v. Hicklin* determined the boundaries and effects of the criminally "obscene"—that is, any material that "would suggest to the minds of the young of either sex, or even to persons of more advanced years, thoughts of a most impure and libidinous character" (Kapur 2001, 343, note 22). This test set by the Hicklin case is still invoked by Indian courts in support of obscenity statutes (5).

10 Regarding Sita's sacred role as an archetype of Hindu feminine moral purity, Sudhir Kakar writes: "The ideal of womanhood incorporated by Sita is one of chastity, purity, gentle tenderness and a singular faithfulness which cannot be destroyed or even disturbed by her husband's rejections, slights, or thoughtlessness. . . . The moral is the familiar one: 'Whether treated well or ill a wife should never indulge in ire' " (1978, 66).

11 Chughtai was a prominent figure in North India's Urdu literary and leftist political scene in the 1930s and 1940s. See Gopinath (2005, 143).

12 In an interview with *Manushi*, she recalls that day: "In 1944 I was charged with obscenity by the Lahore government. A summons arrived: 'George the Sixth versus Ismat Chughtai.' I had a good laugh at the idea that the king had read my story. So we went to Lahore to fight the case" (Chughtai 1983, 5).

13 Another relevant precursor to *Fire* is the collection of short stories by Pandey Bechan Sharma (writing as Ugra) called *Chaklet*, published in 1924. The stories narrated love affairs between men, often with damning (but still ambiguous) editorial comments on the sinful nature of such love. See Vanita (2009) for much more on the Ugra affair.

14 Hindu right-wing activists believed the land was the birthplace of Ram and tore down the mosque with great fanfare. This led to extensive and deadly riots across the country. See Tambiah (1996). The Supreme Court only finally decided on the property's rightful communal ownership in 2010, a decision that was met with controversy.

15 The public sphere in India has always been an elite domain. Early work by the Subaltern Studies collective focused on the numerous ways in which the construction of Indian national identity has been marked by the failure of the indigenous bourgeoisie to posit its universality and mobilize a widespread nationalist movement across boundaries of class, caste, religion, and gender (see Chatterjee 1986; Guha 1997a and 1997b; Amin 1988). One of the effects of this failure has been the marginalization of subaltern participation in the production of a national imaginary. A later effect, manifest in subaltern studies itself, has been a recuperation of these marginalized voices for a revisionist historiography

(Guha 1988). In other words, the Indian public domain has been premised on a division between elite and nonelite discourses, whether in the form of exclusion or recuperation.

16 "*Fire* Referred to Censor Board," *Times of India*, December 5, 1998.

17 In the summer of 1975, Gandhi, then leader of India's powerhouse political party, the Congress Party, had been found guilty of electoral fraud and was facing a new set of elections. Fearing a national uprising against her led by an increasingly powerful opposition leader, Gandhi declared a national Emergency.

18 See the oral history of the effects of Indira Gandhi's Emergency in Delhi in Tarlo (2003).

19 Less explicitly, perhaps, CALERI recalls Walter Benjamin's eighth thesis: that emergency is not an exception but the rule. Furthermore, CALERI suggests that those opposed to fascism must seek to create their own state of emergency (1978, 257).

20 William Mazzarella argues that affect "is not . . . a radical site of otherness to be policed or preserved but rather a necessary moment of any institutional practice with aspirations to public efficacy" (2008, 298).

21 The *Fire* affair, in its ambivalent movement toward identificatory containment, is reminiscent of other major queer emergences such as Stonewall. José Muñoz argues that despite that event's profound importance, it is "equally important to reflect on what was lost by this particular process of formalization. Before this bold rebellion there was another moment in which the countercultural map was perhaps a bit queerer, which is to say more expansive and inclusive of various structures of feeling and habits of being that the relatively restrictive categories of gay and lesbian identities are incapable of catching" (2009, 115).

22 Sangini's help-line logs show a fourfold increase in the number of calls received in the months after the *Fire* protests, and many lesbian activist leaders in the country today trace the beginning of their activism to this critical event.

23 Diasporic Indian queers, too, have had to defend their Indianness. See Gopinath (2005) and Das Gupta (2006) on the battle between the South Asian Lesbian and Gay Association (SALGA) and a group of Indian businessmen called the National Federation of Indian Associations. The latter, in 1995 and 1996, refused to let SALGA march in the New York City India Day Parade. The group responded with banners that read, for example, "Long Live Queer India!" This construction of (queer) Indianness informed CALERI's, though CALERI very consciously worked independently of SALGA in responding to the *Fire* riots (see Kukke, Shah, and Syed 1999, 33–34). Although SALGA allied itself with CALERI from a distance, as Das Gupta shows (2006, 188), SALGA's own critique of Hindu nationalism was still only emerging; the group was hardly in a position to lead or mentor CALERI.

24 CALERI (1999, 71–78) describes these activities in detail in its report.

25 Interview with Vandana, July 3, 2004, New Delhi.

26 Interview with Maya, June 17, 2002, New Delhi.

Chapter 5: To Be Lawful, to Be Just

1 *Naz Foundation v. Government of NCT of Delhi and Others*, WP(C) Civil Writ Petition No. 1009 (1994), 7455/2001 (High Court of New Delhi 2009).

2 On that day I was not in India but on campus in Toronto. Like many people in India, though, I received the news while avidly watching events online and via a surge of text messages and phone calls. My description of the scene is based on those phone calls, photographs, and the draft of an article that Jaya wrote about the event. I refer to the last item in this chapter's conclusion.

3 The mechanism of public interest litigation was developed to more broadly enforce Article 32 of the Indian Constitution. That article gives citizens the right to bring a case directly to the Supreme Court if their fundamental rights have been violated. (PIL are filed at the High Court level as well, as was the case with the Naz petition.) In practice, however, this right is limited by literacy and social position; many do not even know when their rights are being violated. The litigation became a fixture in Indian jurisprudence in the early 1980s through a range of Supreme Court decisions (see Jain 2000, 76–86). This movement was influenced by 1970s legal aid activism as well as by a spirit of atonement for the judiciary's capitulation to the executive during the Emergency (see Desai and Muralidhar 2000).

4 Akshay's privileging of the right to live exemplifies what Miriam Ticktin calls the "sacred place of biological integrity" (2006, 33) in contemporary transnational moral regimes of medical humanitarianism and human rights.

5 See E. Cohen (1993) on the history of British sodomy law and Bhaskaran (2002) for its relationship to Indian colonial sodomy law.

6 For thorough analyses of the uses and abuses of s.377 since its inception, see Bhaskaran (2004) and Gupta (2001).

7 Vidya Deshpande, "Tihar Officials' Dilemma over Condoms," *Pioneer*, February 10, 1994.

8 Suparna Bhaskaran writes that Jai filed his petition "supporting the official position" (2002, 15). This is not quite accurate. The purpose of Jai's petition was to find out, unambiguously, what the "official position" on condom distribution was.

9 *Dr. Janak Raj Jai v. Delhi Administration and Others*, Civil Writ Petition No. 1009 (1994). In a separate press release, Jai argued: "Our country is proud of having the richest religious and cultural heritage in the world and small and petty brains in power, who don't wish to see beyond their nose, shall not be allowed to take this our motherland for a ride. If need be, we are ready to fight a legal battle

up to the apex Court, to save the dignity, honour, religious sentiments of each and citizen [sic] of the country." This press release is in Shobha Aggarwal's private archive. I thank her for the access she gave me to this and other material.

10 ABVA v. *Union of India and Others*, Civil Writ Petition No. 1784 (1994). The group named eight respondents: the Union of India [the judicial term for what is now the Republic of India]; Delhi Administration; the District and Sessions Judge [of Delhi]; the Inspector General of Prisons [of Tihar Jail, Kiran Bedi]; the Superintendent of [Tihar] Jail; the National AIDS Control Organization; the Indian Council of Medical Research; and the All India Institute of Medical Sciences. The petition was filed by Shobha Aggarwal, a lawyer and activist with ABVA, through the group's advocate, Rajesh Talwar. Talwar's claim to a place in gay Indian history is not limited to this petition; he also published a gay-themed play called *Inside Gayland* (Talwar 1995).

11 Under Article 13 of the Constitution, any law found to be inconsistent with, or in derogation of, a fundamental right, such as the ones ABVA cites here, must be declared void.

12 ABVA v. *Union of India and Others*, p. 9.

13 Dr. Janak Raj Jai v. Delhi Administration, Counter-Affidavit on Behalf of the Respondents to the Above Writ Petition, Affidavit Kiran Bedi (1009). AIDS Bhedbhav Virodhi Andolan v. Union of India and Others, Counter-Affidavit Kiran Bedi (1784).

14 At the time of this debate, Tihar Jail had a maximum capacity of 2,000 inmates, but was housing approximately 3,500. These figures come from Bedi's counter-affidavit to Jai's petition. The quote is on page 4 of that counteraffidavit.

15 From a posting on the LGBT-India e-list by a representative of the Milan Project, June 18, 2001, post #8090.

16 From a posting on the LGBT-India e-list by the International Gay and Lesbian Human Rights Commission (IGLHRC), July 10, 2001, post #8257.

17 Complaint # 3920 to the National Human Rights Commission.

18 Anuradha Varma, "NHRC Comes Down on Gay Rights," Pioneer, August 2, 2001.

19 My account of this comes from Bondopadhyay (2002) and is consistent with a variety of other reports and conversations.

20 NFI stands for Naz Foundation International, but it is a completely separate organization from Naz. This is potentially confusing, so I will only refer to NFI by its acronym. "Naz," "Naz India," or "Naz Foundation" in this book refers only to the organization in Delhi.

21 The newspaper writes: "As a majority of the parent organizations funding these NGOs were based in Canada and Europe, which also has a chunk of Pakistani nationals residing there, the [Intelligence Bureau] was pressed into service to

monitor the inflow of funds and their mode of expenditure in India." ("Gay Culture Started in UP in '98 Itself," *Times of India*, July 10, 2001.)

22 Adding even further intrigue, Shivananda Khan and Ashok Row Kavi were notorious professional enemies. The competition produced by their differing philosophies about gay identity in India often took on Hindu-Muslim overtones, and it was widely rumored that Row Kavi had piqued police curiosity about NFI by exploiting existing suspicion of Khan's religious and national sympathies. See L. Cohen (2005) for more on Khan and Row Kavi's relationship, and on the Lucknow affair more generally.

23 Ronald Hyam (1990) shows how increasing rates of venereal disease among British soldiers in the 1850s led to a heightened concern about miscegenation and Indian sexual perversity. Anjali Arondekar (2000 and 2009) demonstrates how central the Indian Mutiny of 1857 was in leading the British to codify populations along lines of perversity and propriety; s.377 was part of this project of differentiation.

24 *Naz Foundation v. Government of NCT of Delhi and Others.* Naz named five respondents: the Government of Delhi; the Commissioner of Police; the Delhi State AIDS Control Society; the National AIDS Control Organization; and the Union of India. All quotes in the text are from this document. I will refer to the case as *Naz v. Govt. of Delhi* hereafter.

25 Interview with Vivek Divan, September 18, 2003, Bombay.

26 Naz also argued that the statute is in violation of Article 15 of the Constitution, which prohibits discrimination on several grounds, including "sex"—which Naz took to include sexual orientation. The group also claimed that the rights to speech, movement, assembly, and association, guaranteed under Article 19, are violated by the homophobic targeting of s.377.

27 The legal and political language of "rights," "fundamental rights," and "human rights" is common in India. India's 1950 Constitution drew on language from the UN's 1948 Declaration of Human Rights. The specific idea of a right to privacy, however, is both new and not explicitly mentioned in the Constitution.

28 Indeed, feminist and queer scholars more generally have been concerned with the politics and ethics of privacy claims. For example, Carol Smart (1989) views privacy claims as being appropriable by the strong against the weak once they are instituted. Nicholas Bamforth (1997, 90–92) agrees, showing that the decriminalization of private same-sex sex in Britain led to a dramatic increase in convictions of gay men under other statutes. Furthermore, for Bamforth, right to privacy arguments focus too narrowly on the sexual lives of gays and lesbians, reducing queerness to sex acts and doing little to mitigate discrimination in work, education, and politics (219).

29 Bamforth argues: "Any justification for law or law reform invokes a vision of

how law should be used in a legitimate system of government. Such a vision will rest on a theory of justice—that is, a theory concerning rightful and wrongful distributions of entitlements among members of society—which is closely connected with a theory of political morality, concerning the principles which should guide the exercise of public power by state institutions" (1997, 108).

30 Shobha John, "Gay Activists May Win the Battle but the Cost May Be High," *Times of India*, January 19, 2003.

31 "Legalizing Homo-Sexuality," unpublished outline of issues for a Prayas Institute of Juvenile Justice discussion, February 1, 2003.

32 PRISM, "Gay Perspective," *Times of India*, January 26, 2003.

33 *Naz Foundation v. Government of NCT of Delhi and Others*, Counter-Affidavit Respondent 5 (200). I will refer to the counteraffidavit as *GoI* hereafter.

34 At the center of the PIL movement was liberalizing the requirements for locus standi. The Supreme Court recognized this throughout the early 1980s and relaxed the standards for citizen representation, especially on behalf of classes of people disadvantaged by poverty, illiteracy, or other social constraints (Desai and Muralidhar 2000, 162–64). Nonetheless, representatives (like Naz) must prove they have sufficient interest, and the courts have also been wary of over-liberalizing the requirements for standing. Progressives and other critics, like C. J. Nirmal, argue that the state deploys a strict reading of locus standi to "prevent the redress of violation of human rights of the poor and disadvantaged" (1999, xxx).

35 The case law on the question of consent is interesting. Bhaskaran (2002) argues that consent was moot in cases dealing with homosexual sodomy because the courts treated homosexual sodomy as unnatural and thus irrational, so not available to (necessarily rational) consent. In one case dealing with heterosexual sodomy, however—*Grace Jeyaramani v. EP Peter*, in Karnataka in 1982—the court declared that a husband could be guilty of sodomy against his wife only if she is not a consenting partner (A. Gupta 2001), thereby introducing the question of consent into sodomy law. What the case law suggests is that the supposedly unnatural act of sodomy is only unnatural or irrational (and thus unavailable to consent) when it occurs outside of conjugal relationships.

36 Minutes of the 377 Activism Campaign Planning Meeting, September 13–14, 2003. In my possession. All quotes from that meeting are derived from these minutes.

37 See Thoreson (2008) on the extraordinary, and seemingly unlikely, success of the South African GLB movement.

38 Members of PRISM would describe Voices as a "concrete manifestation of PRISM's politics of intersectionality" (Sharma and Nath 2005, 96).

39 The case is *Sudesh Jakhoo v. K. C. J. and Others*.

40 Sakshi, IFSHA, and AIDWA later drafted a Criminal Law Amendment Bill in 2000

based on the Law Commission of India's recommendations. The National Commission for Women had drafted a bill similar to this one in 1993 called the "Sexual Violence against Women and Children Bill." That bill also advocated for the substitution of rape with sexual assault and the deletion of s.377. Although the bill referred to the victim as "person" in some instances, suggesting gender neutrality, in other places it referred to the victim as "woman" or "child." Nothing came of the bill legislatively (see Agnes 2002a and 2002b; Menon 2004).

41 172nd Report on Review of Rape Laws, 2000, p.7. One way in which this document departed from Sakshi's recommendations was in the area of marital rape. The Law Commission of India writes: "Representatives of Sakshi wanted us to recommend the deletion of the Exception ['Sexual intercourse by a man with his own wife, the wife not being under sixteen years of age, is not sexual assault'], with which we are unable to agree. . . . We are not satisfied that this Exception should be recommended to be deleted since that may amount to excessive interference with the marital relationship" (13).

42 The Law Commission of India recognized that deleting s.377 would also decriminalize intercourse with animals. The commission shrugged this off, saying, "We may leave such persons to their just deserts" (19).

43 There was one additional objection. Flavia Agnes faulted Sakshi for "mindlessly aping the mistakes committed by western feminists" (2002b, 847). Agnes might have seen Sakshi as being beholden to Western interests because of the sources of funds for its gender neutrality efforts: the MacArthur Foundation, Ford Foundation, and UNIFEM (see N. Menon 2004, 221).

44 Letter to Law Minister 2001. For further expressions of this sentiment, see Agnes (2002b) and N. Menon (2004, 137). These arguments in favor of gender specificity departed from feminist trends in the United States and Canada in the mid-1970s and early 1980s (see Chunn and Lacombe 2000). In these North American cases, feminist coalitions successfully lobbied to shift the legal understanding of rape from a crime with a uniquely sexual nature to a crime enacting several forms of violence. The Indian feminists in the group of thirty-two organizations, however, were asserting the gender- and sex-specific realities of adult rape.

45 J. Sharma and Nath (2005, 89–90), both members of PRISM, discuss the group's long conflicts over gender neutrality. The authors attribute their initial support for a gender-specific law (a support that later "evolved") to their not yet having an intersectional approach to understanding oppression and to their still being attached to identity politics.

46 This argument for a "foot in the door" was taken to heart by those few queer groups that supported gender neutrality, Bombay's Aanchal and Humsafar Trust among them. The argument reminds me of Mary John and Janaki Nair's comments about the courtroom and sexuality. They praise the courtroom for at

least providing "legitimate spaces for the most detailed and unembarrassed discussions of male and female sexuality" (1998, 23). They are right, but their argument stems from the presumption that sexuality in India has primarily been a "question of silence," which makes all frank discussion about sexuality a positive "foot in the door." It is always worth asking what consequence the foot will have, and through what means.

47 PRISM to Bombay meeting against gender-neutral sexual assault laws, December 17, 2001. A copy of the letter is in my possession, and it is also in the archives of Naz and PRISM.

48 Indian criminal law holds that "any person who is aware of an offence being committed" can legitimately file a complaint. (As an aside, the letter points out that one of the few exceptions to this principle applies within the institution of marriage. A magistrate cannot take cognizance of an "offence against marriage" complaint unless it is filed by the husband or the wife.)

49 PRISM to Bombay meeting. The letter also advanced other objections to the recommendations of the Law Commission of India. For instance, the letter writers argued that this was a terrible moment to try to achieve progressive change through legislative acts. Not only had a center-right-dominated Parliament "mutilated" ostensibly prowomen bills, but the lengthy process of comments, amendments, and further modifications might well result in the decision to retain s.377, despite the commission's recommendations. If so, Indian sexual minorities could "land in the same nightmare" as their counterparts in Sri Lanka. There, similar legislative recommendations to delete the antisodomy statute in favor of a broadened sexual assault law had resulted in a broadened antisodomy law instead. The Sri Lankan Parliament amended the statute to include women. They also modernized the statute's language, from "carnal intercourse against the order of nature" to "gross indecency with any person." See Narrain (2004).

50 Those recommendations remained stalled until March 31, 2010. After nearly nine years of inaction on the Law Commission of India's 172nd Report, the Minister for Home Affairs circulated a new draft bill called the "Criminal Law (Amendment) Bill 2010." This bill is very much in line with the report and would enact the same two major changes: the definition of rape would be expanded to all forms of sexual assault, and sexual assault itself would be a gender-neutral crime. The topic is being discussed on the LBGT-India e-list, but without the passions generated in 2001 and 2002 and with almost no reference to those earlier debates. A few activists have suggested, however, that the government is now more willing to move on the commission's recommendations (which included dropping s.377 in favor of a gender-neutral sexual assault law) after seeing that s.377 was likely to fall anyway through judicial action. As of March 2012, the bill has not yet been voted on.

51 Letter to Law Minister 2001.

52 What Anish interrogates here is something that Otto Kahn-Freund calls a "magic belief in the efficacy of the law in shaping human conduct and social relations" (1969, 311). It is also reminiscent of Stuart Scheingold's position on the "mythic" quality of law (2004, xviii).

53 *Naz Foundation v. Government of NCT of Delhi and Others*, 103–4.

references

Agnes, Flavia. 1992. "Protecting Women against Violence? A Review of a Decade of Legislation." *Economic and Political Weekly* 27 (17): 19–33.

———. 2002a. "Gender Neutrality in Rape Law." *Combat Law* 1 (1): 44–51.

———. 2002b. "Law, Ideology and Female Sexuality: Gender Neutrality in Rape Law." *Economic and Political Weekly* 37 (9): 844–47.

Agrawal, Arun. 2005. *Environmentality: Technologies of Government and the Making of Subjects.* Durham: Duke University Press.

Alonso, Ana Maria, and Maria Teresa Koreck. 1989. "Silences: 'Hispanics,' AIDS and Sexual Practices." *differences* 1 (1): 101–24.

Althusser, Louis. 1972 (1970). *Lenin, and Philosophy, and Other Essays.* New York: Monthly Review Press.

Altman, Dennis. 1996. "The Internationalization of Gay Identity." *Social Text* 14 (3): 77–94.

Amin, Shahid. 1998. "Gandhi as Mahatma: Gorakhpur District, Eastern UP, 1921–22." In *Selected Subaltern Studies*, edited by Ranajit Guha and Gayatri Chakravorty Spivak, 280–342. New York: Oxford University Press.

Anderson, Benedict. 1991. *Imagined Communities: Reflections on the Origin and Spread of Nationalism.* New York: Verso.

Appadurai, Arjun. 1988. "Putting Hierarchy in Its Place." *Cultural Anthropology* 3 (1): 36–49.

———. 1996. *Modernity at Large: The Cultural Aspects of Globalization*. Minneapolis: University of Minnesota Press.

Arendt, Hannah. 1968. *Men in Dark Times*. New York: Harcourt, Brace, and World.

Arondekar, Anjali. 2000. "A Perverse Empire: Victorian Sexuality and the Indian Colony." PhD diss., University of Pennsylvania.

———. 2009. *For the Record: On Sexuality and the Colonial Archive in India*. Durham: Duke University Press.

Arora, Dooley. 1999. "Structural Adjustment Program and Gender Concerns in India." *Journal of Contemporary Asia* 29 (3): 328–61.

Asad, Talal. 2004. "Where Are the Margins of the State?" In *Anthropology in the Margins of the State*, edited by Veena Das and Deborah Poole, 279–88. Santa Fe, NM: School of American Research Press.

Austin, J. L. 1976 (1962). *How to Do Things with Words*. New York: Oxford Paperbacks.

Bacchetta, Paola. 1999. "When the (Hindu) Nation Exiles Its Queers." *Social Text* 17 (4): 141–66.

———. 2002. "Rescaling Transnational 'Queerdom': Lesbian and 'Lesbian' Identitary Positionalities in Delhi in the 1980s." *Antipode* 34 (5): 947–73.

Bachmann, Mona. 2002. "After the Fire." In *Queering India: Same-Sex Love and Eroticism in Indian Culture and Society*, edited by Ruth Vanita, 234–43. New York: Routledge.

Bamforth, Nicholas. 1997. *Sexuality, Morals and Justice: A Theory of Lesbian and Gay Rights Law*. London: Cassell.

Basu, Amrita. 1992. *Two Faces of Protest: Contrasting Modes of Activism in India*. Berkeley: University of California Press.

Baviskar, Amita. 2004 (1995). *In the Belly of the River: Tribal Conflicts over Development in the Narmada Valley*. New Delhi: Oxford University Press.

Benjamin, Walter. 1978. *Illuminations: Essays and Reflections*. Translated by Harry Zohn. New York: Schocken.

Bhaiya, Abha. 2009. "The Spring That Flowers between Women." In *Women's Sexualities and Masculinities in a Globalizing Asia*, edited by Evelyn Blackwood, Abha Bhaiya, and Saskia Weiringa, 69–76. New York: Palgrave Macmillan.

Bhan, Gautam. 2006. "Seeking Chaos: The Birth and Intentions of Queer Politics." In *The Sarai Reader 06: Turbulence*, edited by Monica Narula et al., 401–6. New Delhi: Centre for the Study of Developing Societies.

Bhasin, Kamla, and Nighat Said Khan. 2005. "Some Questions on Feminism and Its Relevance in South Asia." In *Feminism in India*, edited by Maitrayee Chaudhuri, 3–7. New York: Zed.

Bhaskaran, Suparna. 2002. "The Politics of Penetration: Section 377 of the Indian Penal Code." In *Queering India: Same-Sex Love and Eroticism in Indian Culture and Society*, edited by Ruth Vanita, 15–29. New York: Routledge.

———. 2004. *Made in India: Decolonizations, Queer Sexualities, Trans/National Projects.* New York: Palgrave Macmillan.

Blackwood, Evelyn. 1984. "Sexuality and Gender in Certain Native American Tribes: The Case of Cross-Gender Females." *Signs* 10 (1): 27–42.

Blackwood, Evelyn, Abha Bhaiya, and Saskia Wieringa, eds. 2009. *Women's Sexualities and Masculinities in a Globalizing Asia.* New York: Palgrave Macmillan.

Blasius, Mark. 2001. "An Ethos of Lesbian and Gay Existence." In *Sexual Identities, Queer Politics,* edited by Mark Blasius, 143–77. Princeton: Princeton University Press.

Bob, Clifford. 2005. *The Marketing of Rebellion: Insurgents, Media, and International Activism.* Cambridge: Cambridge University Press.

Boellstorff, Tom. 2005a. "Between Religion and Desire: Being Muslim and Gay in Indonesia." *American Anthropologist* 107 (4): 575–85.

———. 2005b. *The Gay Archipelago: Sexuality and Nation in Indonesia.* Princeton: Princeton University Press.

Bondopadhyay, Aditya. 2002. "Where Saving Lives Is a Crime." *Combat Law* (April–May): 51–53.

Bourdieu, Pierre. 1975. "The Specificity of the Scientific Field and the Social Conditions of the Progress of Reason." *Social Science Information* 14 (6): 19–47.

———. 1979. "Public Opinion Does Not Exist." In *Communication and Class Struggle,* edited by Armand Mattelart and Seth Siegelaub, 124–30. New York: International General.

———. 1991. *Language and Symbolic Power,* edited by John B. Thompson. Translated by Gino Raymond and Matthew Adamson. Cambridge: Harvard University Press.

Butler, Judith. 1993. *Bodies That Matter: On the Discursive Limits of "Sex."* New York: Routledge.

———. 1997. *The Psychic Life of Power: Theories in Subjection.* Stanford: Stanford University Press.

CALERI. 1999a. *Lesbian Emergence: Khamosh! Emergency Jaari Hai. A Citizen's Report.* Delhi: CALERI.

———. 1999b. "Introduction." In *Lesbian Emergence: Khamosh! Emergency Jaari Hai. A Citizen's Report.* Edited by CALERI. 4. Delhi: CALERI.

———. 1999c. "Press Release of Lesbian Groups." In *Lesbian Emergence: Khamosh! Emergency Jaari Hai. A Citizen's Report.* Edited by CALERI. 22–24. Delhi: CALERI.

Carrillo, Hector. 2002. *The Night Is Young: Sexuality in Mexico in the Time of AIDS.* Chicago: University of Chicago Press.

Chakrabarty, Dipesh. 1992. "Postcoloniality and the Artifice of History: Who Speaks for 'Indian' Pasts?" *Representations* 37 (Winter): 1–26.

———. 2000. *Provincializing Europe: Postcolonial Thought and Historical Difference.* Princeton: Princeton University Press.

Chari, Sharad, and Henrike Donner. 2010. "Ethnographies of Activism: A Critical Introduction." *Cultural Dynamics* 22 (2): 75–85.

Chatterjee, Partha. 1986. *Nationalist Thought and the Colonial World: A Derivative Discourse?* Minneapolis: University of Minnesota Press.

——. 1990. "The Nationalist Resolution of the Women's Question." In *Recasting Women: Essays in Colonial History*, edited by Kumkum Sangari and Sudesh Vaid, 233–53. New Brunswick, NJ: Rutgers University Press.

Chaudhuri, Maitrayee, ed. 2005. *Feminism in India*. New York: Zed.

Chughtai, Ismat. 1983. "Interview with Ismat Chughtai." *Manushi* 19: 5–7.

——. 1990 (1942). "Lihaaf." In *The Quilt and Other Stories*, edited by Ismat Chughtai. Translated by Tahira Naqvi and Syeda S. Hameed. Delhi: Kali for Women.

Chunn, Dorothy E., and Dany Lacombe, eds. 2000. *Law as a Gendering Practice*. Don Mills, Ontario: Oxford University Press.

Cohen, Edward. 1993. *Talk on the Wild Side: Towards a Genealogy of a Discourse on Male Sexualities*. New York: Routledge.

Cohen, Lawrence. 2005. "The Kothi Wars: AIDS Cosmopolitanism and the Morality of Classification." In *Sex and Development: Science, Sexuality, and Morality in Global Perspective*, edited by Vincanne Adams and Stacy Leigh Pigg, 269–303. Durham: Duke University Press.

Cooke, Bill, and Uma Kothari, eds. 2001. *Participation: The New Tyranny?* New York: Palgrave.

Cooper, Fredrick, and Ann Laura Stoler, eds. 1997. *Tensions of Empire: Colonial Cultures in a Bourgeois World*. Berkeley: University of California Press.

Corie, Hammers. 2009. "An Examination of Lesbian / Queer Bathhouse Culture and the Social Organization of (Im)Personal Sex." *Journal of Contemporary Ethnography* 38 (3): 308–55.

Cornell, Drucilla. 1992. "The Philosophy of the Limit: Systems Theory and Feminist Legal Reform." In *Deconstruction and the Possibility of Justice*, edited by Drucilla Cornell, Michel Rosenfeld, and David Gray Carlson, 68–91. New York: Routledge.

Curtis, Debra. 2004. "Commodities and Sexual Subjectivities: A Look at Capitalism and Its Desires." *Cultural Anthropology* 19 (1): 95–121.

Cvetkovich, Ann. 2003. *An Archive of Feelings: Trauma, Sexuality, and Lesbian Public Cultures*. Durham: Duke University Press.

Das, Veena. 2006. *Life and Words: Violence and the Descent into the Ordinary*. Berkeley: University of California Press.

Das, Veena, and Deborah Poole. 2004. "State and its Margins: Comparative Ethnographies." In *Anthropology in the Margins of the State*, edited by Veena P. Das and Deborah Poole, 3–34. Santa Fe, NM: School of American Research Press.

Das Gupta, Monisha. 2006. *Unruly Immigrants: Rights, Activism, and Transnational South Asian Politics in the United States*. Durham: Duke University Press.

Dave, Naisargi N. 2006. "Between Queer Ethics and Sexual Morality: Lesbian and Gay Activism in New Delhi, India." PhD diss., University of Michigan.

——. 2010. "To Render Real the Imagined: An Ethnographic History of Lesbian Community in India." *Signs: Journal of Women in Culture and Society* 35 (3): 595–619.

——. 2011a. "Abundance and Loss: Queer Intimacies in South Asia." *Feminist Studies* 37 (1): 1–15.

——. 2011b. "Activism as Ethical Practice: Queer Politics in Contemporary India." *Cultural Dynamics* (23) 1: 3–20.

——. 2011c. "Indian and Lesbian and What Came Next: Affect, Commensuration, and Queer Emergences." *American Ethnologist* 38 (4): 650–65.

——. 2011d. "Ordering Justice, Fixing Dreams: An Ethnography of Queer Legal Activism." In *Law Like Love: Queer Perspectives on Law*, edited by Arvind Narrain and Alok Gupta, 25–42. New Delhi: Yoda Press.

Davidson, Arnold I. 2005. "Ethics as Ascetics: Foucault, the History of Ethics, and Ancient Thought." In *The Cambridge Companion to Foucault*, edited by Gary Gutting, 123–48. 2nd ed. Cambridge: Cambridge University Press.

de Certeau, Michel. 1984. *The Practice of Everyday Life*. Translated by Steven Rendall. Berkeley: University of California Press.

Deleuze, Gilles. 2001. *Pure Immanence: Essays on a Life*. Translated by Anne Boyman. New York: Zone.

Deleuze, Gilles, and Felix Guattari. 1987. *A Thousand Plateaus: Capitalism and Schizophrenia*. Translated by B. Massumi. Minneapolis: University of Minnesota.

D'Emilio, John. 1993. "Capitalism and Gay Identity." In *The Lesbian and Gay Studies Reader*, edited by Henry Abelove, Michèle Aina Barale, and David Halperin, 467–76. New York: Routledge.

Derrida, Jacques. 1992. "Force of Law: The 'Mystical Foundation of Authority.'" In *Deconstruction and the Possibility of Justice*, edited by Drucilla Cornell, Michel Rosenfeld, and David Gray Carlson, 3–67. New York: Routledge.

Desai, Ashok H., and S. Muralidhar. 2000. "Public Interest Litigation: Potential and Problems." In *Supreme but Not Infallible: Essays in Honour of the Supreme Court of India*, edited by B. Kirpal et al, 159–92. New Delhi: Oxford University Press.

Diaz-Cotto, Juanita. 2001. "Lesbian-Feminist Activism and Latin American Feminist Encuentros." In *Sexual Identities, Queer Politics*, edited by Mark Blasius, 73–95. Princeton: Princeton University Press.

Duggan, Lisa. 2002. "The New Homonormativity: The Sexual Politics of Neoliberalism." In *Materializing Democracy: Toward a Revitalized Cultural Politics*, edited by Russ Castronovo and Dana D. Nelson, 175–84. Durham: Duke University Press.

Duggan, Lisa, and José Esteban Muñoz. 2009. "Hope and Hopelessness: A Dialogue." *Women & Performance: A Journal of Feminist Theory* 19 (2): 275–83.

Edelman, Lee. 2004. *No Future: Queer Theory and the Death Drive*. Durham: Duke University Press.

Elliston, Deborah. 2002. "Anthropology's Queer Future: Feminist Lessons from

Tahiti and Her Islands." In *Out in Theory: The Emergence of Lesbian and Gay Anthropology*, edited by Ellen Lewin and William Leap, 287–315. Urbana: University of Illinois Press.

——. 2005. "Erotic Anthropology: 'Ritualized Homosexuality' in Melanesia and Beyond." In *Same-Sex Cultures and Sexualities: An Anthropological Reader*, edited by Jennifer Robertson, 91–115. Malden, MA: Blackwell.

Escobar, Arturo. 2008. *Territories of Difference: Place, Movements, Life, Redes*. Durham: Duke University Press.

FAOW. 2002. "Another Challenge to Patriarchy." In *Humjinsi: A Resource Book on Lesbian, Gay, and Bisexual Rights in India*, edited by Bina Fernandez, 161–64. Bombay: Combat Law Publications.

Faubion, James. 2001. "Toward an Anthropology of Ethics: Foucault and the Pedagogies of Autopoiesis." *Representations* 74 (1): 83–104.

——. 2011. *An Anthropology of Ethics*. Cambridge: Cambridge University Press.

Fausto-Sterling, Anne. 2005. "The Bare Bones of Sex: Part 1—Sex and Gender." *Signs* 30 (2): 1491–527.

Ferguson, James. 1990. *The Anti-Politics Machine: "Development," Depoliticization, and Bureaucratic Power in Lesotho*. Cambridge: Cambridge University Press.

Fernandez, Bina, ed. 2002. *Humjinsi: A Resource Book on Lesbian, Gay, and Bisexual Rights in India*. Bombay: Combat Law.

Fernandez, Bina, and N. B. Gomathy. 2005. "Voicing the Invisible: Violence Faced by Lesbian Women in India." In *Because I Have a Voice: Queer Politics in India*, edited by Gautam Bhan and Arvind Narrain, 89–104. New Delhi: Yoda.

Fifth National Conference of Women's Movements in India. 1994. *Report on the Fifth National Conference of Women's Movements in India, Tirupati, 1994, January 23–26*.

Fiske, John. 1989. *The John Fiske Collection: Understanding Popular Culture*. New York: Routledge.

Forbes, Geraldine. 1996. *Women in Modern India*. Cambridge: Cambridge University Press.

Foucault, Michel. 1980. *Herculine Barbin (Being the Recently Discovered Memoirs of a Nineteenth Century French Hermaphrodite)*. Translated by Richard McDougall. New York: Pantheon.

——. 1985. *The Use of Pleasure*. Vol. 2. *The History of Sexuality*. Translated by Robert Hurley. New York: Penguin.

——. 1988 (1977). "Power and Sex." In *Politics, Philosophy, Culture: Interviews and Other Writings, 1977–1984*, edited by Lawrence D. Kritzman, 110–24. New York: Routledge.

——. 1990 (1978). *The History of Sexuality*. Vol. 1. *An Introduction*. New York: Vintage.

——. 1994 (1981). "Friendship as a Way of Life." In *Ethics: Subjectivity and Truth*, edited by Paul Rabinow, 135–40. Translated by Robert Hurley. New York: New Press.

Gal, Susan. 1995. "Language and the 'Arts of Resistance.'" *Cultural Anthropology* 10 (3): 407–24.

Garlough, Christine Lynn. 2008. "On the Politics of Folklore: Performance and Grassroots Feminist Activism in India." *Journal of American Folklore* 121 (480): 167–91.

Geetha, V. 1998. "On Bodily Love and Hurt." In *A Question of Silence? The Sexual Economies of Modern India*, edited by Mary E. John and Janaki Nair, 304–31. New Delhi: Kali for Women.

Ghosh, Shohini. 2000. "Queering the Family Pitch: Sexual and Textual Practices in Indian Fiction." *little magazine*, Nov.—Dec. 2000: 38–45.

Gopinath, Gayatri. 1998. "On *Fire*." *GLQ* 4 (4): 631–36.

——. 2005. *Impossible Desires: Queer Diasporas and South Asian Public Cultures*. Durham: Duke University Press.

Gould, Deborah. 2009. *Moving Politics: Emotion and Act Up's Fight against AIDS*. Chicago: University of Chicago Press.

——. 2010. "On Affect and Protest." In *Politcal Emotions: New Agendas in Communication*, edited by A. C. Janet Staiger and Ann Reynolds, 18–44. New York: Routledge.

Grewal, Inderpal. 1996. *Home and Harem: Nation, Gender, Empire, and the Cultures of Travel*. Durham: Duke University Press.

Guha, Ranajit. 1988. "Chandra's Death." In *A Subaltern Studies Reader, 1986–1995*, edited by Ranajit Guha, 34–62. Minneapolis: University of Minnesota Press.

——. 1997a. *An Indian Historiography of India: A Nineteenth Century Agenda and Its Implications*. Calcutta: K. P. Bagchi.

——. 1997b. *Dominance without Hegemony: History and Power in Colonial India*. Cambridge: Harvard University Press.

——. 1997c. Introduction to *A Subaltern Studies Reader, 1986–1995*, edited by Ranajit Guha, ix–xxii. Minneapolis: University of Minnesota Press.

Guidry, John A., Michael D. Kennedy, and Mayer N. Zald. 2000. "Globalizations and Social Movements." In *Globalizations and Social Movements: Culture, Power and the Transnational Public Sphere*, edited by John A. Guidry, Michael D. Kennedy, and Mayer N. Zald, 1–32. Ann Arbor: University of Michigan Press.

Gupta, Akhil. 1998. *Postcolonial Developments: Agriculture in the Making of Modern India*. Durham: Duke University Press.

Gupta, Alok. 2001. "The History and Trends in Application of Section 377 in the Indian Courts." *Lawyers Collective*, July, 9–12.

——. 2005. "Englishpur ki Kothi." In *Because I Have a Voice: Queer Politics in India*, edited by Gautam Bhan and Arvind Narrain, 123–42. New Delhi: Yoda.

Gupta, Charu. 2001. *Sexuality, Obscenity, Community: Women, Muslims, and the Hindu Public in Colonial India*. New Delhi: Permanent Black.

Haksar, Nandita. 1986. *Demystifying the Law for Women*. New Delhi: Lancer.

———. 1999. "Human Rights Layering: A Feminist Perspective." In *Engendering Law: Essays in Honor of Lotika Sarkar*, edited by Amita Dhanda and Archana Parasher, 71–88. Lucknow, India: Eastern.

Hall, Stuart. 2000. "Who Needs 'Identity'?" In *Identity: A Reader*, edited by Paul Du Gay, Jessica Evans, and Peter Redman, 15–30. London: Sage.

Halperin, David. 1995. *Saint Foucault: Towards a Gay Hagiography*. New York: Oxford University Press.

Hansen, Thomas Blom. 1999. *The Saffron Wave: Democracy and Hindu Nationalism in Modern India*. Princeton: Princeton University Press.

Haraway, Donna. 1988. "Situated Knowledges: The Science Question in Feminism and the Privilege of Partial Perspective." *Feminist Studies*, 14 (3): 575–99.

Herdt, Gilbert. 1984. *Ritualized Homosexuality in Melanesia*. Berkeley: University of California Press.

Hirschkind, Charles. 2006. *The Ethical Soundscape: Cassette Sermons and Islamic Counterpublics*. New York: Columbia University Press.

Hoagland, Sara Lucia. 1988. *Lesbian Ethics: Towards New Value*. Palo Alto: Institute of Lesbian Studies.

Hull, Gloria T., Patricia Bell Scott, and Barbara Smith, eds. 1982. *All the Women Are White, All the Blacks Are Men, But Some of Us Are Brave: Black Women's Studies*. New York: Feminist.

Hyam, Ronald. 1990. *Empire and Sexuality: The British Experience*. Manchester, England: Manchester University Press.

J. B. 1999. "March 8." In *Lesbian Emergence: Khamosh! Emergency Jaari Hai. A Citizen's Report*, edited by CALERI, 73. New Delhi: CALERI.

Jagori. 1992. *Tu Ekal, Main Ekal*. New Delhi: Jagori.

———. 1999. "Silence." In *Lesbian Emergence: Khamosh! Emergency Jaari Hai. A Citizen's Report*, edited by CALERI, 43–44. New Delhi: CALERI.

Jain, M. P. 2000. "The Supreme Court and Fundamental Rights." In *Fifty Years of the Supreme Court in India: Its Grasp and Reach*, edited by S. K. Verma and Kusum, 1–100. New Delhi: Oxford University Press.

Jean-Klein, Iris, and Annelise Riles. 2005. "Anthropology and Human Rights Administrations: Expert Observation and Representation after the Fact." PoLAR 28 (2): 173–202.

John, Mary E. 1998. "Introduction: A Question of Silence? The sexual economies of modern India." In *A Question of Silence? The Sexual Economies of Modern India*, edited by Mary John and Janaki Nair, 1–51. New York: St. Martin's Press.

———. 2005. "Feminism, Poverty, and the Emergent Social Order." In *Social Movements in India: Poverty, Power, and Politics*, edited by Raka Ray and Mary Fainsod Katzenstein, 107–34. Lanham, MD: Rowman and Littlefield.

——, ed. 2009. *Women's Studies in India: A Reader.* New York: Penguin.

John, Mary E., and Tejaswani Niranjana. 1999. "Mirror Politics: *Fire*, Hindutva, and Indian Culture." *Economic and Political Weekly* 34 (10–11): 581–84.

Joseph, Miranda. 2002. *Against the Romance of Community.* Minneapolis: University of Minnesota Press.

Joseph, Sherry. 1996. "Gay and Lesbian Movement in India." *Economic and Political Weekly* 31 (33): 2228–33.

Kahn-Freund, Otto. 1969. "Industrial Relations and the Law: Retrospect and Prospect." *British Journal of Industrial Relations* 7 (301, 307).

Kakar, Sudhir. 1978. *The Inner Worlds: A Psycho-analytic Study of Childhood and Society in India.* New Delhi: Oxford University Press.

Kamat, Sangeeta. 2002. *Development Hegemony: NGOs and the State in India.* New Delhi: Oxford University Press.

Kapur, Ratna. 2001. "Postcolonial Erotic Disruptions: Legal Narratives of Culture, Sex, and Nation in India." *Columbia Journal of Law and Gender* 10 (2): 333–57.

——. 2002. "Too Hot to Handle: The Cultural Politics of *Fire*." In *Translating Desire: The Politics of Gender and Culture in India*, edited by Brinda Bose, 182–98. New Delhi: Katha.

Kapur, Ratna, and Brenda Cossman. 1996a. *Subversite Sites: Feminist Engagements with the Law in India.* New Delhi: Sage Books

——. 1996b. "Women, Familial Ideology and the Constitution: Challenging Equality Rights." In *Feminist Terrains in Legal Domains: Interdisciplinary Essays on Women and Law in India*, edited by Ratna Kapur, 61–99. New Delhi: Kali for Women.

Karim, Lamia. 2008. "Demystifying Micro-Credit: The Grameen Bank, NGOs, and Neoliberalism in Bangladesh." *Cultural Dynamics* 20 (1): 5–29.

Kasturi, Leela, and Vina Mazumdar. 1994. Introduction to *Women and Indian Nationalism*, edited by Leela Kasturi and Vina Mazumdar, xxv–lxvii. New Delhi: Indian Association of Women's Studies.

Katyal, Akhil. 2009. "Interrupting the Legacy of the Homosexual." Paper presented at the State of Sexuality, Feminist Preconference to the annual conference on South Asia, October 22, Madison, WI.

Keane, Webb. 2007. *Christian Moderns: Freedom and Fetish in the Mission Encounter.* Berkeley: University of California Press.

Keck, Margaret, and Kathryn Sikkinik. 1998. *Activists without Borders: Advocacy Networks in International Politics.* Ithaca: Cornell University Press.

Khanna, Akshay. 2005. "Beyond 'Sexuality.'" In *Because I Have a Voice: Queer Politics in India*, edited by Gautam Bhan and Arvind Narrain, 89–104. New Delhi: Yoda.

Khayal, Utsa, and Sesan Heske. 1986. "There Are, Always Have Been, Always Will Be Lesbians in India." *Conditions* 13: 135–46.

King, Katie. 2002. "'There Are No Lesbians Here': Lesbianisms, Feminisms, and Global Gay Transformations." In *Queer Globalizations: Citizenship and the Afterlife of Colonialism*, edited by Arnaldo Cruz-Malave and Martin F. Manalansan, 33–48. New York: New York University Press.

Kishwar, Madhu. 1998. "Naive Outpourings of a Self-Hating Indian: A Review of Deepa Mehta's 'Fire.'" http://www.infinityfoundation.com/mandala/s _es/s_ es_kishw_naive_frameset.htm.

———. 2005. "A Horror of 'Isms': Why I Do Not Call Myself a Feminist." In *Feminism in India*, edited by Maitrayee Chaudhuri, 26–51. New York: Zed.

Kukke, Surabhi, Svati Shah, and Javid Syed. 1999. "Fire in New York: A Report." In *Lesbian Emergence: Khamosh! Emergency Jaari Hai. A Citizen's Report*, edited by CALERI, 33–34. New Delhi: CALERI.

Kumani, Ginu. 1995. "Waxing the Thing." In *Junglee Girl*, edited by Ginu Kumani, 117–24. San Francisco: Aunt Lute.

Kumar, Radha. 1993. *The History of Doing: An Illustrated Account of Movements for Women's Rights and Feminism in India, 1800–1990*. New Delhi: Kali for Women.

Laidlaw, James. 2002. "For an Anthropology of Ethics and Freedom." *Journal of the Royal Anthropological Institute* 8 (2): 311–32.

Lambek, Michael, ed. 2010. *Ordinary Ethics: Anthropology, Language, and Action*. New York: Fordham University Press.

Lara, Maria Pia. 1998. *Moral Textures: Feminist Narratives in the Public Sphere*. Berkeley: University of California Press.

Law Commission of India. 2000. *One Hundred and Seventy Second Report on Review of Rape Laws*, March 2000. Law Commission of India.

Lewis, David, and David Mosse, eds. 2006. *Development Brokers and Translators: The Ethnography of Aid and Agencies*. Bloomfield, CT: Kumerian.

Li, Tania. 2007. *The Will to Improve: Governmentality, Development, and the Practice of Politics*. Durham: Duke University Press.

Liechty, Mark. 2001. "Women and Pornography in Kathmandu: Negotiating the 'Modern Woman' in a New Consumer Society." In *Images of the "Modern Woman" in Asia: Global Media / Local Meanings*, edited by Shoma Munshi, 34–54. London: Curzon.

Lingam, Lakshmi. 2005. "Limits to Women's Empowerment: Micro-Credit Groups in South India." Paper presented at the University of Michigan Department of Women's Studies Lecture Series, March 8, Ann Arbor, MI.

Lorway, Robert. 2008. "Defiant Desire in Namibia: Female Sexual-Gender Transgression and the Making of Political Being." *American Ethnologist* 35 (1): 20–33.

Mahmood, Saba. 2005. *Politics of Piety: The Islamic Revival and the Feminist Subject*. Princeton: Princeton University Press.

Manalansan, Martin F. 2002. "A Queer Itinerary: Deviant Excursions into Modernities." In *Out in Theory: The Emergence of Lesbian and Gay Anthropology*, edited by Ellen Lewin and William Leap, 246–63. Urbana: University of Illinois Press.

———. 2003. *Global Divas: Filipino Gay Men in the Diaspora*. Durham: Duke University Press.

———. 2006. "Queer Intersections: Sexuality and Gender in Migration Studies." *International Migration Review* 40 (1): 224–49.

Mani, Lata. 1990. "Contentious Traditions: The Debate on Sati in Colonial India." In *Recasting Women: Essays in Indian Colonial History*, edited by Kumkum Sangari and Sudesh Vaid, 88–126. New Delhi: Kali for Women.

Massad, Joseph. 2007. *Desiring Arabs*. Chicago: University of Chicago Press.

Massey, Doreen. 1994. *Space, Place, and Gender*. Minneapolis: University of Minnesota Press.

Massumi, Brian. 2002. *Parables for the Virtual: Movement, Affect, Sensation*. Durham: Duke University Press.

Mayo, Katherine. 2000 (1927). *Mother India*. Ann Arbor: University of Michigan Press.

Mazzarella, William. 2003. *Shoveling Smoke: Advertising and Globalization in Contemporary India*. Durham: Duke University Press.

———. 2008. "Affect: What Is It Good For?" In *Enchantments of Modernity: Empire, Nation, Globalization*, edited by Saurabh Dube, 291–309. New Delhi: Routledge India.

McCall, Leslie. 2005. "The Complexity of Intersectionality." *Signs* 30 (3): 1771–800.

Mehra, Sunil. 1998. "Nuances of Loneliness." *Outlook*, November 30.

Menon, Nivedita. 2004. *Recovering Subversion: Feminist Politics beyond the Law*. New Delhi: Permanent Black.

———. 2005. "How Natural Is Normal? Feminism and Compulsory Heterosexuality." In *Because I Have a Voice: Queer Politics in India*, edited by Gautam Bhan and Arvind Narrain, 33–39. New Delhi: Yoda.

Menon, Ritu, and Kamla Bhasin. 1998. *Borders and Boundaries: Women in India's Partition*. New Brunswick, NJ: Rutgers University Press.

Merry, Sally Engle. 2005. "Anthropology and Activism: Researching Human Rights across Porous Boundaries." *PoLAR* 28 (2): 240–57.

———. 2006. *Human Rights and Gender Violence: Translating International Law into Local Justice*. Chicago: University of Chicago Press.

Metcalf, Thomas. 1994. *Ideologies of the Raj*. New York: Cambridge University Press.

Mindry, Deborah. 2001. "Nongovernmental Organizations, 'Grassroots,' and the Politics of Virtue." *Signs* 26 (1): 1187–211.

Misra, Geetanjali, and Radhika Chandiramani. 2005. *Sexuality, Gender, and Rights: Exploring Theory and Practice in South and Southeast Asia*. Newbury Park, CA: Sage.

Misra, Kavita. 2003. "A Safe Space: AIDS and New Sociality in an Indian Setting." PhD diss., Princeton University.

———. 2006. "Politico-Moral Transactions in Indian AIDS Service: Confidentiality, Rights and New Modalities of Governance." *Anthropological Quarterly* 79 (1): 33–74.

Mittermaier, Amira. 2010. *Dreams That Matter: Egyptian Landscapes of the Imagination.* Berkeley: University of California Press.

Mohanty, Chandra Talpade. 1991. "Under Western Eyes: Feminist Scholarship and Colonial Discourses." In *Third World Women and the Politics of Feminism*, edited by Chandra Talpade Mohanty, Ann Russo, and Lourdes Torres, 51–80. Bloomington: Indiana University Press.

Mohanty, Chandra Talpade, Ann Russo, and Lourdes Torres, eds. 1991. *Third World Women and the Politics of Feminism.* Bloomington: Indiana University Press.

Moore, Donald. 2005. *Suffering for Territory: Race, Place, and Power in Zimbabwe.* Durham: Duke University Press.

Moraga, Cherrie, and Gloria Anzaldua, eds. 1983. *This Bridge Called My Back: Writings By Radical Women of Color.* New York: Kitchen Table/Women of Color.

Muñoz, José Esteban. 2009. *Cruising Utopia: The Then and There of Queer Futurity.* New York: New York University Press.

Muraleedharan, T. 2005. "Crisis in Desire: A Queer Reading of Cinema and Desire in Kerala." In *Because I Have a Voice: Queer Politics in India*, edited by Gautam Bhan and Arvind Narrain, 70–88. New Delhi: Yoda.

Nanda, Serena. 1986. "The Hijras of India: Cultural and Individual Dimensions of an Institutionalized Third Gender Role." In *Anthropology and Homosexual Behavior*, edited by Evelyn Blackwood, 35–54. New York: Haworth.

———. 1990. *Neither Man nor Woman: The Hijras of India.* Belmont, CA: Wadsworth.

Nandy, Ashis. 1999. "Indian Popular Cinema as a Slum's Eye View of Politics." In *The Secret Politics of Our Desires: Innocence, Culpability and Indian Popular Cinema*, edited by Ashis Nandy, 1–18. New Delhi: Zed.

Narrain, Arvind. 2004. "There Are No Short Cuts to Queer Utopia: Sodomy, Law, and Social Change." *Lines* 2 (4): 1–13. http://issues.lines-magazine.org/textfeb04/arvind.htm.

Narrain, Arvind, and Gautam Bhan. 2005. "Introduction." In *Because I Have a Voice: Queer Politics in India*, edited by Gautam Bhan and Arvind Narrain, 1–30. New Delhi: Yoda.

Narrain, Arvind, and Vinay Chandran. 2005. "It's Not My Job to Tell You That It's Okay to Be Gay: Medicalization of Homosexuality; A Queer Critique." In *Because I Have a Voice: Queer Politics in India*, edited by Gautam Bhan and Arvind Narrain, 49–69. New Delhi: Yoda.

Narrain, Arvind, and Alok Gupta, eds. 2011. *Law Like Love: Queer Perspectives on Law.* New Delhi: Yoda.

Nash, June. 2005. "Introduction: Social Movements and Global Processes." In *Social Movements: An Anthropological Reader*, edited by June Nash, 1–26. Malden, MA: Blackwell.

Naz. 1999. "History's Flirtation with *Fire*: Documenting the Controversy." In *Lesbian Emergence: Khamosh! Emergency Jaari Hai. A Citizen's Report*, edited by CALERI, 10–17. New Delhi: CALERI.

Nirmal, C. J. 1999. "Introduction." In *Human Rights in India: Historical, Social, and Political Perspectives*, edited by C. J. Nirmal, xxvii–xxxvi. New York: Oxford University Press.

Padmanabhan, Mukund. 1988. "The Love That Dare Not Speak Its Name." *Sunday*, July 31.

Pandian, Anand. 2009. *Crooked Stalks: Cultivating Virtue in South India*. Durham: Duke University Press.

Pandian, Anand, and Daud Ali. 2010. *Ethical Life in South Asia*. Bloomington: Indiana University Press.

Patel, Geeta. 2002. "On Fire: Sexuality and Its Incitements." In *Queering India: Same-Sex Love and Eroticism in Indian Culture and Society*, edited by Ruth Vanita, 222–44. New York: Routledge.

——. 2004. "Homely Housewives Run Amok: Lesbians in Marital Fixes." *Public Culture* 16 (1): 131–58.

Patton, Cindy. 1990. *Inventing AIDS*. New York: Routledge.

Pellegrini, Ann. 2002. "Consuming Lifestyle: Commodity Capitalism and Transformations in Gay Identity." In *Queer Globalizations: Citizenship and the Afterlife of Colonialism*, edited by Arnaldo Cruz-Malave and Martin F. Manalansan, 134–48. New York: New York University Press.

Phelan, Shane. 1989. *Identity Politics: Lesbian Feminism and the Limits of Community*. Philadelphia: Temple University Press.

Povinelli, Elizabeth A. 2001. "Radical Worlds: The Anthropology of Incommensurability and Inconceivability." *Annual Review of Anthropology* 30: 319–34.

——. 2002. *The Cunning of Recognition: Indigenous Alterities and the Making of Australian Multiculturalism*. Durham: Duke University Press.

——. 2006. *The Empire of Love: Toward a Theory of Intimacy, Genealogy, and Carnality*. Durham: Duke University Press.

Povinelli, Elizabeth A., and George Chauncey. 1999. "Thinking Sexuality Transnationally." *GLQ* 5 (4): 439–50.

Prasad, Leela. 2006. *Poetics of Conduct: Oral Narrative and Moral Being in a South Indian Town*. New York: Columbia University Press.

Puar, Jasbir. 1998. "Transnational Sexualities: South Asian Trans/Nationalisms and Queer Diasporas." In *Q & A: Queer in Asian America*, edited by David L. Eng and Alice Y. Hom, 405–22. Philadelphia: Temple.

——. 2007. *Terrorist Assemblages: Homonationalism in Queer Times*. Durham: Duke University Press.

Puri, Jyoti. 1999. *Woman, Body, Desire in Post-Colonial India: Narratives of Gender and Sexuality*. New York: Routledge.

Raheja, Gloria Goodwin, and Ann Grodzins Gold. 1994. *Listen to the Heron's Words: Reimagining Gender and Kinship in North India*. Berkeley: University of California Press.

Rao, Arati. 1996. "Right in the Home: Feminist Theoretical Perspectives on International Human Rights." In *Feminist Terrains in Legal Domains: Interdisciplinary Essays on Women and Law in India*, edited by Ratna Kapur, 100–21. New Delhi: Kali for Women.

Ray, Raka. 1999. *Fields of Protest: Women's Movements in India*. Minneapolis: University of Minnesota Press.

Reagon, Bernice Johnson. 1983. "Coalition Politics: Turning the Century." In *Home Girls: A Black Feminist Anthology*, edited by Barbara Smith, 343–56. New Brunswick, NJ: Rutgers University Press.

Reddy, Gayatri. 2005. *With Respect to Sex: Negotiating Hijra Identity in South India*. Chicago: University of Chicago Press.

Rege, Arati. 2002. "A Decade of Lesbian Hulla Gulla." In *Humjinsi: A Resource Book on Lesbian, Gay, and Bisexual Rights in India*, edited by Bina Fernandez, 143–46. Bombay: Combat Law.

Riley, Denise. 1988. *"Am I That Name?" Feminism and the Category of "Women" in History*. Minneapolis: University of Minnesota Press.

Robertson, Jennifer. 1998. *Takarazuka: Sexual Politics and Popular Culture in Modern Japan*. Berkeley: University of California Press.

——. 1999. "Dying to Tell: Sexuality and Suicide in Imperial Japan." *Signs* 25 (1): 1–35.

Rofel, Lisa. 1999. "Qualities of Desire: Imagining Gay Identities in China." *GLQ* 5 (4): 451–74.

Roy, Kumkum. 1998. "Unravelling the Kamasutra." In *A Question of Silence? The Sexual Economies of Modern India*, edited by Mary E. John and Janaki Nair, 52–76. New Delhi: Kali for Women.

S. L. 1999. "Fire! Fire! It's the Lesbians!" In *Lesbian Emergence: Khamosh! Emergency Jaari Hai. A Citizen's Report*, edited by CALERI, 17–19. New Delhi: CALERI.

Saisuresh. 1988. "Two's Company." *Illustrated Weekly of India*. March 20.

Sakhi. 1994. "Don't Look Away." In *Pravartak*, vol. 1.

Sangtin Writers and Richa Nagar. 2006. *Playing with Fire: Feminist Thought and Activism through Seven Lives in India*. Minneapolis: University of Minnesota Press.

Sarkar, Tanika. 1992. "The Hindu Wife and the Hindu Nation: Domesticity and Nationalism in Nineteenth Century Bengal." *Studies in History* 8 (2): 213–35.

——. 1996. "Colonial Lawmaking and Lives/Deaths of Indian Women: Different Readings of Law and Community." In *Feminist Terrains in Legal Domains: Interdisciplinary Essays on Women and Law in India*, edited by Ratna Kapur, 210–42. New Delhi: Kali for Women.

———. 2001. *Hindu Wife, Hindu Nation: Community, Religion and Cultural Nationalism*. London: Hurst.

Scheingold, Stuart A. 2004. *The Politics of Rights: Lawyers, Public Policy, and Political Change*. 2nd ed. Ann Arbor: University of Michigan Press.

Scott, James. 1985. *Weapons of the Weak: Everyday Forms of Peasant Resistance*. New Haven: Yale University Press.

———. 1990. *Domination and the Arts of Resistance: Hidden Transcripts*. New Haven: Yale University Press.

Scott, Joan. 1988. *Gender and the Politics of History*. New York: Columbia University Press.

Seabrook, Jeremy. 1999. *Love in a Different Climate: Men Who Have Sex with Men in India*. New York: Verso.

Sedgwick, Eve Kosofsky. 1992. *Epistemology of the Closet*. Berkeley: University of California Press.

Seidman, Steven. 1993. "Identity and Politics in a 'Postmodern' Gay Culture: Some Historical and Conceptual Notes." In *Fear of a Queer Planet: Queer Politics and Social Theory*, edited by Michael Warner, 105–42. Minneapolis: University of Minnesota Press.

Shah, Alpa. 2010. *In the Shadows of the State: Indigenous Politics, Environmentalism, and Insurgency in Jharkand, India*. Durham: Duke University Press.

Shah, Chayanika. 2005. "The Roads That E/Merged: Feminist Activism and Queer Understanding." In *Because I Have a Voice: Queer Politics in India*, edited by Gautam Bhan and Arvind Narrain, 143–54. New Delhi: Yoda.

Sharma, Aradhana. 2008. *Logics of Empowerment: Development, Gender, and Governance in Neoliberal India*. Minneapolis: University of Minnesota Press.

Sharma, Jaya, and Dipika Nath. 2005. "Through the Prism of Intersectionality: Same Sex Sexualities in India." In *Sexuality, Gender, and Rights: Exploring Theory and Practice in South and Southeast Asia*, edited by Geetanjali Misra and Radhika Chandiramani, 82–97. New Delhi: Sage.

Sharma, Maya. 2006. *Loving Women: Being Lesbian in Unprivileged India*. New Delhi: Yoda.

Sharpe, Jenny. 1993. *Allegories of Empire: The Figure of Woman in the Colonial Text*. Minneapolis: University of Minnesota Press.

Sinha, Mrinalini. 1995. "Nationalism and Respectable Sexuality in India." In *Forming and Reforming Identity*, edited by Carol Siegel and Ann Kibbey, 30–57. New York: New York University Press.

Sinnott, Megan. 2004. *Toms and Dees: Transgender Identity and Female Same-Sex Relationships in Thailand*. Honolulu: University of Hawaii Press.

Sivaramakrishnan, K. 2006. "Some Intellectual Genealogies for the Concept of Everyday Resistance." *American Anthropologist* 107 (3): 346–55.

Smart, Carol. 1989. *Feminism and the Power of Law*. London: Routledge.

——. 1995. *Law, Crime and Sexuality*. London: Sage.

Spivak, Gayatri Chakravorty. 1988. "Can the Subaltern Speak?" In *Marxism and the Interpretation of Culture*, edited by Cary Nelson and Lawrence Grossberg, 271–316. London: Macmillan.

Stree Sangam. 2002. "Women Coming Together." In *Humjinsi: A Resource Book on Lesbian, Gay, and Bisexual Rights in India*, edited by Bina Fernandez, 147–50. Bombay: Combat Law.

Sukthankar, Ashwini. 1999. *Facing the Mirror: Lesbian Writing from India*. New Delhi: Penguin.

——. 2000. "For People Like Us." *New Internationalist*, October. http://www.newint .org/features/2000/10/05/likeus/.

——. 2005. "Complicating Gender: Rights of Transsexuals in India." In *Because I Have a Voice: Queer Politics in India*, edited by Gautam Bhan and Arvind Narrain, 164–74. New Delhi: Yoda.

Sullivan, Gerard, and Peter Jackson. 2001. *Gay and Lesbian Asia: Culture, Identity, Community*. New York: Routledge.

Sunder Rajan, Rajeswari. 2001. "Representing Sati: Continuities and Discontinuities." In *Postcolonial Discourses: An Anthology*, edited by Gregory Castle, 167–89. Malden, MA: Blackwell.

Swarr, Amanda Lock, and Richa Nagar. 2003. "Dismantling Assumptions: Interrogating 'Lesbian' Struggles for Identity and Survival in India and South Africa." *Signs* 29 (21): 491–516.

Sweet, Michael J., and Leonard Zwilling. 1993. "The First Medicalization: The Taxonomy and Etiology of Queerness in Classical Indian Medicine." *Journal of the History of Sexuality* 3 (4): 590–607.

Talburt, Susan. 2004. "Intelligibility and Narrating Queer Youth." In *Youth and Sexualities: Pleasure, Subversion, and Insubordination in and out of Schools*, edited by Mary Louise Rasmussen, Eric E. Rofes, and Susan Talburt, 17–40. New York: Palgrave Macmillan.

Talwar, Rajesh. 1995. *Inside Gayland*. New Delhi: ABVA.

Tambiah, Stanley J. 1996. "Hindu Nationalism, the Ayodhya Campaign, and the Babri Masjid." In *Leveling Crowds: Ethnonationalist Conflicts and Collective Violence in South Asia*, edited by Stanley J. Tambiah, 244–65. Berkeley: University of California Press.

Tarlo, Emma. 2003. *Unsettling Memories: Narratives of Emergency in Delhi*. Berkeley: University of California Press.

Taylor, Harry. 2001. "Insights into Participation from Critical Management and Labor Process Perspectives." In *Participation: The New Tyranny?*, edited by Bill Cooke and Uma Kothari, 122–38. New York: Palgrave.

Tellis, Ashley. 2003. "Ways of Becoming." *Seminar* (April) http://www.india-seminar .com/2003/524/524%20ashley%20tellis.htm.

Thadani, Giti. 1996. *Sakhiyani: Lesbian Desire in Ancient and Modern India.* New York: Cassell.

Tharu, Susie, and K. Lalita. 1993. "Empire, Nation and the Literary Text." In *Interrogating Modernity: Culture and Colonialism in India,* edited by Tejaswani Niranjana, P. Sudhir, and Vivek Dhareshwar, 199–219. Calcutta: Seagull.

Thayer, Millie. 1997. "Identity, Revolution, and Democracy: Lesbian Movements in Central America." *Social Problems* 44 (3): 386–407.

"The Two that Got Away." *Sunday Mail,* March 25–31, 1990.

Thoreson, Ryan Richard. 2008. "Somewhere over the Rainbow: Gay, Lesbian, and Bisexual Activism in South Africa." *Journal of Southern African Studies* 34 (3): 678–97.

Ticktin, Miriam. 2006. "Where Ethics and Politics Meet: The Violence of Humanitarianism in France." *American Ethnologist* 33 (1): 33–49.

Tomlinson, John. 1991. *Cultural Imperialism: A Critical Introduction.* Baltimore: Johns Hopkins Press.

Trawick, Margaret. 1992. *Notes on Love in a Tamil Family.* Berkeley: University of California Press.

Tsing, Anna Lowenhaupt. 2004. *Friction: An Ethnography of Global Connection.* Princeton: Princeton University Press.

Upadhyay, Ushma. 2000. "India's New Economic Policy of 1991 and Its Impact on Women's Poverty and AIDS." *Feminist Economics* 6 (3): 105–22.

V. S. 1999. "A Lesbian Critique of *Fire.*" In *Lesbian Emergence: Khamosh! Emergency Jaari Hai. A Citizen's Report,* edited by CALERI, 7–8. New Delhi: CALERI.

V.T. 1999. "Regal Cinema." In *Lesbian Emergence: Khamosh! Emergency Jaari Hai. A Citizen's Report,* edited by CALERI, 72. New Delhi: CALERI.

Valentine, David. 2007. *Imagining Transgender: An Ethnography of a Category.* Durham: Duke University Press.

Vanita, Ruth. 2005. "A Rose by Any Other Name: The Sexuality Terminology Debates." In *Gandhi's Tiger and Sita's Smile,* edited by Ruth Vanita, 60–69. New Delhi: Yoda.

——. 2009. *Chocolate and Other Writings on Male Homoeroticism.* Durham: Duke University Press.

Vanita, Ruth, and Saleem Kidwai. 2001. *Same-Sex Love in India: Readings From Literature and History.* New York: St. Martin's Press.

Vasan, Sudha. 2004. "NGOs as Employers: Need for Accountability." *Economic and Political Weekly* 39 (22): 2197–208.

Visweswaran, Kamala. 2010. *Un/Common Cultures: Racism and the Rearticulation of Cultural Difference.* Durham: Duke University Press.

Warner, Michael. 2002. "Publics and Counterpublics." *Public Culture* 14 (1): 49–90.

Weston, Kath. 1991. *Families We Choose: Lesbians, Gays, Kinship.* New York: Columbia University Press.

——. 1993. "Lesbian/Gay Studies in the House of Anthropology." *Annual Review of Anthropology* 22: 339–67.

Williams, Raymond. 1977. *Marxism and Literature*. New York: Oxford University Press.

Williams, Walter. 1986. *The Spirit and the Flesh: Sexual Diversity in American Indian Culture*. Boston: Beacon.

Wright, Timothy. 2001. "Gay Organizations, NGOs, and the Globalization of Sexual Identity: The Case of Bolivia." *Journal of Latin American Anthropology* 5 (2): 89–111.

Ziarek, Ewa Plonowska. 1995. "'Straying Afield of Oneself': Risks and Excesses of Foucault's Ethics." In "The Histories of Michel Foucault," edited by Jeffrey R. Di Leo. *Symploke* 3 (2): 179–99.

Grover, Anand, 178, 179, 184, 190
Guautam, Siddhartha, 156, 172, 196, 198. *See also* ABVA
Gupta, Charu, 144, 225n9

Haksar, Nandita, 180, 201–2
Hall, Stuart, 217n27
Halperin, David, 20
help lines, 24, 71–72, 73, 76–80, 155, 226n22. *See also* Aanchal; Sangini
Herculine Barbin, 215n6
hierarchies: elites/elitism among queer activists and, 41–42, 54–56, 122–24, 182; in legal rights discourse, 170, 182, 185–86; of oppression and worthiness in the women's movement, 98–99, 102, 109–10, 122–23, 135; of political competence, 46–47, 55, 59–60, 74–75, 91, 158, 160, 171, 184, 185, 214n53
hijras, 28, 120, 131, 134, 206, 208n8, 222n43, 223n55
Hindus/Hinduism: becoming "Indian" and, 18, 38, 162; communalism and, 146–47, 151, 177, 209n17, 225n14, 229n22; *Fire* and, 141–44, 144–46, 150, 151–55, 160–63, 224n6; Hindu Marriage Act of 1955 and, 43, 212n22; national identity and, 152; nationalism and, 141, 143, 145–46, 149–50, 224n6, 225n8; women's movement and, 101
HIV/AIDS: funding and, 177, 178, 229n21; lesbians' relationship with gay men and, 27–28, 39–40, 71–72, 78–79, 85–86, 169, 175, 186–87, 211n12; Lucknow affair and, 90, 176–78, 186; *Mr. X v. Hospital Z* and, 178; repeal of Section 377 efforts and, 169, 172–73, 179, 227n4. *See also specific organizations*

homosociality, 4, 19, 48, 63, 150
Humjinsi, 134, 135
humjinsi, as term of use, 18
Hyam, Ronald, 229n23

identity: "becoming Indian" and 160–63, 227n27; "becoming lesbian" and, 155–60, 165; as freedom, 69; politics of naming and, 17–21, 18, 35, 37, 40, 56–57, 90, 94, 104, 107–9, 120, 132, 146–47, 156–57, 208n13, 208n15, 209n18, 209nn20–21; queer critiques of, 4, 7, 8, 14–15, 16, 91–96; subject formation/interpellation and, 62–68, 139, 151, 153, 154, 160, 163, 164; visuality and, 57–58
IFSHA, 193, 231n40
imagination: imagined community and, 34–36, 57, 58–59, 78, 210n2; queerness as imagined and, 20–21, 181–82
inclusion, as deferral of life, 87–89; politics of, 68, 87–89, 91, 94, 203, 217n25, 226n21, 232n46. *See also* containment
incommensurability, 15, 138–39, 141, 151–55, 159–61, 163, 223n2, 226nn20–21. *See also* becoming and being; commensuration; containment
India Centre for Human Rights and Law, 134, 223n57
Indian Penal Code, 146, 167, 171–72. *See also* Section 377 of the Indian Penal Code
International Women's Day, March 8th, 103, 110–11, 119–20, 119–21, 221n41, 223n53
intersectionality, 20, 93, 98, 192, 218n28, 231n38
invention, 3, 7–9, 12–14, 36, 44, 47, 60, 203, 208nn9–10

activism; Section 377 of the Indian Penal Code

lesbians: affect and, 35–36, 126–27, 163; ascendance of dialogue and, 54–55, 56; class and, 55–56, 132; community and, 34–36, 38, 44–46, 51–53, 53–60; field of immanence and, 139–40, 155, 165; foreigners and NRIs and, 59–60, 64–65, 70, 77, 83; hierarchies of political competence and, 46–47, 55, 59–60, 74–75, 91, 158, 160, 171, 214n53; marriage and, 43–44, 51, 52, 104–7, 112, 116–17, 143, 211n20, 220n17; mirror metaphor and, 58–59; naming and, 17–21, 33–34, 35, 36–37, 38, 40, 58, 67, 93, 94, 104, 107–9, 112, 115, 121, 155–60, 163, 164, 219n9, 220n19; race and, 25, 59, 71, 113–14, 215n9, 221n28; relationship with gay men and, 27–28, 39–40, 71–72, 78–79, 85–86, 169, 175, 186–87, 211n12; relationship with women's movement and, 41, 71, 74, 89, 97–99, 110, 112–15, 115–18, 119–22, 124–26; rights and, 55, 74, 107, 115, 116, 119–20, 156–57, 160–63, 164; rural and, 20, 28, 49, 98, 104–5, 109, 210n27, 219n11; sex and, 35–36, 46–47, 47–53, 60, 85–87, 87–89, 155–160, 181; subject formation and, 42–46, 57–59, 61–68, 72, 73, 139, 151, 153, 154, 155–60, 163, 164, 211nn19–20, 212n22, 212n24, 215n11; as "Western," 70, 113, 116, 141–43, 156. *See also specific organizations*

Less Than Gay, 156, 172

LGBT-India (e-list), 176, 183, 187, 188, 222n43, 228n15, 229n16

"Lihaff" (short story), 147–49, 225nn11–12

Lucknow affair, 90, 176–78, 186, 217n25, 229n22

Mahmood, Saba, 7, 208n5

Manalansan, Martin, 16

Manushi (journal), 104, 224n4, 225n12

marriage/s: compulsory heterosexual and, 4, 5, 39, 63, 95, 125, 180–81; feminist and queer critiques of, 94, 180, 200; Hindu Marriage Act of 1955 and, 43, 212n22; legal rights and law and, 43, 162–63, 232n48; lesbian, 43–44, 51, 52, 104–7, 112, 116–17, 143, 211n20, 220n17; policewomen and, 43–44, 104–7, 112, 116–17, 143, 211n20, 220n17; "single women" and, 108

Martina Club, 111–12

Massad, Joseph, 15–16

mass mediation, 42–46, 72, 73, 153, 211nn19–20, 212n22, 212n24, 215n11

Massumi, Brian, 9–10, 140, 155, 165

MASUM (Mahila Sarvangeen Utkarsh Manda), 124–27, 129, 131–32, 135, 206, 222n50, 222n53. *See also* Pune controversy

Mathura campaign, and politics of representation, 102–3, 104, 106, 112, 219n8

Mayo, Katherine, 145, 147, 225n8

Mazzarella, William, 24, 155, 163, 226n20

McCall, Leslie, 218n28

Mehta, Deepa, 140, 145–48, 152, 224nn3–4. *See also* Fire

Menon, Nivedita, 180, 198

men who have sex with men (MSM). *See* MSM

Mindry, Deborah, 98, 123

mirror metaphor, 58–59, 66–68, 78, 214n59

morality, as undone by ethics, 6, 84–85, 207n2. *See also* ethics

moral virtue of poverty, 98, 99, 102, 118–19, 123–24

MSM (men who have sex with men), 19, 39–40, 71–72, 78, 175, 176–78

Muñoz, José Esteban, 9, 20, 181, 226n21

Muslims/Islam: communalism and, 146–47, 151, 152, 177, 191, 201, 209n17, 219n8, 225n14, 229n22; *Fire* and, 151, 152–53, 161–62, 224n6; obscenity campaigns and, 148–49; queer activism and, 28, 164, 177, 191, 201, 229n22; queer historiography and, 38, 147, 161–62; "queering" of Others and, 143, 146, 146–47, 152; women's movement and, 101

Narmada Bachao Andolan, 11

Narrain, Arvind, 176, 201–2

National Conference of Women's Movements (NCWM), 108–9, 112–18, 220n21, 221n26

National Federation of Indian Women (NFIW), 116, 117

National Human Rights Commission (NHRC), 175–76. *See also* aversion therapy

nationalism, 141, 143, 145–46, 149–50, 224n6, 225n8

Naz (Naz Foundation (India) Trust or Naz India or Naz Foundation): aversion therapy case and, 175–76; help line for men and kothis and, 72, 77; *Naz v. Govt of Delhi* and, 30, 168–70, 178, 179–81, 182–93, 227n3–4, 229n24, 229n26, 230n34; relationship with PRISM and, 90, 183; relationship with Sangini and, 72, 73, 75, 77, 79; supporter of smaller groups and, 71, 90

Naz Foundation International (NFI), 176–77, 229n20, 229n22. *See also* Lucknow affair

Naz Foundation v. Government of NCT of Delhi and Others (Naz v. Govt of Delhi), 30, 168–70, 178, 179–81, 182–93, 203–4, 227nn3–4, 229n24, 229n26, 230n34. *See also* legal rights and law; Section 377 of the Indian Penal Code

NCWM (National Conference of Women's Movements), 108–9, 112–18, 220n21, 221n26

Network for Sexual Rights (NSR), 131–36

NFI (Naz Foundation International), 176–77, 229n20, 229n22

NFIW (National Federation of Indian Women), 116, 117

NGOs and NGO-ization: lesbian dependence on, 73, 75, 124–36; political competence and incompetence and, 46, 75; politics of funding and, 4, 135, 184; queer critiques of, 127–29; scholarship on, 11–12, 129–31; women's movement and, 100, 110, 122–23, 124–36. *See also specific organizations*

NHRC (National Human Rights Commission), 175–76. *See also* aversion therapy

nonresident Indians (NRIS) and foreigners, 57, 59–60, 114, 156, 214n54, 221n28, 226n23. *See also* diasporic queer activists

NSR (Network for Sexual Rights), 131–36

obscenity, 146–51, 225nn9–13

OLAVA (Organized Lesbian Alliance for Visibility and Action), 124–27, 129,

queer, definition of, 20–21

queer activism: becoming and, 1–2, 6, 7–8, 60, 192; elites/elitism and, 41–42, 54–56, 122–24, 182; as ethical practice and, 6–9, 13, 20, 36, 75, 82, 83–87, 95–96, 99, 131, 135, 139, 140, 182, 196–99, 201, 202, 203, 207n2, 208nn5–6, 214n59; fieldwork and, 21–22, 24–27, 209n24, 209n25; gender neutrality in sexual assault law and, 169–70, 182, 193–99, 231nn40–44, 232nn45–46, 232nn48–49, 233n50; hierarchies of political competence and, 46–47, 55, 59–60, 74–75, 91, 158, 160, 171, 184, 185, 214n53; as invention, 3, 7–9, 12–14, 36, 44, 47, 60, 203, 208nn9–10; language definition of queer and, 20–21; NGOs and, 126–29, 223n55; overview of, 1–3; politics of funding and, 14, 26, 46, 48, 73, 75, 82, 91, 135; publications and, 26–27, 38–39, 43, 44, 48, 72, 74, 111, 153–54, 156, 172, 209n25, 210n26, 211n8, 220n22, 228n10; radical worlds and, 14, 133, 138, 203, 207n4; religion/communalism and, 28, 152, 164, 182, 191, 201; Section 377 and, 30, 168–70, 172–74, 178, 179–81, 182–93, 203–4, 227nn3–4, 228n10, 229n24, 229n26, 230n34; transnationalism and, 10–12, 22, 29, 34, 110, 156, 208n6. *See also* class and sexuality; legal rights and law; LGBT-India; protests, marches, and celebrations; publics, public sphere, and counterpublics; rights and rights-based activism; *specific organizations*

queer anthropology, 14–17, 208nn11

queer historiography, 18–20, 33, 38, 161–62

queer language, 17–21, 132, 208n13, 208n15, 209n18, 209nn20–21. *See also* language

queer theory: ethics and, 7–8, 20, 85; homonationalism and, 173; narcissism and, 58–59, 214n59; passionate attachment and, 69; "queer" and, 20–21; queerness and futurity and, 20, 85, 181, 214n59; sex as radical and, 86

race, 25, 59, 71, 113–14, 215n9, 221n28

Radhakrishnan, Mita, 118–19, 221n38

radical ethics, 8, 36, 207n4. *See also* ethics

radical and liberal feminisms, 114, 118–19, 221nn38–39, 221n41, 222n43. *See also* feminisms; poetics of silence

radical worlds, 14, 133, 138, 203, 207n4

Raheja, Gloria Goodwin, 12–13

Rakesh, Shaleen, 178–79, 222n43

rape and sexual violence: against children, 187–88, 193, 231n40; Indian feminism and, 100, 102–3, 104, 106, 107, 108, 117–18, 219n8; law and, 193–96, 219n7, 231nn40–41, 231n44, 233n50; same-sex and, 83, 170, 195–96, 198–99. *See also* gender neutrality in sexual assault law; legal rights and law; Mathura campaign; Section 377 of the Indian Penal Code

Rashtriya Swayamsevak Sangh (RSS), 141–44

Reagon, Bernice Johnson, 82

Rege, Arati, 54, 211n4, 213n47

representation, politics of, 102–3, 105–7, 111–12, 219n8, 220n17

resistance, in contrast to invention, 12–14

rights and rights-based activism: aversion therapy and, 175–76; children

Urmila and Leela (marriage, of two policewomen), 43–44, 104–7, 112, 116–17, 143, 211n20, 220n17

Vanita, Ruth, 19, 201, 209n18
Vasan, Sudha, 130, 131
Vimla Faroqui episode, 115–18
Visweswaran, Kamala, 208n6
Voices against 377 (Voices), 192, 206, 231n38
vulnerability, and legal rights, 170–71, 196, 198

Warner, Michael, 164
the "West" as counterpoint, real and imagined, to India, 14–17, 19, 37, 39, 70, 83, 86, 91, 101–2, 113, 116–17, 123, 138, 141–43, 146, 150, 157, 161–62, 200, 214n2, 218n2, 219n11, 224n4, 224n6, 231n43
Weston, Kath, 4, 14–15, 58, 59
Williams, Raymond, 9, 36
women's movement: affiliated versus autonomous and, 100–102; economic liberalization and, 109–10; hierarchies of worthiness and, 98–99, 102, 109–10, 122–23, 135; historic context for, 101–2, 219nn5–6; lesbians' dependence on, 30, 99–100, 211n12; marriage of two police-

women and, 43–44, 104–7, 112, 116–17, 143, 211n20, 220n17; Mathura campaign and, 102–3, 219n8; National Conference of Women's Movements (NCWM), 108–9, 112–18, 220n21, 221n26; NGO-ization and, 108–10, 126–31; overview and use of term, 30, 98–100, 131–36, 218nn2–3, 219n4; poetics of silence and, 104, 115, 121, 156, 219n9; politics of representation and, 102–3, 105–7, 111–12, 219n8, 220n17; protests and marches and, 5, 103, 110, 119–21, 221n41, 223n53; rape and sexual violence focus in, 106, 107, 117–18, 220nn18–19; "single women" and, 19, 36–37, 107–9, 112, 220n19; Western perceptions of, 101–2. See also feminists/feminism; specific organizations
Women to Women/Stree Sangam (now LABIA or Lesbians and Bisexuals in Action). See Stree Sangam/Women to Women (now LABIA or Lesbians and Bisexuals in Action)
World Social Forum (WSF) in 2004, 131, 132–33, 134

"xenophobic queerphobia," 141–44, 152

Ziarek, Ewa Plonowska, 6–7

Naisargi Dave is an assistant professor of
anthropology at the University of Toronto.

Library of Congress Cataloging-in-Publication Data
Dave, Naisargi N. (Naisargi Nitin), 1975–
Queer activism in India : a story in the anthropology
of ethics / Naisargi N. Dave.
p. cm.
Includes bibliographical references and index.
ISBN 978-0-8223-5305-8 (cloth : alk. paper)
ISBN 978-0-8223-5319-5 (pbk. : alk. paper)
1. Lesbian activists—India. 2. Lesbianism—India.
I. Title.
HQ75.6.I4D38 2012
306.76′630954—dc23
2011053091

www.ingramcontent.com/pod-product-compliance
Lightning Source LLC
Chambersburg PA
CBHW050343270326
41926CB00016B/3583